TRAVELING
SOLO

Help Us Keep This Guide Up to Date

Every effort has been made by the author and editors to make this guide as accurate and useful as possible. However, many things can change after a guide is published—establishments close, phone numbers change, hiking trails are rerouted, facilities come under new management, etc.

We would love to hear from you concerning your experiences with this guide and how you feel it could be made better and be kept up to date. While we may not be able to respond to all comments and suggestions, we'll take them to heart and we'll also make certain to share them with the author. Please send your comments and suggestions to the following address:

The Globe Pequot Press
Reader Response/Editorial Department
P.O. Box 480
Guilford, Connecticut 06437

Or you may e-mail us at:

editorial@GlobePequot.com

Thanks for your input, and happy travels!

TRAVELING SOLO

{
Advice and Ideas
for More than 250 Great Vacations
}

Fifth Edition

ELEANOR BERMAN

INSIDERS' GUIDE®

GUILFORD, CONNECTICUT
AN IMPRINT OF THE GLOBE PEQUOT PRESS

The information in this guidebook was confirmed at press time. We recommend, however, that you contact establishments before traveling to obtain current information. The author and The Globe Pequot Press assume no liability for accidents happening to, or injuries sustained by, readers who engage in the activities described in this book.

INSIDERS' GUIDE®

ISSN 1544-4562
ISBN 0-7627-3697-6

Manufactured in the United States of America
Fifth Globe Pequot Edition/First Printing

Contents

Introduction

The first time I traveled by myself, I was newly divorced and scared to death. I never dreamed at that point that travel writing was to become my profession, almost forcing me to become adept at getting around on my own. I was just a travel lover determined that lack of a companion was not going to keep me at home. Happily, I discovered that the excitement of my first visit to San Francisco overcame my qualms. I did meet people along the way—not every day or for every meal, but often enough to keep me from feeling totally alone. I discovered to my surprise that there were unique pleasures to being completely on my own. And I had a wonderful time.

That was a long time ago, but I still remember my initial fear, and I have special empathy when someone asks me plaintively, "But where can I go alone?"

Having now traveled extensively for both business and pleasure, I've learned that there are many happy answers to that question; that, in fact, solo travel can have special advantages simply because you can tailor it exactly to your own tastes.

The purpose of this book is to point out some of the myriad possibilities for rewarding solo vacations, as well as offer some of the know-how that makes for more confident travel on your own. My aim is to help you discover that you don't always need a traveling companion to have a wonderful time—that alone need not mean lonely.

No one asked or paid to be included in this book. I chose programs and tours strictly because they represented a wide range of activities that seemed to offer an opportunity for comfortable and exciting singular vacations. I tried to stay with those that have been around long enough to have a proven record. The basic information was provided by the operator of each program, as were the names of most of the references quoted. The comments were requested because the trips I could experience personally were necessarily limited (you will find my remarks under E.B.). Wherever possible, I wanted to hear from travelers who could give firsthand reports.

The best way to ensure that any vacation is successful is to gather as much information as possible before you make a choice. That is doubly true when you are planning a trip alone, without a companion to help cushion disappointments. Use the listings in this book as a guide and a starting point only, to be followed up by research with travel agents, friends, and specialized magazines. If you're considering a particular group trip or activity, ask for current information and *references,* and phone directly to clear up unanswered questions before you sign on. You might follow my example and ask for names of past solo participants who can tell you whether they felt comfortable as part of such a group.

I've tried to give the cons as well as the pros for some of these trips in the hope that they will be of value to you in making a choice. Inevitably, these are personal assessments, and my tastes may not always match your own.

The pages that follow present only a sampling of trips, and I may have omitted some equally rewarding possibilities for solo travel. If you know of any, please write to me care of The Globe Pequot Press and share them for a future edition.

If this book gives you new ideas, encourages you to overcome your fears of traveling by yourself, and helps you to make the right choices for *you,* my mission will have been accomplished.

On Your Own: The Rewards

N OT VERY LONG AGO IN NEW YORK CITY, A LECTURE WAS HELD that packed the auditorium. The topic: vacations for singles.

The turnout was not surprising. We are living in a world where the number of single people is increasing dramatically. According to the U.S. Census Bureau, the number of unmarried adults nearly doubled from 1970 to 1999, growing from 54 to 101 million. The 2000 census, which measured people beginning at age 15, found over 221 million single, separated, divorced, or widowed Americans.

And 22 percent of all trips were taken by single-member households, according to a 2002 report from the United States Travel Data Center, the research arm of the Travel Industry Association of America (TIA). Seventy-one percent of these solo travelers' trips were strictly for pleasure.

Married or single, 2004 statistics from the TIA show that nearly one-quarter of U.S. travelers, 34.8 million adults, report that they have taken a vacation by themselves in the past three years. Yet information for those who want to plan a vacation alone has been hard to come by. Most people know about Club Med and some of the tours designed for single travelers. But there is also a world of exciting travel to be enjoyed on your own that is not labeled "For singles only."

Many people are at a loss when it comes to finding these vacations because information is scattered. The occasional lecture or article may not be available when you really need it. Few guidebooks look at travel issues from the point of view of a single traveler. Travel agents also are limited by this lack of reference material.

The aim of *Traveling Solo* is to fill that gap, to bring together in one sourcebook the wide range of rewarding vacations that can be enjoyed without a traveling companion.

Today no one, young or old, needs to stay at home for lack of company. The exciting possibilities for travel are as varied as the ages, budgets, and interests of those millions of singles. And while that old stickler, the single supplement, still makes it more expensive to travel alone, for those who need to economize there are ways to match up with compatible roommates to share the costs.

One chapter ahead will include the range of programs exclusively for singles, but most of the options in this book are not limited by marital status. They are choices based on personal interests, places, and programs where you can feel equally comfortable with or without a partner. Many of them include family-style meals, eliminating the need to eat alone, a prospect that is daunting to many travelers.

The first chapters are divided into various categories of vacation experiences, from shaping up your body to stretching your mind, from active adventure to relaxing in the sun. There is something here for everyone, from travelers in their 20s to adventure-seekers over age 50.

Many of these ideas can be found in other guides. The difference here is that the information was compiled with the single traveler in mind—single in this case meaning simply traveling alone.

The data supplied by the organizer of each trip is supplemented wherever possible by firsthand accounts from past solo travelers—including myself. If there are no reports, it is because no references were made available. Big tour companies and cruise lines in particular were generally unwilling to give out names of past clients.

Exact prices change rapidly, so the trips here are designated by general price categories as follows:

I = $150 a day or less including meals

M = $151–$200 daily

E = $201–$250 daily

EE = More than $250 per day

Transportation is not included in these estimates except for tours or unless it is specifically mentioned.

For your information, "single supplement" refers to the common practice of adding a surcharge for solo travelers. Though it is a source of expense and annoyance to everyone who travels alone, the supplement has a practical reason; it is an attempt to make up for the lost revenue of a second person in the room. Some wise hoteliers and tour operators have realized that single travelers are valuable customers and have minimized or eliminated the supplement. Many offer guaranteed "shares," which means that they will provide you with another single person of your sex as a roommate or they will waive the supplement if they cannot find someone to share the room.

The term "homestay" means an arrangement of accommodations in another person's home.

The last section of the book is for those who want to travel completely on their own, with ideas and guidance for doing so safely and comfortably.

One issue should be stressed from the start. This is not a book about how to find Mr. or Ms. Right on your vacation. Cupid is notoriously unreliable about where and when he aims his arrows, and there is no surer way to doom your trip than to base its success on whether or not you find romance on your travels.

The trips here encourage you to look at solo travel not as a way to find someone else, but as a time to find yourself. That is the secret of a truly successful solo vacation.

Certainly there are challenges in traveling by yourself. Dining alone is a big one, and successful solo travel requires more advance research, more careful planning, and more resourcefulness than a trip for two. All these topics will be covered in the pages ahead.

But what stops most people from traveling alone is less logistics than attitude. If you've never traveled by yourself, it may seem frightening. It's easy to feel nervous, shy, self-conscious, and even self-pitying when you seem to be one in a world of twos. The tendency is to imagine that people will look at you and say, "Poor thing—all alone."

In truth, traveling alone says nothing about you whatever except that you have a spirit of independence and adventure. Who's to say you don't have a wonderful friend at home who can't get away for this particular trip?

Furthermore, rather than feeling sorry for you, many of the couples you are envying may be jealous of your spirit and your freedom. Travel shared can be wonderful—but it can sometimes pose its own problems. Neither friends nor lovers are always in harmony in their enthusiasm or energy levels. If she loves Gothic cathedrals but he'd rather scuba dive, tensions can loom. Nothing is more frustrating than a companion who wants to use up all of your free time shopping—unless it is a travel mate who taps a foot impatiently every time *you* want to browse in a store. Travel partners may sometimes lack your stamina, or, even worse, may keep up a pace that wears you out.

So, travel with a partner means compromises. Solo travel, on the other hand, can be the ultimate self-indulgence, the chance to tailor a vacation strictly to your own tastes, energies, and timetable—to go where you please, do exactly what you want when you want, and meet interesting new people of all ages and both sexes, married and single, in the process.

Without the insulation of a partner, you may find that you are more open to experiencing a new environment. You notice more, impressions are more vivid, you can take time to linger—and reactions are completely your own, uncolored by someone else's opinions.

By yourself you can feel freer to broaden your horizons and try out new roles, to live out a few fantasies perhaps, like riding a horse or rafting a river or painting a sunset—activities you might hesitate to attempt in front of the folks back home.

Because there is far more incentive to meet other people when you are by yourself, you tend to become more outgoing, to seek out new friends—and to find them.

What's more, many travelers who set out a bit shaky about traveling solo return feeling very good about themselves, with a stronger sense of competence, self-assurance, and independence for having proved that they can make it on their own.

Traveling alone has its challenges, but it can also be a wonderful opportunity. In the pages ahead you'll find a world of ideas for rewarding adventures. Make the most of them by selecting those that are uniquely right for you.

Making Choices

In planning a successful solo vacation, the first and most important tip to keep in mind is a simple one: Know yourself.

You may consider literally thousands of possibilities for vacations, from tennis camps and museum tours to cruising the Nile or trekking in Nepal. Or you may choose to explore a great city on your own. One of the pitfalls of planning a trip alone is the temptation to choose what you think other single people are doing rather than doing the research to find something suited to your own tastes.

Yes, lots of people go on rafting trips by themselves, but if you hate camping and would be terrified by swirling rapids, it makes little sense to head for a river. Remember that the greatest advantage to traveling by yourself is the freedom to do exactly what you like best.

And while trips for "singles" may seem more comfortable than being a single among couples, it is a mistake to limit yourself only to this category. Consider these trips, certainly, but if you sign up for a trip solely for single company and discover that all you have in common with your fellow travelers is your marital status, the trip will be a washout.

The first question to ask yourself, then, is what you want from your vacation. Here are some points to consider:

- Do you need to relax and wind down or do you want a pick-me-up, a totally new adventure to spice up your life?
- What kind of physical shape are you in—and how much physical challenge do you want on your trip?
- Do you want to expand your present hobbies or interests or develop a new one?

- Is there some particular area you want to visit? If so, do you prefer seeing a little bit of a lot of places or spending time getting to know one destination in depth?
- Are you seeking a warm climate?
- How important is the quality of the food and lodging?
- Will you be happier making arrangements on your own and moving at your own pace, or would you be more secure as part of a group with all the planning done for you?

The more carefully you analyze what you are hoping for, the more likely you are to find it. Suppose, for example, that you want to visit the south of France. Your goals are to see the countryside, get some exercise, meet other people ages 30 to 40, and sample gourmet food. Many luxury tours could supply the gourmet part of the formula, but they would provide little exercise and probably attract an older clientele. An upscale biking or hiking trip might fill all of the requirements. What remains then is to research who offers such trips in this area and contact each with the right questions.

If you have the same destination in mind, but want a less strenuous trip, you might look into a learning vacation—one that stresses cooking, learning a foreign language, architecture, photography, or art. For a younger scene, consider tours geared to those under 35.

When your sights are set on sunshine, beware. A Caribbean island or the Mexican Riviera can hold perils for single travelers. Romantic resorts naturally attract loving couples, and there is nothing more depressing than feeling like an odd man out in a lovers' hideaway. Look for other possibilities instead. Depending on your tastes, a trip to the Yucatan ruins in Mexico, a tennis camp in Florida, or painting lessons in the Caribbean are warm-weather options that should offer companions whose enthusiasms match your own. Windjammer sailing cruises attract lots of active, sociable people in the Caribbean, or you could check into a sunny spa resort, which tends to draw many solo participants, married and single alike.

Researching a trip is easier than ever, since so many programs and resorts now maintain pages on the Internet. Even if you don't own a computer, you can still use this resource; most public libraries provide Internet access.

Should you join a tour or take off on your own? A lot depends on your travel experience and disposition. Do you dislike regimentation and prefer setting your own pace? Are you content to amuse yourself at home on occasion with solo walks, shopping expeditions, or museum visits? Are you able to talk to strangers? Are you willing to spend time and effort researching and planning your trip? Most of all, are you an optimist, ready to make the most of what you have rather than pining about what is missing? If the answers are yes, don't hesitate to try a trip by yourself; often going solo is the most rewarding way to go.

A good way to test the waters is to join a group or a tour, then afterward spend extra time in a city on your own. Or you might break up a solo city visit with short group tours to nearby attractions, providing a chance for a day or two of companionship.

Browse through all of the categories of vacations included in this book, including suggestions for travel on your own. You should find enough ideas to get you happily to almost any part of the world that intrigues you, and inspiration to try some new travel experiences as well. The key to traveling happily on your own is simply to do it in the way that will be most comfortable and enjoyable for *you*.

Section ONE

GREAT
Group Vacations
for
Solo Travelers

Learn a Sport

SPORTS ARE THE PERFECT VACATION ICEBREAKER WHEN YOU ARE ALONE. It is easy to get to know others when you are learning new techniques together. Whether you improve your old game or pick up a new one, you'll also be adding a valuable dimension to your life when you get home. On a sports vacation, everyone is a winner.

Which sports are offered? Almost any you can name. From tennis and golf to scuba diving or mountain climbing, if you want to learn it, you can find someone to teach you on your vacation. You can learn to cross-country ski, canoe, ride a horse—or even live out your fantasy of being a major leaguer at a spring training baseball camp.

Tips for Enjoying Sports Camps

- Try to avoid blisters. If you buy new shoes for the trip, leave plenty of time to break them in at home before you go.
- Be prepared for hours out-of-doors with proper protection—sunscreen, sunglasses or a visor, and a protective hat.
- Start an exercise routine at home, stressing aerobics, for about a month before you go. Beginner or expert, you'll get more out of sports instruction if you build up your stamina in advance.

Here's a survey of the sporting vacation world.

Tennis

Tennis camp is one of the most popular sports vacations. Since there is a wide variation in facilities and rates, your first decision in choosing a tennis camp should be based on its ambience—resort versus campus dormitory-style living. This is often a matter of budget as well as preference, since resorts are obviously more expensive. Locations with group dining are often more sociable for single participants, but tennis instruction at resorts can provide a way to meet people on a resort vacation that might otherwise be lonely.

Your next decision depends on how intensive an instructional program you prefer. Finally, the season will make a difference. Decide whether you want to head for the mountains or the sunshine—or maybe let tennis camp solve the problem of planning a Caribbean vacation on your own.

A terrific resource for tennis camp recommendations is the Web site www .tennisresortsonline.com. The information on this site is compiled by Roger Cox, one of America's top tennis writers, who has visited almost every resort and describes each program and its ambience in depth. Viewers who have attended these programs are invited to rate them for accommodations, cuisine, staff, programs, dollar value, and suitability for solo travelers.

Cox was kind enough to provide his own "top ten" list for solo tennis enthusiasts. These range from college campus programs with dorm accommodations to luxury resorts. All include meals in their tennis packages, and offer either group dining or a staff that funnels those who are alone to tables with other vacationers.

Here are his picks, in order of preference:

1. John Newcombe Tennis Ranch, New Braunfels, Texas
2. Nike Amherst Tennis Camp, Amherst, Massachusetts
3. Total Tennis, Saugerties, New York
4. New England Tennis Holidays, North Conway, New Hampshire
5. Killington Tennis at Cortina Inn and Resort, Killington, Vermont
6. Sweet Briar College/Van der Meer Tennis, Sweet Briar, Virginia
7. Swarthmore Tennis Camp, Swarthmore, Pennsylvania
8. Inn at Manitou, McKellar, Ontario, Canada
9. Gardiner's Resort, Carmel Valley, California
10. Gunterman Tennis Schools, Stratton Mountain, Vermont

While the lodgings and atmosphere may vary, the essential teaching programs all are much like the program I experienced some years ago at the Topnotch resort in Stowe, Vermont.

The instruction began with an orientation session and a few minutes of individual play with instructors who graded and divided us by ability into groups of four. Then we spent about an hour learning the right way to volley at the net.

During the next few days, we moved on to forehand, backhand, serve, overhead, and short strokes, with special drills devised to work on each stroke. Each day began with about fifteen minutes of warm-up exercises. One morning we were videotaped and got to see firsthand what we were doing right and wrong. Another day we got a private half-hour lesson to work on individual problems. On the last day we received an honest but upbeat evaluation sheet, with tips as to what to watch out for at home. The pros were excellent—outgoing, encouraging, and fun as well as fine teachers.

Tennis Tips

Before you sign up for any tennis program, you should know the answers to the following questions:

- What is the instructor/student ratio? It should be no higher than one instructor per four students.
- How long has the program been running?
- What are the qualifications of the pros—are they certified by the U.S. Tennis Association and/or the U.S. Professional Tennis Association?
- Are there ample indoor courts so your vacation won't be washed out if it rains?

Will tennis camp work miracles on a mediocre tennis game? Unfortunately, you can't radically change your game in a few days, and most camps don't try. Instead they work on improving your existing strokes. With such concentrated practice, you do see encouraging improvement—and at the same time meet many people who share your interest in the sport.

Following is a listing of a variety of tennis camps:

The most spartan—those on school campuses—attract the most singles because everyone dines together.

TOTAL TENNIS

Box 28, Saugerties, NY 12477;
(800) 221–6496 or (845) 247–9177;
www.totaltennis.com (M–E)

Years in business:	20+
Age range:	20–60
Most common age:	30–45
Percent alone:	50
Number of participants:	60
Male/female ratio:	50/50
Will try to arrange shares, but the single supplement, when rooms are available, is modest	

This year-round facility devoted to tennis is on the sixty-seven-acre grounds of a former resort overlooking the northern Catskill Mountains.

Facilities include thirteen red clay courts, seven all-weather courts, and five indoor courts. Participants are divided by ability into groups of four for five hours of daily instruction. Juice and fruit are served during breaks. Programs last from two to seven days; all include at least one private lesson.

Forty-three guest rooms in renovated buildings have air conditioning and private bathrooms. Most rooms have terraces and mountain views.

The congenial Main Lodge features fireplaces in the reception area, living room and library, dining, TV/movie and card rooms, and fabulous views. A sociable cocktail hour precedes dinner on Wednesday and Saturday. A newly constructed day spa offers massage therapy rooms and a hot tub—nice for soothing aching muscles.

A swimming pool cools guests in summer, and in winter, a golf club ¼ mile down the road provides change-of-pace cross-country skiing for those who bring along their skis. For those who still have energy when the clinics end at 4:00 P.M., Saugerties is an antiquing center, and 10 miles away a host of shops beckon in charming Woodstock.

COMMENTS **Male, 30s:** *You have to work to get the most from this, but being serious about a game is an escape. Though hours of instruction seems like hard work, the atmosphere is friendly, and everyone has fun. Evenings can be social but are usually laid-back and quiet. There is a wide range of ages, with most people in their 20s and 30s and others up to their 60s. There are always many singles, a good mix of men and women, and no one has to worry about finding people at compatible levels of play.*
Female, 30s: *Low-key, friendly, and open. Good instruction. I felt perfectly comfortable alone.*

SWARTHMORE TENNIS CAMP

Swarthmore College, 500 College Avenue, Swarthmore, PA 19081; c/o 444 East 82nd Street, Suite 31D, New York, NY 10028; (212) 879-0225 or (800) 223-2442; www.swarthmoretenniscamp.com (I–M)

Years in business:	Since 1980
Age range:	30–65
Most common age:	35–45
Percent alone:	80
Number of participants:	24 per week
Male/female ratio:	50/50
Late June to mid-August; no single supplement in dorm lodging	

Held on the manicured acres of Swarthmore College, 12 miles from Philadelphia, this summer program attracts many singles. Five-day clinics include five hours of instruction (with a 4:1 student-to-instructor ratio) and one to three half-hour private lessons, depending on the length of the stay. Twelve outdoor courts and six indoor courts ensure ample space for instruction. Best bets for singles are the hotel-type accommodations in Strathaven, where guests have all their meals together on campus, or Ashton House, a Victorian B&B where those who pay a modest upgrade supplement receive breakfast and lunch, but are on their own for dinner. Strathaven has an outdoor pool, and everyone has the use of the school's indoor pool and Nautilus equipment. In addition to one-week programs, three-day clinics from Tuesday to Friday or Thursday to Sunday are available.

COMMENTS **Female, 50s:** *I've gone for four successive summers and plan to go back. I choose the singles weeks since more people come alone. It is very relaxed, and there's a variety of people, from early 20s to 70s, about evenly divided between male and female, and backgrounds vary from a housewife to an ex-marine. You can be alone if you want, but someone is always looking for company for dinner or a movie. The staff really goes out of its way to make everyone comfortable, and they are good about getting people together. They suggest places to eat and often go along.* **Male, 30s:** *The instruction is terrific, and you get a lot of tennis—six hours a day. I don't play regularly, and I liked this because there was enough playing time to re-inforce what we were learning. My game improved a lot. There was a wide mix in ages, 20s to 60s, a good mix of men and women. Most of the other people were ei-ther couples or friends who came together, but it was very easy being alone because every day had a focus. The instructors were enthusiastic and helpful and very socia-ble. On Saturday night a whole group, including the instructors, went into Philadelphia for dinner. It was a very good experience.*

NIKE AMHERST TENNIS CAMP
Amherst College, Amherst, MA
c/o U.S. Sports Camps, Inc., 4470 Redwood Highway, San Rafael, CA 94903;
(800) NIKE CAMP;
www.ussportscamps.com (I–M)

Years in business:	Since 1972
Age range:	20–70
Most common age:	mid-30s
Percent alone:	50
Number of participants:	50 per week
Male/female ratio:	50/50
Early June to mid-August; one singles week each month	

Serious tennis in sociable surroundings marks this pioneer program, the first tennis camp in the Northeast. Amherst is hard to beat for value, friendliness, and the quality of instruction. This is a demanding program—five hours on the court each day, plus private lesson time and lots of free play. But the setting on a beautiful old college campus and the set-up, with everyone dining to-gether at long tables, makes for easy camaraderie. There's something going on every night, from round-robins to lectures to informal gatherings at a local pub. Another big bonus: Double and single dorm rooms are clustered around a sitting area, and there's no extra charge for single rooms! One week each month is des-ignated for singles.

Adults play on six clay and fourteen hard courts (juniors have their own upper complex) and have the use of three indoor courts at Amherst and eight more available at neighboring schools Smith, Holyoke, and Hotchkiss. Full and weekend programs are available. For those who have extra energy, the college athletic center is available with an indoor lap pool, running track, and well-equipped fitness center, and there are nature and bike trails and a local golf course nearby. The most telling statistic: Nearly half of the attendees are return visitors.

Amherst is one of a host of Nike adult tennis camps held around the country, both in school settings and at resorts, under the auspices of U.S. Sports Camps. Campus locations include the University of Illinois, the University of California at Santa Cruz, Michigan State University, Stanford University, and Lawrenceville School in New Jersey. Resort locations include the Trail Racquet Club in Florida; Eagle Crest Resort in Oregon; Lake Tahoe, California; and The Boulders in Colorado. For more information, write to U.S. Sports Camps, 4470 Redwood Highway, San Rafael, CA 94903, phone (800) 645–3226, or go to www.ussports camps.com.

SWEET BRIAR COLLEGE/VAN DER MEER TENNIS
Route 29, Sweet Briar, VA 24595;
(800) 845–6138;
www.vandermeertennis.com (I)
June–August

Another college campus option, this well-established program begun in 1979 is run by Dennis Van der Meer, a pro well known for his year-round tennis academy in Hilton Head, South Carolina. Because it offers group meals, this is a more sociable choice for singles. The scenic campus 15 miles north of Lynchburg, Virginia, is set on 3,300 acres in the Blue Ridge Mountain foothills and offers fourteen hard courts, four with lights, and three grass courts, plus a gym, two lakes, an olympic-size indoor pool, and trails for walking, hiking, or jogging. Campers stay in air-conditioned dorms and dine on better-than-average cafeteria food. The demanding program has campers on court for five to six hours daily. Adult sessions typically draw thirty to forty campers. There is also a large junior camp on campus.

Van der Meer has newer summer adult campus programs in Pennsylvania at Mercersburg Academy, and the Westtown School outside Philadelphia.

TOPNOTCH AT STOWE RESORT AND SPA

4000 Mountain Road, P.O. Box 1458,
Stowe, VT 05672;
(802) 253–8585 or (800) 451–8686;
www.topnotch-resort.com
two-hour program (M)
four-hour program (E, no meals)

Years in business:	25+
Age range:	35–65
Most common age:	35–65
Percent alone:	Varies
Number of participants:	Varies
Male/female ratio:	Varies
Year-round	

Topnotch is exactly that: a beautiful setting in the Green Mountains and a first-class resort offering horseback riding, mountain biking, indoor and outdoor pools, and a lovely spa as well as tennis. A tennis-spa package is available. The Tennis Academy is consistently rated among the top in the Northeast by tennis magazines. The outdoor courts are supplemented by four all-weather indoor courts, allowing for a year-round program.

Topnotch no longer holds a regular organized tennis week like the one I attended, although a few camp sessions are offered; check the Web site for details and dates. Though there is a minimum stay of three days, you can begin on any day, and the participants will vary from day to day, even during singles weeks. Programs last three hours on the courts, and everyone gets a half-hour private lesson for every three-day stay.

COMMENTS E.B.: *Topnotch has been doing this for a long time, and they do it very well. Be prepared for a lot of tennis, even if you choose just two hours of instruction. What with playing with fellow campers in the afternoon, practicing my serve, working on strokes with the ball machine, and taking part in friendly tournaments, four hours of tennis was the average every day.*

But our group was on its own after the day's lessons ended, and many couples chose to eat at area restaurants rather than in the dining room. It was harder getting to know people well than if one were in a group that shares meals. A social singles week is a better choice. During those weeks, everyone gathers for cocktails late in the day and almost naturally stays together for dinner with planned activities at night. There is no predicting male/female ratio. Some groups have even had the unusual problem of too many men!

Female, 20s: *The social week was very congenial, with an equal number of men and women. Ages were from early 20s to late 40s. We all went out to dinner and the bars together. The program was very well run. The people were interesting, from all over the United States and Canada. The accommodations were wonderful.*

Male, 30s: *The tennis program is staffed by pros of exceptional ability in tennis and also in dealing with people. To a man, they are polite, supportive, and lots of fun to be with. Their acute observations of my strokes and personalized attention were much appreciated. What is so nice is that after a very short time at Topnotch, you feel you really know the pros and other players.*

JOHN NEWCOMBE TENNIS RANCH

P.O. Box 310469, New Braunfels, TX 78131;
(830) 625-9105 or (800) 444-6204;
www.newktennis.com (M–E)

Years in business:	30+
Age range:	30–60s
Most common age:	Varies each week
Percent alone:	20
Number of participants:	Maximum of 80
Male/female ratio:	30/70
Year-round weekly and weekend programs	

Australian John Newcombe, former U.S. Open and Wimbledon champion, believes that tennis should be fun. When "Newk" and his partners converted this former dude ranch in the Texas hill country, the program they created reflected his philosophy of good tennis and good times. The ambience is informal and friendly, and the excellent facilities include twenty-four outdoor courts, four of which are clay, and four indoor courts.

The program begins with tips from the various pros. Then come two and a half hours of drill work on the courts, developing shot techniques, reflexes, concentration, and conditioning. Video replays and a roving coach reinforce the teaching. Each group of four moves from court to court and from pro to pro.

If you choose the intensive program, afternoon brings more drills, strategy sessions, and supervised match play. Otherwise you can relax at the pool or in the Jacuzzi. Late day brings a sociable doubles round-robin.

Good food and lots of it is one of the big attractions here. Accommodations are in courtside condominiums, rustic casitas, or cottages. Unfortunately, there is no matching program, so there is no way around a single supplement—possibly the reason why singles are in the minority. Given the Texas climate, the best times to come are spring and fall. Avoid school vacation weeks, when the resort fills up with families.

RAMEY TENNIS SCHOOL

5931 Highway 56, Owensboro, KY 42301;
(501) 771-4723; www.rameycamps.com
Two-, three-, and five-day programs (I–M)

Years in business:	30+
Age range:	19–70
Most common age:	35–55
Percent alone:	75
Number of participants:	21
Male/female ratio:	Varies
Year-round, week-long, and weekend programs; will try to arrange shares	

This "total immersion" program, located in a pleasant country setting among farms and orchards, is geared to high achievers, with the day planned from 9:00 A.M. to 9:00 P.M. Tennis takes up to six hours daily or can be extended for diehards. Strategy sessions, stroke presentations, tennis videos, and plenty of instruction are on the full agenda. Four campers work with one pro and also get to work individually with director Joan Ramey, a U.S. Professional Tennis Association Master Professional. Campers are housed in cottages or in nearby motels. Facilities include three indoor and three outdoor tennis courts, an outdoor pool, a Nautilus fitness room, sauna, and racquetball courts. A masseuse can be arranged to ease tired muscles. Horseback instruction is available at the Ramey Equestrian School.

COMMENTS **Male, 40s:** *The ages varied from teens to 50s; people were mainly from the Midwest. You naturally get to know people, especially those in your tennis group, but we all ate meals as a group, making it even easier. Food was excellent, the accommodations fine, the program well run. It was a great experience.*
Male, 40s: *There were some singles, but mostly couples or two friends who came together. But I was alone, and I didn't feel lonely. It was easy to meet people, even though I stayed at a motel in town, because we all ate together. The food was the high point of the trip. I was very impressed also by the structure of the lessons. We worked for eight hours a day, but it was spaced so that you didn't get worn out.*

NEW ENGLAND TENNIS HOLIDAYS

P.O. Box 1648, North Conway, NH 03850; (800) 869-0949; www.netennisholidays.com (M–E)

Years in business:	Since 1987
Age ranges:	20s–70s
Most common age:	40
Percent alone:	Over 50
Number of participants:	up to 24; 10–15 on average
Male/female ratio:	Roughly 50/50
May through September	

The Cranmore ski area in North Conway, New Hampshire, is the summer headquarters for this program. Participants are housed in inns or condos near the mountain, many with pools and other amenities. Breakfast is at the lodging, lunch at the courts; the group goes out together for meals in area restaurants.

Players are evaluated, divided by ability into groups of four for instruction on all types of strokes, and taught singles and doubles strategies. Videos of each individual on the court help reinforce instruction. Indoor courts ensure play, rain or shine. *Tennis Magazine* rates this program highly.

KILLINGTON TENNIS AT CORTINA INN AND RESORT

Cortina Inn, Route 4, Killington, VT 05751;
(802) 773-3331 or (800) 451-6108; www.killingtontennis.com
Late May–late September
Full-day (E); half-day (M)

This is a program initiated in 1998, when the old Killington School for Tennis moved off the mountain. Packages at the Cortina Inn include meals and evening activities. The comfortable, contemporary ninety-six-room inn also has sociable lounges for mingling—including the Centre Court Library, where afternoon refreshments are served—making this a good choice for singles who like inn ambience with their tennis.

Half-day and full-day instruction is offered on eight clay courts, with videotaping and private lessons included in tennis packages. Instruction places special emphasis on teaching ball control using top spin, aiming to give you a "secret weapon" on the court. A unique feature is station training. An instructor is positioned at every court, each one focusing on a different stroke or drill. You choose the aspects of your game that need practice and work as long as you like—or move from court to court for an overall workout.

The inn also offers an indoor pool and whirlpool, saunas, a fitness center, and hiking trails from the property. Golf and fly-fishing schools are available, as well.

GARDINER'S RESORT

P.O. Box 228, Carmel Valley, CA 93924;
(408) 659–2207; www.gardiners-resort.com (EE)

The number of solo participants is small, but this facility, formerly known as John Gardiner's Tennis Ranch, deserves mention as it is the ultimate luxury in tennis programs. Gardiner was a pioneer in offering instruction when he began the camp in 1957. Since his death in 2000 at age 92, his wife, Monique, and the staff have continued his traditions. Clinics with a 4:1 pro to student ratio have three-hour instructional sessions in the morning, followed by two hours of drills and matches in the afternoon. Whether participants stay in one of six individual guest rooms or one of five two-bedroom homes, each accommodation comes with a private patio and fireplace. A sauna, Jacuzzi, and massages are available in the new fitness center. Three gourmet meals are part of the tennis package, including buffet-style poolside lunch and a five-course dinner. Since there are no tables for two, it is easy to get to know other guests. They may range from Texas ranchers to feminist lawyers, but all tend to be interesting and well-heeled people.

INN AT MANITOU

McKellar, Ontario, Canada POG ICO;
(705) 389–2171 or (800) 571-8818;
www.manitou-online.com (EE)
Early May to mid-October

This is another luxurious tennis vacation possibility, a cozy inn on a beautiful lake 150 miles north of Toronto, surrounded by forest and rocky shoreline. The tennis-minded inn has a dozen hard and clay courts and one indoor court for just thirty-five rooms. Popular three-, four- and seven-day tennis clinics for all abilities offer three hours of excellent instruction each day; afternoons are open for play, which sometimes means doubles with the pros or a round-robin match. The pros give exhibitions before dinner most evenings.

Spacious rooms come with fireplaces, terraces, and whirlpool tubs, and some have private saunas. Rates include three sumptuous meals a day, plus daily afternoon tea, and you can have breakfast or dinner delivered to your room. Juice and coffee are placed outside the door early every morning, one of the many amenities that have earned the inn membership in the prestigious Relais and Chateaux group of hotels. Because exchange rates with Canada are favorable for Americans at present, the rates are not quite as steep as they might otherwise be. Other facilities include a spa and a golf teaching academy.

The inn is a favorite of tennis guru Roger Cox, who rates it among his top choices for solo travelers.

GUNTERMAN TENNIS SCHOOLS

P.O. Box 1633, Manchester Center, VT 05255;
(800) 426–3930 or (802) 867–0382
P.O. Box 300, Amelia Island, FL 32035; (888) 261–6161; www.greattennis.com (M)

Kelly Gunterman, who taught for many years with John Newcombe, has had his own program at Stratton Mountain Resort in southern Vermont since 1991, held from May through October. He also conducts clinics almost year-round at Amelia Island Resort Plantation in Florida. Gunterman offers an intensive five-hour-a-day program as well as a three-hour morning choice midweek to allow for enjoying the resorts and nearby attractions. He teaches basics as well as advanced techniques and uses a lot of videotaping to help students see their mistakes and improve. Tennis guru Roger Cox says that Gunterman has a relaxed approach that makes his school fun and a popular choice, especially in Vermont, where he may draw as many as twenty campers during the week and nearly thirty on some weekends. However, Cox cautions that this is a school recommended for the quality of instruction, but with a caveat for solo travelers. These are spread-out resorts with a range of lodgings, and there is no central location for getting together. And most people tend to come with a companion. That said, the locations are appealing and the program does include lunch and usually one cocktail get-together, which allows for socializing and hopefully making plans to meet other participants for dinner.

Other resorts with large tennis instructional programs include:

THE BROADMOOR, 1 Lake Circle, Colorado Springs, CO 80901; (719) 634–7711 or (800) 634–7711.

NAPLES BATH AND TENNIS CLUB, 4995 Airport Road North, Naples, FL 33942; (813) 261–5777 or (800) 225–9692.

HOPMAN TENNIS PROGRAM, Saddlebrook Resort, 5700 Saddlebrook Way, Wesley Chapel, FL 33543 (near Tampa); (813) 973–1111 or (800) 729–8383.

COLONY BEACH AND TENNIS RESORT, 1620 Gulf of Mexico Drive, Longboat Key, FL 34228; (941) 383–6464 or (800) 282–1138.

BOCA RATON TENNIS CENTER, Boca Raton Resort and Club, 501 East Camino Real, Boca Raton, FL 33432; (561) 447–3000 or (888) 498–BOCA.

THE POINTE SOUTH MOUNTAIN RESORT, 777 South Pointe Parkway, Phoenix, AZ 85044; (602) 438–9000 or (877) 800–4888.

LITCHFIELD BEACH RESORT, P.O. Drawer 320, Pawleys Island, SC 29585; (843) 237–3000 or (888) 766–4633.

WINTERGREEN RESORT, P.O. Box 706, Wintergreen, VA 22958; (434) 325–2200 or (800) 266–2444.

For further listings of tennis schools, consult the following resources:

TENNIS MAGAZINE, 810 Seventh Avenue, New York, NY, 10019; (212) 636–2700. Prints an annual listing of tennis camps and clinics usually in a spring issue. www.tennisresortonline.com. Also see www.tennis.shawguides.com.

Golf

Golf schools based at top resorts give single vacationers a focus to the day and a way to meet people, as well as the chance to improve their game. With locations from coast to coast, they provide opportunities for a comfortable resort vacation year-round.

There are dozens of programs at resorts throughout the country. Those listed here have a long history. An excellent source of additional recommendations is the current "Top 25" list published by *Golf Magazine*. It can be found on their Web site, www.golfonline.com/instruction/schools.

THE ORIGINAL GOLF SCHOOL

Mount Snow Resort, Mount Snow, VT 05356;
(802) 464–7788 or (800) 240–2555;
www.thegolfschool.com (E)

Years in business:	Since 1978
Age range:	12–80
Most common age:	35–55
Percent alone:	25–30
Number of participants:	25–50
Male/female ratio:	60/40
Offered year-round; suitable for beginners; offers singles weeks	

This popular school is at home at the Mount Snow Golf Club in Vermont from May through September, and also hosts programs at Sugarloaf/USA in Maine in summer and fall and at the Plantation Inn and Golf Resort in Crystal River, Florida, October through May. All locations offer a low teaching ratio—four students per instructor—and instruction that ranges from fundamentals for beginners to fine nuances for the experts. Videotape plus other training aids and classroom instruction are part of the two- to five-day programs offered. Special offerings include women's and spa programs and four "singles-themed" weekends at the beginning of the month, June to September. Balls and clubs are available, so beginners don't have to worry about equipment.

COMMENTS **Female, 40s:** *A special effort is made to make single people feel comfortable, with a get-together party to help you meet people. There were many more single males than females! The small teaching groups mean you get to know people well. A good learning experience, a lot of golf, and a lot of fun.*

GOLF DIGEST SCHOOLS

5520 Park Avenue, Box 395, Trumbull, CT 06611;
(800) 243-6121; www.golfdigestschool.com (EE)

Years in business:	Since 1971
Age range:	25–65
Most common age:	Over 35
Percent alone:	50
Number of participants:	4–12
Male/female ratio:	Varies, but more men

Offered year-round; suitable for beginners; single supplement charged

Schools at resorts around the country operate under the auspices of this golfing magazine. Many top pros are teachers, and instruction is geared to every level from beginner to advanced. Classes are held at the practice tee, the practice bunker, and the putting green. Videotapes are also used. The welcoming cocktail reception and dinner with instructors is a good chance to meet other participants. Among the locations are top resorts in Scottsdale and Tucson, Arizona; Lake Tahoe and Rancho Mirage, California; Las Vegas, Nevada; Palm Beach Gardens, Florida; San Antonio, Texas; Lenox, Massachusetts; and White Sulphur Springs, West Virginia.

COMMENTS **Female, 40s:** *I've attended two schools, with very different lodgings—villas at one, a lodge at another, but both were quite comfortable. Generally there are couples and men alone; women are in the minority. You all start as strangers, then quickly become friendly. Many people get together for dinner. I never ate alone. Ages were from 20s to 70s; the larger group is divided into smaller sections, and you get to know your own group very well.*

CRAFT-ZAVICHAS GOLF SCHOOL

600 Dittmer, Pueblo, CO 81005;
(719) 564-4449 or (800) 858-9633;
www.czgolfschool.com (E–EE)

Years in business:	Since 1968
Age range:	30 and up
Most common age:	55
Percent alone:	30
Number of participants:	15–20
Male/female ratio:	30/70

Year-round; suitable for beginners; will try to arrange shares

The second-oldest golf school in the country holds two- to four-day clinics at Sun River Golf Club in St. George, Utah, and at the Walking Stick Golf Course in Pueblo, Colorado. Groups are divided into classes with a ratio of one pro for every three golfers, with male instructors for the men and female instructors for the women. Instruction takes place in the morning, and course play with the instructors in the afternoon. The atmosphere is friendly, with many meals planned with students and instructors in attendance. The program has been included in a *Golf Magazine* listing of America's top twenty-five golf schools for six years in a row.

COMMENTS **Male, 60s:** *I went alone, and it was fine, though there were hardly any other singles. There are many couples where only one plays golf, so it works out. The people were from all over the United States and about evenly divided between males and females. The program was well organized, with good instruction. Classes are small. The days are full, and I was too tired to worry about doing anything at night. They do a great job.*
Female, 40s: *I've been there twice, first alone and I came back with my sister. About one-third of the people come by themselves. The staff was excellent—I dropped my handicap by seven strokes after my first time there. You get lots of individual attention. The staff really concentrates on you and your game. It's pretty easy to meet people. You all wear name tags, and you meet lots of people at meals. Many people return—over half the people there had been before. I highly recommend the women-only classes—especially to women going alone—since there is no distraction so you concentrate on your golf, which is what you're there to do.*

JOHN JACOBS' GOLF SCHOOLS

7825 East Redfield Road, Scottsdale, AZ 85260;
(480) 991–8587 or (800) 472–5007;
www.jacobsgolf.com
(M–EE; cost varies with the resort chosen)

Years in business:	Since 1971
Age range:	20–70
Most common age:	40–55
Percent alone:	20
Number of participants:	Varies
Male/female ratio:	60/40
Offered year-round; guaranteed shares if requested thirty-one days in advance	

A long-established program that graduates more than 16,000 students annually, the John Jacobs' Golf Schools are found in more than forty locations from Hershey, Pennsylvania, to Napa, California. One- to five-day sessions include a comprehensive teaching program. Longer sessions have opening and closing dinner parties with instructors and classmates. Another "top twenty-five" pick.

For additional golf school possibilities, see the following:

www.shawguides.com, A comprehensive, up-to-date guide to over 600 golf schools and camps worldwide.

Golf Digest Magazine, 5520 Park Avenue, Trumbull, CT 06611; (203) 373–7000; www.golfdigest.com.

Golf Magazine, 2 Park Avenue, New York, NY 10016; (212) 779–5000; www.golfonline.com.

Horseback Riding

Horseback Riding, Western Style

Why don't more single people go to ranches? It's hard to imagine a more informal, relaxing vacation. Everybody is in jeans; nobody puts on airs; "dudes" come from all over the country and are all ages. This is a favorite family vacation, but while solo guests are few, ranches are the best examples I know of why an easy ambience, family-style meals, and a common pursuit are more important for a good vacation than the presence of lots of "singles." I've not met anyone who went to a ranch alone who did not report having a wonderful time.

Besides riding, many ranches offer activities such as river-rafting, short pack trips, and hiking. They are the perfect introduction to the panoramas and pleasures of the American West.

Ranches vary in ambience, but the routines at most of them are similar. Guests mount up the first day so that the wranglers can judge their ability. Beginners get instructions in starting, stopping, turning, and getting to know a horse. Your horse is assigned according to your ability to ride. Each day adult rides are offered morning and afternoon for both beginners and advanced riders.

Since many people arrive with little or no riding experience, lessons also are offered every day to help you sit tall in the saddle. Some wind up the week galloping across the meadows; others are content to stay with the "slow ride" each day, a trek into the wilderness that is no less beautiful when the horses move at a reassuring, steady walk.

Evenings bring informal group activities from nature talks and slides to square dancing. Sometimes there is a trip to a nearby rodeo.

If you want to avoid the family scene, come in spring or fall, when school is in session.

I've visited two very different kinds of ranches, both places that I would recommend to anyone who loves the outdoors and wants to learn to ride.

TANQUE VERDE RANCH

14301 East Speedway, Tucson, AZ 85748;
(520) 296–6275 or (800) 234–DUDE; www.tanqueverderanch.com (E–EE)

In a sublime setting 2,800 feet high in the foothills of three mountain ranges, Tanque Verde Ranch sits amidst millions of acres of national forest and adjoins the Saguaro National Park, a veritable forest of giant cactus. Guests ride over silent, open desert, up rocky canyons, and into towering mountains. The food is plentiful and delicious, especially cookouts over a mesquite fire; almost every belt was out at least a notch by the end of the week. A tradition here is the early morning ride where a chuck-wagon breakfast of eggs and pancakes awaits in the desert, served up against a backdrop of cactus haloed by the glow of the morning sun.

The main building of the ranch is historic, dating to the 1860s, but the seventy-four air-conditioned rooms in modern casitas are downright luxurious. The ranch has Arizona's largest riding stable, with more than 140 mounts. Five tennis courts, indoor and outdoor pools, saunas, whirlpools, and a workout room are available when you are not in the saddle. Nature programs, guided hikes, mountain biking, fishing, and walks are added features for those who are interested.

Despite the comparatively large number of guests here, singles need not feel left out. As the brochure says, "It's easy to be alone, but hard to feel lonely." I met a friendly couple in the van from the airport who invited me to their table at dinner that night, and I never lacked for company the rest of the week. Meals are family style, so each day was an opportunity to meet more people. The other two singles in residence during my stay were a male visitor from Japan, about age 35, and a woman in her 60s.

COMMENTS **Female, 30s:** *I've been there ten times, three or four times alone, and I'd tell anyone to come alone. It's very comfortable, the kind of place where you can feel really safe, relax, and have fun. No one is looking at you because you're there by yourself. I made friends quickly each time, and I got to know the staff, too—they were always good for conversation and companionship. There's always something going on, so you can be alone or with people whenever you want. It is evenly split between men and women, but not many men by themselves. The food is great and plentiful. They have a new chef, and the menu is lighter now, more health oriented.*

Female, 40s: *I first went here with my husband and kids, then was divorced, and I've gone alone for the past four years. There are very few singles, but it's very easy to meet people, starting at meals, which are served family style at tables for ten. A separate kids' program for much of the day means you aren't surrounded by children even though many families do come. I love the fact that it is so quiet, that you can be alone or with people as you choose. I'm planning to go back next year!*

VISTA VERDE RANCH
P.O. Box 770465, Steamboat Springs, CO 80477;
(970) 879–3858 or (800) 526–7433; www.vistaverde.com (EE)

This is an equally stupendous setting in the high meadows north of Steamboat Springs. At 7,800 feet, surrounded by national forest and wilderness areas and the 12,000-foot peaks of the Rockies, the air is crystal clear and the views glorious. Though food and accommodations are upscale and amenities include private hot tubs, a sauna, and fitness equipment, this is a working ranch, with cattle, plenty of farm animals, and its own stable of more than seventy horses. With a maximum of forty guests and a friendly staff, making friends was a snap. Besides enjoying riding, eating, and evening entertainment together, guests share adventures such as white-water rafting trips, hot-air balloon rides, hiking, kayaking, mountain biking, and rock climbing. If you don't feel at home and don't know everyone well by the time the week is over, it's your own fault. Special weeks in early June and after Labor Day featuring cattle drives and fly-fishing are especially recommended for single guests, and the hiking is superb in early June, when wildflowers and waterfalls abound. September, when the kids are back in school, is an excellent time for solo travelers. The owners tell me that they had ten singles one week last September. The ranch is also a popular haven for cross-country skiers in winter.

At both ranches, the guests were well educated, interesting, and went out of their way to include someone who was alone.

COMMENTS **Female, 30s:** *I've been there six times total, with someone and on the cattle drive alone. There aren't many singles—on all my trips I've encountered only two other singles—one male in his 40s and one woman on the cattle drive with me. But it was nice to go alone because it seems like they pay more attention to you to make sure you're having a good time. The staff treated me like family—they were very welcoming and took care of me. It's a great experience that I'd recommend to anyone.*

How to Choose a Ranch

There are enough ranches out West to fill a separate book, and because none attracts a large number of single guests, the best bet is to get a comprehensive listing, narrow the choices by location, and write for brochures. The first determining factor will be price, since ranches can range from $600 to $2,000 a week and from five-star to pure rustic. When you have a few possibilities in mind, call them directly. You'll get a good idea of the flavor of the place just from the way you are received on the telephone. Here are a few considerations you should learn from the brochure or the owner:

- Emphasis: Are single adults welcome? How many came last year? Do more come at certain times of year?
- Rates: Many ranches give a break to single adults with only a modest added supplement.
- Location: To experience the true beauty of the West, pick a ranch with mountain views and access to rides in the wilderness. If you are traveling alone, you may prefer a ranch that provides transportation services or that is easy for you to reach from a major airport.
- Size: Outgoing people will do fine almost anywhere, but on the whole, it is easier to meet people at a smaller ranch.
- Ambience: Is this an authentic working ranch or a resort? Are accommodations modern or rustic?
- Amenities: If you are a new rider, chances are you will soon be a "tender-seat." You may welcome facilities such as whirlpools or the ministrations of a masseuse on the premises—services that can be found even on working ranches these days.
- Facilities: Do you care about a pool or tennis courts in addition to riding? If so, check whether they are available.
- Activities: Are there options beyond the ranch itself—trips to the rodeo, rafting expeditions, fishing, et cetera? Is there an evening program?
- Staff: What is the ratio of staff to guests? Who gives the riding instruction? How much teaching experience do they have?
- Horses: Are there more horses than guests? Will you be assigned the same horse each day?
- References: Every ranch should be able to provide you with the names of guests who have visited recently. Call them before you decide where to go.

LAZY HILLS GUEST RANCH

Box G, Ingram, TX 78025; (830) 367–5600 or
(800) 880–0632; www.lazyhills.com (I)
Will try to arrange shares

In business for more than forty years, this is a family-owned, working ranch in beautiful country, a good choice for those who want to sample Texas-style ranching. Besides riding, the ranch offers swimming, tennis, basketball, volleyball, hiking, fishing, hayrides, cookouts, and a hot tub to soak away any aches or pains. Owners say that it is a good choice for singles, even though they are few in number, because they are included when they want to be, yet are not pressured to participate in activities.

COMMENTS **Female, 30s:** *I've gone a number of times, alone and with my son. It is a working ranch with trail rides, tennis, a pool, a lovely environment. Meals are served family style, so you get to know everyone. Guests come from all over the world and range in age from 20s to 90s. There have been a number of single people on my visits, more women than men.*
Female, 40s: *There were few other singles, but I had a wonderful time. It was easy to be there solo because the owners made sure I was never by myself if I didn't want to be. The area is very beautiful and peaceful. The hayrides were absolutely wonderful. I would recommend this place to anyone.*

Here are sources that can supply ranch listings; some can also offer advice on selection:

COLORADO DUDE AND GUEST RANCH ASSOCIATION

P.O. Box 2120, Granby, CO 80446; (970) 887–3128; www.coloradoranch.com.
Publishes free annual state directory and offers guidance.

THE DUDE RANCHERS ASSOCIATION

P.O. Box 2307, Cody, WY 82414; (307) 587–2339; www.duderanch.org.
Publishes annual directory including over one hundred ranches in twelve states and two Canadian provinces. The association will give advice on choosing a ranch.

GORPTRAVEL.COM

An online resource with links to dozens of ranches throughout the western United States.

ARIZONA DUDE RANCH ASSOCIATION

P.O. Box 603, Cortaro, AZ 85652; www.azdra.com.
Offers a pamphlet on state ranches.

TRAVEL MONTANA

P.O. Box 200533, Helena, MT 59620; (800) 847–4868; www.visitmt.com.
Lists all Montana ranches under "Lodging" with links to individual sites.

WYOMING DUDE RANCH ASSOCIATION

P.O. Box 618, Dubois, WY 83513;
(307) 455–2084; www.wyomingdra.com.
Offers free brochure and links to individual ranches on the Web.

For more information on individual ranches in the West, consult Gene Kilgore's Ranch Vacations, *Avalon Travel Publishing; find information online at www.ranchweb.com.*

Horseback Riding, Eastern Style

For Easterners who can't make the trip out West, here are a few places that teach riding in rustic, informal, and scenic surroundings:

ROCKING HORSE RANCH

Highland, NY 12528; (800) 647–2624 or (845) 691–2927; www.rhranch.com.

PINE GROVE RANCH

Lower Cherrytown Road, P.O. Box 209, Kerhonkson, NY 12446; (845) 626–7345
or (800) 926–6520; www.pinegrove-ranch.com.

ROARING BROOK RANCH & TENNIS RESORT

Lake George, NY 12845; (518) 668–5767 or (800) 882–7665;
www.roaringbrookranch.com.

Baseball

Every guy—or gal—who has ever fantasized about being a major leaguer can make the dream come true at one-week spring training camps where guests become the rookies and former greats of the sport turn coach. Said one participant, "You walk into the clubhouse, grab a cup of coffee, head for your locker, and get your freshly laundered uniform, with your name stitched on the shirt above your number. You look around and you see baseball stars, telling stories about the old days, and you're one of them . . . for one week, you're on the team." This participant, one of three women in the camp, not only got to play but actually got a hit in the final game, a thrill she will never forget.

Baseball camps, aptly named "Dream Weeks" by one promoter, attract as many nonathletes as aces. Nobody under age 30 is allowed. Campers are coached in every phase of the game by former greats. They get drafted for teams, play each other, and sometimes play the pros. Talk is centered on baseball—past, present, and future. Most participants haven't played ball for years—but they have a ball! Who comes to baseball camp? One recent roster included surgeons, lawyers, a dentist, a comic-book distributor, a real estate broker, a bartender, two mailmen, a plumber, and a congressional analyst.

The programs are basically alike, and most will try to arrange shares. All are in the EE price category, but participants find them a once-in-a-lifetime fantasy come true.

COMMENTS **Male, 40s:** *I've attended the Randy Hundley Cubs camp twice. I went alone and was placed with a roommate. You can't help meeting people. Most of the men were over 40, married but traveling on their own, and Cub fans from the Midwest. It is well run.*
Male, 30s: *I've been to baseball camp three times and I am going again. It is so easy to meet people—there is instant "team spirit." The men are mostly married, from 30 to 50; there were very few women. I had a great time each time and am looking forward to returning.*

Baseball camps for adults include:

ALL-STAR ADVENTURES, INC.
2500 East Hallandale Beach Boulevard, Suite #510, Hallandale Beach, FL 33009; (800) 847–2131 or (954) 454–6220; www.allstaradventures.com.
Dream weeks offered with the Florida Marlins, Texas Rangers, Atlanta Braves, Tampa Bay Buccaneers, and a week with the all-stars. The company also offers basketball and hockey dream weeks.

RANDY HUNDLEY'S FANTASY BASEBALL CAMPS, INC.
1935 South Plum Grove Road, #285, Palatine, IL 60067;

(847) 991–9595; www.cubsfantasycamp.com.
Nirvana for Chicago Cubs fans.

LOS ANGELES DODGERS ADULT BASEBALL CAMP
Box 2887, Vero Beach, FL 32961;
(772) 569–4900 or (800) 334–7529; www.ladabc.com.
Former stars from both Brooklyn and L.A. Dodgers take part.

NEW YORK YANKEES FANTASY CAMP
3102 North Himes Avenue, Tampa, FL 33207;
(800) 368–2267; www.yankeesfantasycamp.com.
A chance to mingle with Yankee greats.

*For a listing of other baseball fantasy camps, plus ratings, see www
.hihard1.com or type "baseball fantasy camps" into an Internet search
engine such as Google.*

Sailing

Attending sailing school is a wonderful combination of learning a skill and experiencing the exhilaration of being at sea. In a week you learn the ropes from port to starboard. You start on land, learning what to expect, then head on board with instructors. Pretty soon the crew mates are working as a team, beginning to speak the language of sailing, and getting to know their boat. Friendships come easy working in such close quarters toward a common goal. By the time the week is over, the crew is usually able to chart a course and set out on its own.

Sailing schools are a wonderful way for singles to visit the Caribbean, as well as scenic ports in the United States.

STEVE AND DORIS COLGATE'S OFFSHORE SAILING SCHOOL
16731 McGregor Boulevard, Fort Myers, FL 33908;
(888) 454–8002 or (239) 454–1700;
www.offshore-sailing.com (E–EE)
Three- to seven-day programs, special week for women

Years in business:	40+
Age range:	12–75
Most common age:	30s
Percent alone:	45
Number of participants:	90,000 graduates
Male/female ratio:	50/50
Year-round	

School locations: New York City; Jersey City, New Jersey; Newport, Rhode Island; Fort Myers and St. Petersburg, Florida; the Florida Keys; and Tortola in the

Caribbean. Will try to arrange shares—two per room in Tortola. Single supplement on live-aboard cruises is very small. Meals are included only while cruising.

The four-day "Learn to Sail" program for beginners is based at a resort and kicks off with an optional get-acquainted social. Days are divided into morning classes and afternoons on the water. No more than four students are assigned with an instructor to each Colgate 26 sailboat, and a real bond develops among them. Once the basics are mastered, students can increase their knowledge with more advanced sailing and cruising weeks. A special live-aboard cruising course combines curriculum with a thrilling one-week sail on a 40- to 50-foot boat in some of the world's ultimate sailing destinations—Tortola in the British Virgin Islands and Newport, Rhode Island, depending on the time of year. Graduates can become members of the Offshore Cruising Club, eligible to enjoy cruising vacations in more beautiful locales, and the Offshore Sailing Club, sailing regularly on club-owned boats at offshore branches.

COMMENTS **Female, 40s:** *My St. Lucia classmates, numbering just two, were also female—one slightly younger and one slightly older than me, one married and one divorced, all of us from different walks of life and enrolled for vastly different reasons. By the end of the week we enjoyed a very special breed of friendship based on a combination of shared apprehension, excitement, embarrassment, fear, joy, panic, and amazing mutual support.*
Male, 30s: *On the last day, like kids, you stay out past the allotted time until, finally, the instructor arrives in his launch to see you home. You wish you could spend a month of sailing days like these.*

ANNAPOLIS SAILING SCHOOL

601 Sixth Street, P.O. Box 3334, Annapolis, MD 21403; (800) 638-9192 or (410) 267-7205; www.annapolissailing.com (M–EE, depending on location; meals included only aboard ship)

The nation's largest sailing school boasts over 140,000 graduate sailors. Courses include two, three, or five days of classroom and on-board instruction and supervised sailing to reinforce new skills in a variety of sailing conditions. Once you've

Years in business:	Since 1959
Age range:	16 and up
Most common age:	25–35
Percent alone:	Varies
Number of participants:	3,000 annually
Male/female ratio:	Varies

Year-round; branch in St. Croix, U.S. Virgin Islands; seasonal locations in Annapolis, Maryland, and the Florida Keys; suitable for beginners; will try to arrange shares

mastered the basics, you can elect to continue with a five-day Cruising Course, a cruise vacation at sea that continues your instruction. Courses are also available in St. Croix in the U.S. Virgin Islands.

Package arrangements with nearby inns and hotels can be made by the school at each location.

COMMENTS **Female, 20s:** *I went alone on a two-day program and liked it so much I decided to work there. The age range is about 25 to 50, but most people are in their 20s and 30s and from the Northeast. There are a few couples and many singles, though many are groups of friends who come together.*
Male, 50s: *It was a very good experience. The instruction was excellent, and there was no problem being alone. I learned a lot and had fun, though I stayed in a hotel and there was no real socializing at night. Of nineteen people, there was one couple and all the rest were single. They were quite a diverse group of people, but mostly from the Northeast.*

Scuba Diving

More Americans every year are descending to discover the eerie beauty at the bottom of the sea. Recent statistics show that around 12 million people now have their diving certification, and with it a kinship that makes it easy to find friends on any diving vacation. If you want to join their numbers, the easiest way is to head for Club Med locations in the Bahamas; Sonora Bay, Mexico; or the Turks and Caicos Islands. Each has a dedicated dive center where you can learn and be certified. Many other Club Meds also offer lessons.

Or you can choose one of the great diving spots—Bonaire in the Dutch West Indies or the Cayman Islands—to gain your certification. For the most current list of courses available, as well as a selection of hotel brochures, contact the island tourist offices at the following addresses/telephones.

BONAIRE GOVERNMENT TOURIST OFFICE
10 Rockefeller Plaza, Suite 900, New York, NY 10020; (212) 956–5912
or (800) BONAIRE; www.infobonaire.com

Diving is what Bonaire is all about, and all major hotels have learning programs. The most luxurious accommodations are at the Harbour Village Beach Club, where there is a full-service health spa, and the Plaza Resort Bonaire. Both resorts have fully equipped dive shops offering a variety of courses. The most knowledgeable divers head for the renovated Habitat, originally run by Cap'n Don Stewart, an island legend. Ask the tourist office for dive package information.

CAYMAN ISLANDS DEPARTMENT OF TOURISM

Doral Centre, 8300 Northwest 53rd Street, Suite 103, Miami, FL 33126 (offices are also in Chicago, New York, Houston, and Toronto);
(305) 599–9033 or (800) 346–3313; www.divecayman.ky

Information packets from the Caymans include a long list of dive packages, many based at resorts and almost all including a certification course for beginners.

Fly-Fishing

Fly-fishing is a sport rapidly gaining fans for the challenge of learning to select and tie the right flies as bait and for the enjoyment of the serene beauty of fishing in remote trout streams.

ORVIS FLY-FISHING SCHOOLS

10 River Road, Manchester, VT 05254;
(802) 362–3622 or (800) 235–9763;
www.orvis.com
(I; does not include lodging)

This longtime sports outfitter offered the first organized fly-fishing school in the United States and still sets the standard as the sport grows in popularity. The instructors at the two-day and two-and-a-half-day courses are professionals who give a solid foundation that includes lessons on how to cast, how to make essential knots for tying on flies, how to select the right flies for the right fish, how to read a trout stream, how to wade a stream safely, how to manipulate the lines in tricky currents, and how to play, land, and release a fish. Classes are taught on casting ponds, in an indoor classroom, and on beautiful trout streams. Similar courses are offered in a number of locations, including Sandanona, New York; Cape Cod, Massachusetts; Homestead, Virginia; Coeur d'Alene, Idaho; Ridgedale, Missouri; Grand Traverse Bay, Michigan; Kohler, Wisconsin; and others. Participants make their own lodging arrangements.

Kayaking, Canoeing, and White-Water Rafting

Among the many appeals of these water sports is the opportunity to be out-doors on a river in some of America's most beautiful wilderness country. You can learn some of the necessary skills on a regular rafting trip, but these programs focus on instruction.

NANTAHALA OUTDOOR CENTER

13077 Highway 19, Bryson City, NC 28713; (800) 232–7238; www.noc.com (I–M)

Years in business:	30+
Age range:	8–80
Most common age:	20s, 50–65
Percent alone:	30–50
Number of participants:	Varies
Male/female ratio:	3/1
Year-round. Some classes are for parent-child and for women only. Lodgings are suggested, but participants do the booking on their own	

Located on a mountainside along the Nantahala River near Great Smoky Mountains National Park, this employee-owned center boasts many paddling champions and is a terrific place to learn water skills. *Esquire* magazine called the center "the Oxford of whitewater canoe schools." Courses in canoeing and kayaking run the gamut from beginner to expert, one day to one week. Participants in longer courses try several rivers. The student/teacher ratio is never more than 5:1.

In the evening, participants in multiday clinics gather for dinner and activities such as wine and cheese socials, movies, and bonfires—good places to meet and mingle.

Lodgings are in simple cabins. Reasonable packages include instruction, room, and meals. Restaurants include the River's End on the river and Relia's Garden up the hill, where the tasty, fresh-picked vegetables and herbs come from their own garden.

COMMENTS **Female, 30s:** *I've gone half a dozen times alone, and it was great every time. The program is terrific, the instructors world-class—and it's cheap! There are plenty of singles—in my last group, in fact, there was only one couple out of ten people. There are always more men, usually in their 30s and 40s. There is no social pressure; you eat as a group, and it's easy to get to know people. Cabins are lovely, with wooded views from the balcony. The food is very good, all natural and with homemade bread. I definitely recommend it.*

Male, 40s: *I've been on lots of kayaking trips, and I think this is the best instruction in the country. I've gone several times, alone and with a friend. You feel at home as soon as you get there. Most people come alone; the majority are from the East Coast, but more seem to be coming from all over. The age range is from 20s to 50s, about 2:1 male to female. The lodges have beautiful views; the food is so good they put out their own cookbook. And the instruction is great—five students to one instructor, and very patient, understanding teachers.*

DVORAK'S WHITEWATER PADDLING SEMINARS

17921 U.S. Highway 285, Nathrop, CO 81236;
(800) 824–3795 or (719) 539–6851;
www.dvorakexpeditions.com (I)

Years in business:	Since 1972
Age range:	10–70
Most common age:	20–55
Percent alone:	Majority
Number of participants:	3,200 yearly
Male/female ratio:	More males
Mid-March to October	

The first licensed outfitter in Colorado, this experienced company offers instructional seminars where students begin on flatwater to learn the basic strokes necessary to control a raft, canoe, or kayak, then move down the river to practice their skills in moving water. As skills sharpen, so does the challenge. Instruction varies from half-day sessions to twelve-day paddling trips. More Dvorak information and participants' comments are on page 110.

Downhill Skiing

Downhill skiing attracts everyone—singles, couples, families—because this is one sport everyone can enjoy. Each ski area has special runs designated as easy, intermediate, and expert. The lodge provides a place for everyone to come together at mealtimes and at day's end. Learning the sport is easier than ever with the popular "shaped" skis that make carving turns a snap. Almost every area has programs for the growing number of snowboard enthusiasts. Once you learn to ski or snowboard, you'll actually look forward to winter.

Of all the many types of sports schools available, ski schools are the easiest to find. Almost every slope has midweek five-day learn-to-ski packages at substantial savings over their weekend rates. The most comfortable way to approach this alone is to be part of a package plan by which the group will remain together for the five days; if you simply sign up for individual lessons, you may have different classmates and instructors each day and will have little opportunity to become friendly with those in your class. Ask in advance.

The entire ski-week group generally meets at a welcoming party on arrival, then is divided into smaller groups according to ability. There is the opportunity also for evening get-togethers for ski movies or entertainment. Ski lodges are friendly places anyway, albeit crowded, and it is easy to meet people naturally during the day, at lunch, or at the bar after skiing. Singles are also paired up with other singles in the lift line, though that could as likely mean a ten-year-old child as a possible dinner companion. It's all in the luck of the draw.

Lodgings can be informal meeting places as well, with guests gathering in front of the fire for drinks at the end of the day. If you are in your 20s or 30s, dorm-style accommodations are a good place to find other singles. Many ski area lodging offices will steer you to the right places if you ask. Avoid condominium accommodations if you are alone; they limit your sociability.

Several resorts—including Sun Valley, Idaho; Copper Mountain and Winter Park, Colorado; Northstar-at-Tahoe, California; and Whiteface/Lake Placid, New York—have recently offered special packages for singles. When you call the central reservations number at any resort, it pays to ask whether anything is currently available for solo skiers.

Cross-Country Skiing

Cross-country enthusiasts are growing, lured by the quiet and beauty of the snow-covered countryside and the lack of lift lines. Almost every major area today offers cross-country trails and instruction; a day or two of practice is all it takes to get started. Local chambers of commerce can point you to inns that have cross-country trails outside the door. But lessons won't necessarily guarantee company. If you are looking for a cross-country group, the best bet is to contact outdoor organizations such as the Appalachian Mountain Club or Colorado Mountain School (see the following pages) or check the winter offerings of outdoor trip organizers.

One location that may be of interest is Jackson, New Hampshire, a charming village in the White Mountains with several inns. The Jackson Ski Touring Foundation maintains over 154 kilometers of groomed trails that are among the best in the eastern United States. They conduct group tours every Friday afternoon, with guides who provide tips on technique. Afterward everyone gathers at the base lodge for wine and cheese by the fireplace. On Mondays skiers can meet with a local forest ranger to ski different trails, with wildlife commentary along the way. The Foundation also offers guided snowshoe tours on Saturdays. For more information, phone (603) 383–9355 or see their Web site, www.jacksonxc.org.

Outdoor Skills

The more comfortable and adept you are at outdoor activities, the more you will enjoy and appreciate the outdoors. This kind of enrichment is the goal of these multifaceted programs.

APPALACHIAN MOUNTAIN CLUB

5 Joy Street, Boston, MA 02108;
(617) 523–0655; www.outdoors.org (I)

Years in business:	125+
Age range:	Up to 85
Most common age:	28–55
Percent alone:	35
Number of participants:	90,000 members; groups are small, vary in size
Male/female ratio:	50/50
Year-round	

Founded in 1876, the Appalachian Mountain Club has twelve chapters throughout the Northeast and into the Mid-Atlantic. The organization has three goals: conservation, education, and recreation. A variety of weekend workshops for both beginners and advanced outdoor enthusiasts are held in four lodge locations. They include guided outings as well as the teaching of outdoor skills, with a strong emphasis on the enjoyment of nature. Among the workshop offerings are canoeing, mountain biking, fly fishing, camping, map and compass reading, nature studies, outdoor photography, ecology, hawk watching, and a host of winter programs including cross-country skiing, snowshoeing, and animal tracking. One of the most complete programs is at Pinkham Notch in Gorham, New Hampshire, in the heart of the White Mountains. The newest facility, the Highland Center at scenic Crawford Notch, New Hampshire, has monthly themes that expand the programs with topics such as Healthy Living and Lifestyles, including an introduction to yoga, and Mountain Cultures and Lifestyles around the World. Other lodges with teaching programs include the Cardigan Lodge in New Hampshire's Lakes Region and the Mohican Outdoor Center in Blairstown, New Jersey, along the Appalachian Trail in the Delaware Water Gap.

COMMENTS E.B.: *I'm a longtime AMC member. The lodges are not luxurious, but they are comfortable, the people are outgoing outdoors lovers of all ages, and the club and its program are tops. East Coast singles who love the outdoors should consider joining their local chapters for many congenial activities.*

Singles' Options

As a rule, more single skiers are found at the big, better-known resorts, such as Vail, Colorado, and Killington, Vermont.

*Solo skiers who want to travel with a group should check with Any Mountain Tours. Through **Club Any Mountain** the company offers escorted tours of a dozen ski areas in the western United States and Canada. You'll be with a hosted group of skiers and will be assigned a roommate to avoid single supplement charges. There is a $50 fee to guarantee a shared hotel room or condo match. Phone (888) 292–0200 or check www.clubany mountain.com for upcoming trip schedules.*

***Moguls Ski & Snowboard Tours** organizes an annual National Jewish Singles Ski Trip, a sociable way to visit major mountains. This group also holds women's programs, snowboard camps, and Ski Training vacations for skiers who want to upgrade their skills. Phone (800) 925–8914, ext. 117 or see www.moguls.com/njs for details.*

A well-established British tour operator found on the Internet, www.solosholidays.co.uk, offers trips for singles to Austria, France, Italy, Canada, and the Americas. Participants usually get single rooms with private baths. And O Solo Mio, a U.S. operator (listed on page 181), often schedules ski trips in winter.

Most major ski areas have discovered that females-only ski clinics are popular with women who would rather do their slipping and sliding without a male audience. Contact mountains directly for current schedules.

ADIRONDACK MOUNTAIN CLUB

814 Goggins Road, Lake George, NY 12845;
(800) 395–8080 or (518) 668–4447;
www.adk.org (I)

Years in business:	80+
Age range:	2–80
Most common age:	30–50
Percent alone:	30
Number of participants:	46 beds in lodge
Male/female ratio:	50/50
Year-round	

Educational workshops, field trips to see wildflowers or birds, guided hikes, and winter cross-country skiing are among the programs of this venerable club for outdoorsmen and nature lovers. Classes in outdoor skills include wilderness fishing, paddling, map and compass reading, introductory rock climbing, and basic canoeing and kayaking. There are also workshops in natural history. Accommodations are in the club's comfortable, rustic Adirondak Loj, in private rooms, or coed bunk rooms; family-style, home-cooked meals are served in the pine-paneled dining room.

COMMENTS **Male, 40s:** *There's lots of diversity because accommodations vary from a dorm for eighteen to family rooms for four to six to private rooms. People come from all over; about half are single, and men outnumber women. There are classes in kayaking and winter sports. A family atmosphere makes it easy to strike up conversations, and everyone is friendly. The staff is wonderful. This attracts outgoing, well-educated people and is great for singles who are into the outdoors.*

Mountain Climbing

Are you up for a challenge? Want to prove you can conquer a mountain? Mountain climbing school can teach you the techniques and the right equipment to get to the top!

COLORADO MOUNTAIN SCHOOL

P.O. Box 1846, 341 Moraine Avenue,
Estes Park, CO 80517;
(888) CMS-7783 or (970) 586-5758;
www.cmschool.com
(I; does not include lodging)

Years in business:	20+
Age range:	Wide
Most common age:	Late 20s–30s
Percent alone:	40
Number of participants:	4,000 annually
Male/female ratio:	3/1
Year-round	

Located in the shadow of Rocky Mountain National Park, this group offers three- to six-day Beginning Rock Camps as well as three-day weekends teaching the proper techniques for backpacking, mountaineering, and rock climbing. Longer stays have the advantage of time to hone your skills. Once you've learned the basics, there are intermediate and advanced camps as well as many guided climbs and mountain hikes, both in the Rockies and abroad. Lodging in Colorado is your choice of nearby motels or the dorm-style, inexpensive hostel in Estes Park, where there is plenty of company from other climbers and hikers. Meals are not included. In winter the emphasis shifts to skiing, mountaineering, and ice climbing, and once again there are programs for beginner to advanced.

The owners say: "Many people have met and become good friends through these courses and outings. In mountain travel, there is ample opportunity for a tremendous amount of honest, open discussion, and the mountain atmosphere encourages this. Our participants always exchange addresses, et cetera, at the end of trips and stay in contact with each other afterward."

COMMENTS **Female, 40s:** *I've been once, am going again. It was a lot of fun, there was a lot of instruction, and it was very good. All the participants were from Colorado, and most came alone. I signed up for a more difficult workshop, so there were few women. Ages were 25 to 50.*

Climbing enthusiasts might also consider these other mountaineering schools:

YOSEMITE MOUNTAINEERING SCHOOL
Yosemite National Park, CA 95389; (209) 372–8344; www.yosemiteparktours.com (click on "mountaineering school").

JACKSON HOLE MOUNTAIN GUIDES AND CLIMBING SCHOOL
Box 7477, Jackson, WY 83002; (800) 239–7642 or (307) 733–4979; www.jhmg.com.

Wilderness Skills

Programs teaching wilderness skills aim to do more than give you techniques for outdoor activities like backpacking, canoeing, or climbing. They present mentally and physically challenging situations meant to stretch your ability to the limit. Success means enhanced self-confidence that will carry over into the rest of your life.

OUTWARD BOUND WILDERNESS SCHOOLS
100 Mystery Point Road,
Garrison, NY 10524;
(877) 205–6726 or (866) 467–7651;
www.outwardbound.org. (I–E, depending on location; includes food and camping) Year-round; special classes offered for women and for parent and child

Years in business:	40+
Age range:	14–35+
Most common age:	18–25
Percent alone:	High
Number of participants:	
10–12 per group	
Male/female ratio:	51/49
Suitable for beginners; will try to arrange shares	
Year-round	

Outward Bound courses are in a class by themselves. Those who participate, many of them beginners in outdoor skills, come to be stretched mentally and emotionally as well as physically—with the wilderness as a classroom. If you want to learn about backpacking, canoeing, mountaineering, rock climbing, mountain biking, sailing, kayaking, white-water rafting, ski mountaineering, dogsledding, snowshoeing, or almost any other outdoor adventure, their schools in Colorado, North Carolina, Maine, and Minnesota and in several urban centers are ready to teach you these skills—and much more. Several courses combine skills such as backpacking, canoeing, and mountain climbing.

Most courses include solo time for reflection. Renewal courses are outdoor experiences specially intended for adults wanting to examine more closely their personal or career goals and renew their energies in an outdoor setting.

The courses usually have five parts. Phase one is a training and physical conditioning period, giving instruction in technical skills, safety, first aid, shelter construction, wilderness cooking, environmental awareness and conservation, map and compass reading, et cetera. Next, in phase two, these skills are applied. Groups of eight to twelve are formed, and as participants become more self-reliant, instructors turn the leadership role over to them. The third phase, the solo, is a period of solitude—one to three days in the wilderness alone. Afterward, the group comes together to execute an expedition with a minimum of supervision. Then comes a final event, a last fling with your body that involves running, paddling, cycling, snowshoeing, or skiing—more miles than you may have thought possible. Finally, there is a period of reflection on your experiences, feelings, and personal discoveries during the course.

More than 400,000 alumni, from troubled youths to corporate executives to adults in a period of life transition, testify that meeting the challenges of Outward Bound has helped them to go beyond what they believed they could do and to develop new self-confidence as a result.

NATIONAL OUTDOOR LEADERSHIP SCHOOLS

284 Lincoln Street, Lander, WY 82520; (307) 332–5300; www.nols.edu (I–E, depending on course)

Years in business:	Since 1965
Age range:	14–69
Most common age:	Each course has a suggested age range, from 17–22 to over 50
Percent alone:	High
Number of participants:	12
Male/female ratio:	Varies with the course
Year-round	

Formed to train wilderness leaders and educators, NOLS attracts many who are planning a career in wilderness education, but others attend to learn outdoor skills from experts or to learn leadership skills. Natural history, horsepacking, backpacking, white-water rafting, mountaineering, rock climbing, sea kayaking, sailing, and winter skiing are among the wide range of pursuits offered.

Most adult courses are for two weeks and designed to meet the needs of those age 23 and over.

NOLS has trained over 75,000 outdoor leaders around the globe; typically about 300 of them work for the school each year. Their ages range from 19 to 61.

COMMENTS **Female, 20s:** *I learned that almost all the challenges were fun and that living without the so-called conveniences of everyday life is often more pleasant than living with them.*

Male, 40s: *I was blown away by the beauty; I think heaven must look like the Wind Rivers. I will never forget it. These were the best instructors in the world. They engendered confidence in us all. They were confident, and it rubbed off.*

Stretch Your Mind

EVER WISHED YOU TOOK BETTER VACATION PICTURES . . . OR COULD paint a picture? Would you like a better understanding of the stock market . . . or a wine list . . . or what an archaeologist actually does on a dig? What about a yen to try your hand at quilting or carving or playing the fiddle?

Whatever your interest—or your fantasy—you can indulge it on a learning vacation that stretches your mind and talents in scenic surroundings.

In a situation where everyone is learning together, there is automatically a common interest, a natural bond, and a lot of mutual support. Many programs are set up so that the group eats together, but even when meals are optional, students who have shared classes naturally tend to get together for dinner.

The choices are enormous, as is the range of settings. You can learn to paint in Italy, to cook in Provence, or to twang a banjo in the West Virginia hills. Here are some of the many wonderful options.

Learning Vacations

Learning vacations come in many forms, from formal campus settings to research in the field. Besides the programs listed here, most universities also have a week of "Alumni College," and many also welcome non-alums to share the learning.

CORNELL'S ADULT UNIVERSITY
626 Thurston Avenue, Ithaca, NY 14850–2490;
(607) 255–6260; www.cau.cornell.edu (I)

A getaway for nature enthusiasts, armchair philosophers, art and music lovers, romantics and pragmatists of all persuasions," says the brochure, and indeed this largest of all summer university programs offers something for almost every interest. Classes are taught by university faculty; subject matter runs the gamut. Some recent offerings:

Years in business:	35+
Age range:	30–80
Most common age:	40–60
Percent alone:	35
Number of participants:	150 per week
Male/female ratio:	Varies

July to early August; four 1-week sessions in Ithaca; learning sessions also year-round in various off-campus locations

"Great American Trials of the Twentieth Century," "Architecture from the Ground Up," "Writing Workshop: Reality, Imagination and the Problem of Truth in Autobiographical Writing," "Web Page Design Studio," "The Wine Class," "Painting Studio: Apples and Oranges: Still Life Then and Now," and "The Golf Clinic."

This is a "back-to-school" week of dorm living and cafeteria dining with all the many athletic and cultural facilities on campus open to participants. And while there is a large program for young people, which attracts many families, single adults will find plenty of company. The evaluation sheets at the end of each session are enthusiastic: More than 90 percent of the participants say they plan to return.

Cornell also sponsors interesting year-round programs in the United States and abroad. Some examples recently were "Democracy in Ancient Athens in Greece," "The Gardens of Paris," "The Peruvian Amazon, a River and Rain-Forest Expedition," "April in New York: A Spring Theater Weekend," and "Cape Cod Ecology and the Fall Migrations."

COMMENTS E.B.: *The Cornell campus is magnificent, in the heart of the Finger Lakes, a region of spectacular natural gorges. I chose "Gorgeous Gorges of the Finger Lakes," a course that offered a daily walk of about 3 miles through the gorges, many of them remote locations tourists would ordinarily miss. It didn't feel like class—the instructor was like a knowledgeable friend who could point out a million interesting things you would never have noticed on your own, from birdcalls to the marks of the last glacier. There were no assignments, but readings were available if we wanted to learn more.*

Our group of a dozen ranged in age from 30 to 80, equally divided between men and women. At least half of the group was on its own during class; even couples at the program tend to choose different subjects. Classmates and dorm mates provide a natural base for making friends. The cafeteria food was so-so, but the setting was another congenial place for meeting people. All you have to do is say, "May I join you?" and set down your tray.

The evening schedule included a wine tasting at a nearby vineyard, a cookout, and a campus concert. If these didn't appeal, there were plenty of activities around campus as a substitute. The week ended with a banquet followed by a "graduation" party. Going to college for a week proved to be a congenial and relaxing vacation. The cost was nominal, and, as a bonus, I learned a lot.

Male, age 39: *The combination of camaraderie and intellectual stimulation brought me back twenty years to my days as a student.*

Female, 40s: *I had a splendid time. Although I came by myself, the program is so well organized, the people so friendly, and your time so full, I never felt at loose ends for a moment.*

VACATION COLLEGE

Program in the Humanities and Human Values, College of Arts and Sciences, CB#3425,
1700 Airport Road, University of North Carolina,
Chapel Hill, NC 27599; (919) 962–1544;
www.unc.edu/depts/human
(I; does not include lodging or most meals)

Years in business:	20+
Age range:	15–92
Most common age:	60s
Percent alone:	50
Number of participants:	60–120 per week
Male/female ratio:	Varies with topic
June and July	

Year-round this lovely campus in Chapel Hill offers a changing series of two- to four-day seminars led by university faculty. A new theme each week means a choice of topics that have recently included "Politics and Health in America," "The Age of Reason," "East Asia," "The Swing Era: Jazz of the Big Bands," and "Literature of the American South." Two-day Weekend Seminars are held in the spring and fall, on subjects such as "American Women Writers" and "Politics and the Supreme Court."

In addition to alumni, these programs attract many adults looking for a stimulating change of pace, exploring important cultural and social topics. Lodging can be in residence halls or in local motels. An opening dinner gives a chance to get acquainted; after that, classmates often get together to try the many good restaurants in Chapel Hill. Some seminars include a film or two (with popcorn) in the evening.

SUMMER CLASSICS IN SANTA FE

St. John's College, 1160 Camino Cruz Blanca,
Santa Fe, NM 87505; (505) 984–6117;
www.stjohnscollege.edu (I)

Years in business:	Since 1990
Age range:	20–80
Most common age:	40s
Percent alone:	75
Number of participants:	Maximum of 17 per seminar
Male/female ratio:	40/60
Summer; no single supplement	

Remember those "great books" you were always going to read someday—Shakespeare, Dostoyevsky, or Plato? Each summer, participants in these week-long seminars read and discuss world classics in literature and philosophy. The changing reading list may include such works as Tolstoy's *Anna Karenina*, Greek dramas, Plato's *The*

Apology, or Shakespeare's plays. They also discuss the text of great operas and attend an actual performance by the highly regarded Santa Fe Opera. Participants choose morning, afternoon, or both sessions, from several offered each week, and can stay for one or more weeks. In their free time, students can explore the historic buildings, archaeological sites, and the many art galleries of Santa Fe. Accommodations are in recently built campus dormitories. Rooms are suite-style, with five individual bedrooms sharing a common living room and a large bathroom, which is partitioned for privacy. The beautiful setting of the college, the lures of Santa Fe, and the unique content combine to give this one of the highest return rates among learning programs.

COMMENTS **Male, 40s:** *I can't put into words how this program nurtures me and calls all of my intellect into play. It's magic. There are no lectures—tutors begin with a question about the text, and stimulating discussion follows with fascinating people from every walk of life. We develop together and learn from each other. The attractions of Santa Fe greatly add to the experience. I've hiked at Bandolier National Monument and gone to the Chamber Music Festival and the Santa Fe Opera. It is a total change from my work and home life and has been so rewarding that I've returned three times and this year took a sabbatical to enroll in the college's graduate program.*

Female, 50s: *This is a wonderful place because it combines so many things. The classes provoke exciting discussion that one normally does not get at home on important interesting topics, but never stuffy. The people are very bright, the discussion is lively, and you combine one week of reading with another of opera. There's so much available in Santa Fe, and the location of the college in the hills is simply beautiful. It is a marvelous experience.*

WACHS GREAT BOOKS SUMMER INSTITUTE

Colby College, Waterville, ME; www.colby.edu (click on "Special Programs," then look under "Workshops and Conferences" for Great Books)
Contact: Colby College Special Programs, 4730 Mayflower Hill Drive, Waterville, ME 04901; (207) 872–3386; e-mail: summer@colby.edu (I)

"Great Books," say the sponsors, "is for people who love to think and talk about the world's great ideas, and whose greatest pleasure is to spend time with others who share that joy." Every summer since 1956, readers have come together for one week in August at Colby College in Maine to do just that—to read and discuss provocative writings with other stimulating people. The 2005 topic was "The

Fool," with readings by Erasmus, Cervantes, Cato, Joseph Heller, Philip Roth, and Isaac Bashevis Singer. With everyone living in the Colby dormitories, eating together in a college dining room, and joining together for discussions, friendships are all but guaranteed.

Organized discussions take place in the morning, with free time for relaxation in the afternoon, where the talk often continues over a tennis game or a swim in the lake. Discussion leaders rotate so that, although you will stay with the same discussion group all week, you will have a different leader each day. A wide variety of planned and unplanned activities takes place in the afternoon and evening, from a Maine lobster bake to sing-alongs.

The Great Books Institute takes over a section of the Student Union each night for the "Wachs Works" (named after the founder of the program, Is Wachs), a time for socializing, bridge, and various other activities. Golf, boating, music, and summer theater can be found nearby.

Local chapters of the Great Books Foundation hold many other weekend events around the country. For information, phone (800) 222–5870; www.greatbooks.org.

CHAUTAUQUA INSTITUTION
Chautauqua, NY 14722;
(716) 352–6200 or (800) 836–ARTS;
www.ciweb.org (I–M)

Years in business:	Since 1874
Age range:	2–102
Most common age:	50s
Percent alone:	25–30
Number of participants:	150,000 per season
Male/female ratio:	40/60
Summer	

This is where the idea of learning vacations began. Chautauqua was founded as a training camp for Sunday school teachers and evolved into a nine-week summer feast of arts and education, served up in a period Victorian village. The religious element, while still present, is optional.

The lineup of activities is staggering. Twice-a-day talks by prominent lecturers are on a new theme each week, from arts and humanities to the economy, science, and politics to the environment. The summer school topics include the arts, languages, human relations, public speaking, nutrition, parenting, self-improvement, foreign cultures, and much, much more. Activities such as line dancing, t'ai chi, and aerobics keep the program up to date. Evening entertainment may feature the resident symphony and theater companies, opera, ballet, Shakespeare performances, or guest stars ranging from jazz greats such as Wynton Marsalis to Bill Cosby and the Beach Boys. And for a sporting change of pace by day, golf, tennis, and sailing are available.

Chautauqua lodging includes hotels, inns, guest houses, condominiums, and private homes. The clientele has tended to be on the older side but is changing somewhat as an active children's program has begun to attract young families. For single participants, Joan Fox, a former director of public information at Chautauqua, says, "Chautauqua is a safe haven where cars and cares are outside, a secure gated community where a single vacationer falls in easily with others attending the same lectures, concerts, or classes."

COMMENTS **Female, 40s:** *I've been alone and with friends; I keep going back for the intellectual stimulation. The lecturers are great, and the hotels and food are very good. It's a very special place and is great for singles . . . people are friendly, and it's easy to meet them.*
Female, 50s: *Chautauqua has rounded my personality and sharpened my intellect. How I love it!*
Female, 60s: *The program is wonderful. You buy a gate ticket and can participate in any and all activities. You can stay busy all day long. The group is heavily female and there are many widows, but many families also come and the age range is wide—from children to those in their 70s. There is a good number of singles, and it is very suitable for them. You can stay in a hotel and have meals family style. People come from all over, but most are from the Northeast. The place started as a religious institution and is still highly religious for some, but it doesn't have to be.*

THE CLEARING
P.O. Box 65, Ellison Bay, WI 54210;
(877) 854–3225 or (920) 854–4088;
www.theclearing.org (I)

Years in business:	Since 1935
Age range:	18–85
Most common age:	55–65
Percent alone:	75
Number of participants:	25–35
Male/female ratio:	1/3
Spring through fall; will try to arrange shares	

Inspired by Danish folk schools that stress teaching, learning, and living together in scenic surroundings, this program calls itself "a unique school of discovery in the arts, nature, and humanities." In a setting meant to provide a clearing of the mind, dozens of courses, from watercolors, weaving, and design to ecology, astronomy, writing, and philosophy, are presented. Classes are taught outdoors and in the cathedral-like schoolhouse designed by renowned landscape architect Jens Jensen. It is located in a wooded setting overlooking the water in Wisconsin's scenic Door County. Participants live in charming log-and-stone cabins and enjoy family-style meals at wooden tables. Inexpensive rates, no bar, hassle-free atmosphere, healthful food, time to meet interesting people, and quiet, contemplative time in un-spoiled natural surroundings are part of the experience.

COMMENTS **Female, 60s:** *I have been at least twenty times. The Clearing is quiet, serene, a true retreat with time to think and exchange ideas with new people. It's inspiring. Most people are middle-age and from the Midwest. Accommodations are simple but adequate; meals are not gourmet but good and very social, with lots of lively conversation. The scenery is just beautiful, and you really get to know everyone.*

Male, 60s: *I've been with and without my wife. It is easy to be there alone. The group is mostly professionals, many single people, and many women. There is a tra-dition that you can't sit down at the same place twice at meals, so you're encour-aged to meet everyone. It is quiet and informal, but with a purpose. I recommend it to anyone, single or not.*

STAR ISLAND CONFERENCE CENTER
10 Vaughan Mall, Suite 8, Worth Plaza,
Portsmouth, NH 03801;
(603) 430–6272; www.starisland.org (I)

Years in business:	Since 1916
Age range:	Wide
Most common age:	Varies with week's program
Percent alone:	Varies
Number of participants:	180–260
Male/female ratio:	More females
June to September; will try to arrange shares	

The Star Island Corporation, comprising Unitarian Universalist and United Church of Christ constituencies, owns and op-erates this seasonal religious and educational conference center. Open to all denominations, the center offers discussion/instruction in a variety of weekly themes, such as natural history, art, and international affairs. Outdoor recreation includes swimming, boating, tennis, volleyball, and games. A marine laboratory provides near-natural habitats for native biota, and naturalists lead narrated ecology walks. Evening candlelight services are held in the historic chapel. Living quarters are in a century-old "grand hotel" and a few cottages. Family-style meals and the small size of the island are conducive to meet-ing other people. A list of the coming year's programs is available by sending a stamped, self-addressed envelope to the Portsmouth office.

COMMENTS **Female, 50s:** *This is a place to get in touch with your spiritual side. There are more single people than married, more women than men. It is very comfortable to be alone. The programs are very well organized, and I would recom-mend this to anyone. When you get there, you're not a stranger.*

Male, 40s: *I've gone for seven years, sometimes alone, sometimes with a friend. It's an easy group to get to know—meals are family style, everyone wears a name tag, about a quarter are single, but many married people come without their spouses. All activities are optional. Over half choose to go to morning chapel, even more to evening chapel. Workshops are in photography, painting, dance, music, drama, and writing—no experience necessary. Afternoons are free for trips to nearby islands. At night there are guest artists and folk dancing.*

Similar Unitarian-sponsored retreats are:

THE MOUNTAIN RETREAT AND LEARNING CENTER
3872 Dillard Road, Highlands, NC 28741; (828) 526–5838; www.mountaincenters.org.

ROWE CAMP AND CONFERENCE CENTER
Kings Highway Road, Box 273, Rowe, MA 01367; (413) 339–4954; www.rowecenter.org.

Study Vacations Abroad

A number of short-term study and educational tour programs are available abroad, often sponsored by U.S. universities in association with colleges in other countries. These offer memorable stays in the ivied surroundings of schools such as Oxford and Cambridge as well as the chance to meet interesting people. Some use dorm facilities on campus; others use hotels. The offerings vary from year to year, so it is best to call for current information.

HUMANITIES ABROAD
11 Gloucester Street, Boston, MA 02115;
(617) 266–8091 or (800) 754–9991;
www.humanitiesabroad.com, (I, plus airfare)
No single supplement on most programs; will try to
arrange shares; small single supplement in Florence.

Years in business:	25+
Age range:	25–80
Most common age:	45–60
Percent alone:	80
Number of participants:	20 maximum
Male/female ratio:	1/3

Education and culture are the focus of this varied program for those who want to learn more about the countries they visit. Some classes are based at such institutions as Cambridge and Dublin's Trinity College, where mornings are devoted to lectures and discussion and afternoons are free for exploring the area. These two- to three-week in-depth seminars are equivalent to a short university course. Other trips are less rigorous, but still education-oriented, concentrating on such topics as Dante, foods of Tuscany, or the art and architecture of Italy. Greece and Sicily are other destinations. Each program offers some sightseeing and evening lectures. About 70 percent of the participants are teachers.

COMMENTS **Female, 50s:** *I went alone and was very comfortable. There was a diverse group, ages 30 to 65, heavily female. Mornings were spent in class; in the afternoons there were tours of museums or lectures. There was always something to do. The accommodations were not great, but the trip was inexpensive.*
Female, 70s: *I've been on several trips alone. It is wonderful, and I always make friends. There is a nice mix of people from all over the United States, ages 35 to 70, most in their 40s. Many are married but traveling alone. Meals are as a group and there is lots of discussion, making it easy to get to know people. There is always something to do during the week; weekends are free to do whatever you want.*

UNIVERSITY OF LONDON
Birkbeck College, Faculty of Continuing Education, 26 Russell Square, London, England; 0207–631–6676; www.bbk.ac.uk; e-mail: drama@fce.bbk.ac.uk (I)

Years in business:	20+
Age Range:	25–75
Most common age:	55–65
Percent alone:	99
Number of participants:	25
Male/female ratio:	1/5

This choice program for those who love the theater deserves special mention for its reasonable cost compared to other summer programs abroad and its location in the heart of London. Participants read and discuss three current plays, attend the productions, then discuss them. The seminars end at about 3:45 P.M., leaving a little time for sightseeing, especially on days when no play is on the evening schedule. Directors and actors from the plays participate in a post-production discussion. These are often big names in the theater. The program runs for two weeks, focusing on different plays each week; students can choose to attend one or both sessions. Very basic lodging is offered in school dormitories, though you are free to make other arrangements if you prefer. Tuition covers room, board, breakfast, seminars, and theater tickets. Birkbeck, located in the Bloomsbury section of London not far from the British Museum, is the continuing education arm of the University of London, and offers many other courses in its summer catalog.

COMMENTS **E.B.:** *I loved this program. It was a chance to learn much more about theater and to get to know interesting and intelligent participants from*

Germany, France, Italy, and Spain, all fluent in English, as well as theater lovers from England and the United States. Many who attend are teachers of literature who use what they learn to enrich their courses. Most of the attendees were older, but a young Scottish student and a young teacher from Spain sent by his school, both in their 20s, seemed quite comfortable and happy in the group. The two instructors have been doing this for years and seem to know everyone in the London theater world. We had tickets to sold-out productions such as Michael Frayn's Democracy, *a revival of Harold Pinter's* Old Times *starring Jeremy Northam, and the Royal Shakespeare Company production of* Othello. *Frayn, Northam, and a beautiful young actress, Lisa Dillon, who played Othello's Desdemona, came to our seminars after we saw their plays. All were wonderfully articulate and interesting, and happy to answer any and all questions. It must be said that London dormitories are old, and rooms are small and stark, with a sink, desk, and small closet the only amenities. Breakfast, however, was adequate, and since the whole week cost less than $900, it was hard to complain. Those who want slightly more upscale lodgings might consider the Tavistock Hotel, which is just a short block from the school's location and is a bit over $100 per night for a small single room with private bath and breakfast. You must then add about $600 for tuition and tickets to your tab, but the cost is still less than most university programs. Wherever you stay, you are a fifteen-minute walk or a five-minute tube (subway) ride from SoHo and the heart of London.*

More options:

TRAVEL WITH SCHOLARS, UNIVERSITY OF CALIFORNIA, BERKELEY EXTENSION CENTER

1995 University Avenue, Berkeley, CA 94720; (888) 209–7344, ext. 221 or (510) 642–3824; www.unex.berkeley.edu/travel (EE)

The University of California at Berkeley offers two- and three-week travel-study programs in Paris, Oxford University in England, and changing destinations from Spain and Portugal to Italy to Ireland. A special program in London with distinguished drama critics gives an in-depth look at the London theater scene.

CAMBRIDGE UNIVERSITY INTERNATIONAL SUMMER SCHOOL

Madingley Hall, Madingley, Cambridge CB3 8AQ, United Kingdom; 44 (0)–1954–280–398; www.cont-ed.cam.ac.uk (E–EE)

The ivied halls of Cambridge, England, are open to summer students for two- to four-week programs. Participants can choose from a variety of themes— history, literature, and art, to name a few—or a mix of courses across several categories. Lodging and meals are in campus dorms. There are ample opportunities for exploring the area, including optional weekend excursions to Stratford-on-Avon and London, and the school offers add-on travel programs, such as a week-long architectural tour of England. Students make their own air arrangements. Ages of summer enrollees range anywhere from college students to seniors in their 70s. The college offers weekend programs as well; they fill up early, so don't dally if you are interested.

UNIVERSITY OF CAMBRIDGE SUMMER STUDY PROGRAM
c/o Office of Co-operating Colleges,
5441 Thomas Road, Fairview, PA 16415; (814) 456–0757; www.cssp.net (E–EE)

For over twenty years, this renowned university has offered a two-week summer adult education program expressly for Americans, administered through cooperating colleges in the United States. Five courses are taught in small seminars limited to no more than fifteen participants. Subjects include history, literature, and art and cover topics such as evolution of British gardens. Students are housed at atmospheric Downing College, set on fifteen acres, the most spacious of the central colleges of the university. Optional weekend excursions are available.

UNIVERSITY VACATIONS
3660 Bougainvillea Road, Miami, FL 33133;
(800) 792–0100; www.universityvacations.com (E–EE)

This twenty-year-old organization sponsors a series of one-week learning vacations at Cambridge University as well as the Sorbonne and universities in Dublin, Bologna, Rome, Berlin, Edinburg, and other cities. Lodgings are upscale; all lectures are in English.

More information on study opportunities for adults abroad can be obtained from:

THE ALTERNATIVE TRAVEL DIRECTORY
Transitions Abroad Publishing, Inc., P.O. Box 1300, Amherst, MA 01004;
(800) 293–0373; www.transitionsabroad.com.

Volunteer Programs

Assisting scientists and archaeologists in their work or helping people in need is a wonderful way to widen your horizons and get a new perspective on an area. As a side benefit, many of these trips are tax deductible. The cost is considered a donation.

EARTHWATCH INSTITUTE
3 Clock Tower Place, Maynard, MA 01754;
(978) 461–0081 or (800) 776–0188;
www.earthwatch.org (I–EE)

Years in business:	30+
Age range:	16–85
Most common age:	35–55
Percent alone:	50
Number of participants:	4,000 per year; divided into 700+ individual projects
Male/female ratio:	40/60

More than 50,000 volunteers have gone out on Earthwatch vacation-learning experiences in the United States and fifty other countries around the globe, helping scientists and researchers in field projects ranging from anthropology to zoology. Groups are generally small, with between four and fifteen people. Most participants have college degrees and are a well-traveled lot: professionals, scientists, managers, students, retirees, and teachers. A large percentage of them come alone.

Would-be volunteers learn about the projects in the annual catalog or by becoming members of Earthwatch. They can send for a more detailed briefing of the projects that interest them. Among the hundreds of possibilities each year are archaeological excavations; surveys of plants, birds, or animals; underwater and environmental impact studies; and research in agriculture, public health, and art history. Some recent projects: tracking widlife in Alaska's rain forest; excavating an ancient Andes settlement in Peru; monitoring wild dolphins in Florida; studying black bears in China, elephants in Ghana, and octopuses in Costa Rica; collecting stories and songs of Russia; documenting maternal healthcare in Zimbabwe; and tracking dinosaur footprints in Britain. Costs vary widely, depending on distance, length of stay, and living conditions.

COMMENTS Female, 50s: *For two weeks we lived in splendid isolation studying honey eaters on Australia's Kangaroo Island. I shared a bunkroom with four other women. Just outside my door were kangaroos, koalas, emus, and other creatures people seldom encounter outside a zoo. We did simple but necessary jobs such as hand-pollinating blooms and marking and bagging clusters of flowers for breeding studies. We also observed honey eaters and bees as they collected nectar and pollinated—or failed to pollinate—the plants. We got two days off for sightseeing. In the evenings, we played games, sang folk songs, talked a lot. The group, ages 25 to 60, had a wide range of occupations. We were a motley and congenial crew.*

Male, 40s: *I've gone on six trips, each time alone. It was hard the first time, then became easy. There was about an equal mix of men and women, single and married, from varied backgrounds. How well the program runs depends on the "Principal Investigator," the person in charge. One of my trips was not so well run. I would recommend this type of vacation to other singles, but I would also say that you have to really want to do it. This is not a leisure vacation. There is work involved.*

UNIVERSITY RESEARCH EXPEDITIONS PROGRAM (UREP)

UC Davis Extension, 1333 Research Park Drive, Davis, CA 95616; (530) 752-8811; www.extension.ucdavis.edu/urep (I–EE)

Years in business:	25+
Age range:	16–75
Most common age:	30–50
Percent alone:	High
Number of participants:	5–10 per project
Male/female ratio:	Varies

Like Earthwatch, UREP programs provide the opportunity to be part of a team doing actual research in the field (this time assisting University of California scholars), while gaining new knowledge, new friends, and insights into another culture. Tax-deductible contributions pay project costs and participants' expenses. The only requirements for participation are curiosity about the world and a willingness to invest in learning. Recent projects have included excavation of a pre-Inca mound site in Bolivia, a Middle Stone Age excavation in Serengeti National Park in Tanzania, and studying festivals, costumes, and textiles of Oaxaca, Mexico.

COMMENTS **Female, 50s:** *It was a positive and interesting experience that enabled me to see places and have experiences that I probably would not have had traveling with a tour group or alone. It was eye-opening, energy-expending, socially cooperating, native-appreciating, and thoroughly enjoyable—the most highly concentrated two weeks of learning and cultural immersion that I've experienced in many years of travel. The experience exceeded my expectations. It was one of new understanding of another people and of personal growth.*

Male, 40s: *I've been on four trips with them, to Easter Island, to the High Sierras twice, and to the Sierra Nevadas—all really great programs because you* *see things that a tourist would never see. Most people do come alone—couples are rare. The leaders help to get the group to bond together. You have to work together and get along because the trips tend to be in isolated places without bathrooms or other comforts. You get to know one another really well. Everyone has a sincere interest in the project and that brings them together right off the bat. I've met a lot of interesting people, everyone from a physicist to a cop to grad students. It's a great program if you're into learning and being outside in interesting places. But it is work, not for the weak!*

GLOBAL CITIZENS NETWORK
130 North Howell Street, St. Paul, MN 55104;
(651) 644–0960 or (800) 644–9292;
www.globalcitizens.org (I, plus airfare)

Volunteers with this nonprofit group have helped with projects ranging from building wells, roads, and schools to assisting at village clinics and schools. In Guatemala, they have taught in the primary school, helped install a water system, and painted the community center; in New Mexico volunteers helped build a community youth center for the Navajo Nation. A current project is helping with Tibetan refugee settlements in Nepal. Groups of six to ten volunteers are accompanied by a trained team leader and spend one, two, or three weeks on-site. Along with assisting with community projects, a main focus of the programs is a cross-cultural exchange. People of all skill levels and talents are welcome to participate. The organization makes a strong effort to keep its projects affordable for volunteers.

COMMENTS **Female, 50s:** *This was probably the best vacation I **ever** had. I was not a tourist. I became part of the village, learned to love its people, to care about the welfare of the village. . . . I learned a lot about working and living in a foreign culture. I learned a lot about myself.*
Male, 40s: *Most of my traveling, I'm a spectator, sitting in a coffee shop, watching life go by. Here in the Yucatan, I was a doer, a part of the action, a being within the community, and the sense of sharing and intimacy was overwhelming. It's a whole different thing.*

GLOBAL VOLUNTEERS
651 Little Canada Road, St. Paul, MN 55117;
(651) 407–6100 or (800) 487–1074;
www.globalvolunteers.org (I–M, plus airfare)

This nonprofit organization was founded in 1984 to work toward peace and mutual understanding among nations. It has special consultive status with the United Nations Economic and Social Counsel. When requested by local authorities, the organization sends teams of volunteers to live and work with people in the country on projects that contribute to the nation's long-term development. That could mean teaching English to children in Italy, Hungary, the Ukraine, or Peru, or building a community center or church in Jamaica, Ireland, Ecuador, or Tanzania. About 150 teams go out each year.

COMMENTS **Female, 50s:** *This week we have worked hard teaching English to college students and a very mixed group of community members. All of the students seem to work hard. Mostly, we have talked to them about ourselves, U.S. students and colleges, and Durham. We try to loosen them up, and then encourage them to ask us questions. Our main job is to get them to speak English and to help with their pronunciation. They respond with bravery and courage. I think my main problem may be in falling seriously in love with them, as you can imagine. They seem to realize that, which is so sweet. Yesterday, the students applauded when I came in. There are thirty to fifty students in each of my classes. I am totally worn out after each class, but it's very exhilarating.*

HABITAT FOR HUMANITY INTERNATIONAL
121 Habitat Street, Americus, GA 31709;
(229) 924–6935 or (800) 422–4828; www.habitat.org (I)

In the Global Village program operated by this group, volunteers pay a small fee for one- to three-week work stints helping to build decent, affordable housing for the needy. The fee covers participants' housing and meals. International trips provide a unique opportunity to become active partners with people of another culture, working alongside members of the host community. Locations have covered all fifty states and more than forty countries, from Armenia to New Zealand. Schedules of current work projects are posted on the Web site and are available from the main office in Americus.

PASSPORT IN TIME CLEARINGHOUSE

P.O. Box 31315, Tucson, AZ 85751;
(520) 722-2716 or (800) 281-9176; www.passportintime.com
No set fees; volunteers pay only their own expenses

No experience is necessary to join this program, which places volunteers as assistants to Forest Service archaeologists and historians in their research on national forest lands across the nation. Participants have helped to stabilize ancient cliff dwellings in New Mexico, excavate a 10,000-year-old village site in Minnesota, restore a historic lookout tower in Oregon, and clean vandalized rock art in Colorado. Projects vary in length from a weekend to a month, and facilities vary widely. Some projects involve backcountry camping where volunteers are responsible for their own food and gear; others offer meals prepared by a camp cook, often for a small fee. Sometimes volunteers can stay in local hotels and travel to the site each day. There are dozens of interesting opportunities. To learn about current projects and how to enroll, check the Web site or write or call for the free newsletter published each March and September.

AMERICAN HIKING SOCIETY VOLUNTEER VACATIONS

1422 Fenwick Lane, Silver Spring, MD 20910;
(301) 565-6704, ext. 206; www.americanhiking.org
No fees except a registration fee; volunteers pay their own expenses and transportation

Years in business:	25+
Age range:	18–80
Most common age:	20–80
Percent alone:	65
Number of participants	700 per year
Male/female ratio:	60/40

The American Hiking Society organizes as many as one hundred one- and two-week working Volunteer Vacations into remote and beautiful backcountry areas in the continental United States, Hawaii, and Alaska. Sessions are held year-round, except for the month of December. Teams of ten to twelve volunteers armed with shovels and rakes help to renovate and clear existing trails and build new ones. Everyone works hard in the morning, but afternoons are spent relaxing or exploring. Volunteers should be able to hike 5 miles or more a day and supply their own camping equipment.

The **Sierra Club** (see page 90) conducts week-long service trips for volunteers who help maintain trails and preserve the beauty of wilderness locales. **The Nature Conservancy** (see page 118) holds volunteer programs assisting conservation biologists with bird and wildflower inventories or riparian restoration at the Tensleep Conservation Project site in Wyoming.

Sources for additional volunteer trips are *Volunteer Vacations* by Bill McMullin, Chicago Review Press (800–888–4741) and *International Directory of Voluntary Work,* Peterson's Guides (800–338–3282).

Archaeology

Ever fantasized about being an archaeologist and going on a dig? Here's your chance!

CROW CANYON ARCHAEOLOGICAL CENTER
23390 County Road K, Cortez, CO 81321;
(970) 565–8975 or (800) 422–8975;
www.crowcanyon.org (I)

Years in business:	20+
Age range:	18–80
Most common age:	35–55
Percent alone:	85
Number of participants:	420 per year
Male/female ratio:	40/60

Here in the rugged terrain of the "four corners" where Arizona, New Mexico, Utah, and Colorado meet, adults join archaeologists searching for evidence of the ancestral Pueblo culture in the Mesa Verde region of southwestern Colorado. They learn the process of excavation, artifact identification, and interpretation by working on a dig, at the same time gaining firsthand understanding of the environment in which these people thrived. Participants live in round log cabins that resemble Navajo hogans and share hot meals at the lodge and sandwiches in the field. One-week programs begin on Sunday and end on Saturday throughout the summer.

Crow Canyon also offers a travel program focusing on archaeology and culture. See page 93.

COMMENTS **Female, 40s:** *I went alone for the first time, have gone back five times, and know a lot of people now. This is the best program I've ever found. The group is warm, with amazing backgrounds and levels of intelligence. The ages ranged from 18 to 80, about evenly divided between male and female, and last time there were only three couples out of twenty-four people. You have classes in the morning, go to the dig site in the afternoon and early evening, and have lectures after dinner. The food was family style and excellent. This program has caused several people to decide to go back to school for a master's degree.*
Male, 30s: *I've been going alone for five years. This is not Club Med, not a summer camp or play time—you are actually contributing to the archaeological work in progress. Accommodations and food are great. It's wonderful for anyone who is into archaeology or Southwestern art.*

CENTER FOR AMERICAN ARCHEOLOGY

CAA Educational Program, P.O. Box 366, Kampsville, IL 62053;
(618) 653–4316; www.caa-archeology.org (I)

An educational and research institution, the CAA offers one- to four-week adult field schools throughout the summer and fall, providing on-site training in archaeological excavation and analysis at sites in the Illinois River Valley. Newcomers as well as experienced diggers are welcome. Evenings are occupied with lectures, classroom activities, and experimental archaeology sessions. Meals are served cafeteria style, and lodging is a dormitory setting.

C O M M E N T S   **Female, 30s:** *This is mostly doing, not classes. It's an intense, very involving program, working all day, with planned activities at night. Accommodations are comfortable though not luxurious; the food was substantial and good.*

A good source of information on other archaeology vacation opportunities:

ARCHAEOLOGY FIELDWORK OPPORTUNITIES BULLETIN

Archaeological Institute of America, 655 Beacon Street, Boston, MA 02215;
(617) 353–9361; www.archaeological.org. A listing of almost 300 excavations and field schools worldwide with openings for volunteers and students.

Foreign Language Workshops

Learning a new language will allow you to travel abroad with more confidence and may widen your horizons at home as well.

LANGUAGE IMMERSION INSTITUTE

State University of New York at New Paltz,
JFT 214, 75 South Manheim Boulevard,
New Paltz, NY 12561; (845) 257–3500;
www.newpaltz.edu/lii or
www.giveusaweekend.com
(I, program only)

Years in business:	Since 1981
Age range:	15–80
Most common age:	45
Percent alone:	75
Number of participants:	6–15 per workshop group
Male/female ratio:	40/60

This innovative language department sponsors year-round weekend "total immersion" workshops at the New Paltz campus and in New York City, plus weekends and a one-week session at the beautiful Mohonk Mountain House resort outside New Paltz. Two-week intensive programs are held in summer at the New Paltz campus.

The approach here is to speak only the new language from day one, perfect for travelers who want to increase their vocabularies and learn conversation quickly. Only enough grammar is taught to give a needed foundation. Up to 200 people may enroll for weekend seminars; they are divided into small groups according to ability. The two-week summer classes include fifty hours of instruction and leave plenty of time for recreation. Twenty languages are offered, Arabic to Yiddish. Students arrange their own lodging in area motels or inns. Dormitory rooms on campus are available in June and July.

Overseas students can choose homestay, hotel, or apartment accommodations. The LII also sponsors year-round learning vacations in Costa Rica, Mexico, Spain, the Dominican Republic, Canada, Italy, and France in conjunction with local language schools.

COMMENTS E.B.: *My weekend at SUNY was a delight. Teachers are chosen for their outgoing personalities as well as language fluency, and they conduct classes with flair and a sense of fun. A typical assignment: "Pick a French character and describe yourself so that the class can guess who you are." Everybody gets into the spirit, and there's lots of laughter as well as learning. The class stayed together at lunch, still speaking French. Most of us chose to have dinner together as well, though we did give ourselves an English break. The approach dredged up every word of my forgotten college French—I was amazed. It left me in much better shape to tackle a trip to France.*

Male, 50s: *It's easy to come to this program alone. Everyone is learning, and we all make mistakes—alone or with a friend, you'd still have to get up in front of everyone and speak a foreign language. Most people do come alone, but everyone bonds quickly in the class. I've also gone on several trips to Costa Rica. I love the homestay program. I've spent an hour at the dinner table with my homestay family after the dishes were cleared, just talking about life in our different countries, family structure, politics—anything. No class can give you that.*

ECOLE DES TROIS PONTS

c/o Learning Destinations, P.O. Box 640713,
Oakland Gardens, NY 11364; (718) 631–0096;
www.learningdestinations.com (M–E).
Single rooms are available; includes lessons and all
meals.

Years in business:	10+
Age range:	20–70
Most common age:	Over 40
Percent alone:	40
Number of participants:	Maximum of 6 per class
Male/female ratio:	35/65

This is a chance to learn French in the setting of a lovely eighteenth-century chateau where cooking lessons are also offered. The general course consists of nineteen hours of French per week Monday through Friday, with weekends free to explore the area. A holiday course offers fifteen class hours per week, with more time to relax. Those who wish can combine the week with cooking classes (see page 71). This is a total immersion experience, with the chance to speak French constantly in a supportive atmosphere.

Both language and cooking students live, take classes, and dine in the Chateau de Matel in Roanne, a small town on the border of the Beaujolais and Burgundy wine areas that is best known for Troisgros, its three-star restaurant. The chateau, typical of the early 1700s, is set on thirty-two acres of park and woodland. The grounds include a pool and the chance for walks or bike rides along a canal at the foot of the grounds. Hosts are Rene Doral, a Frenchman, and his Australian wife, Margaret O'Loan, both of whom speak English. They get high marks from past participants for their hospitality. Prices seem quite fair for what is offered.

C O M M E N T S   **Female, 30s:** *It was terrific. The setting is lovely, the hosts create a family atmosphere, with everyone dining together, and the food was wonderful. Most of the people had come alone, and I made many friends from around the world, places like Japan and New Zealand. Three years later, we are still in touch. I had lived in France a long time ago, and in one week, I was able to bring back all the French I had known.*
Female, 40s: *The hosts are wonderful, the food is superlative, and the guests are so-phisticated and interesting and come from around the world. The chateau itself is lovely, though guest rooms are simple. Many people come alone. I researched well before I chose this school, and I go back year after year.*

Other options:

Several other language programs offer rewarding vacations in conjunction with language schools abroad, many with the option of homestays that provide an insider's look at the culture of the country. Prices vary widely according to the lodging and the country chosen. Here are some of the possibilities:

NATIONAL REGISTRATION CENTER FOR STUDY ABROAD (NRCSA)

P.O. Box 1393, Milwaukee, WI 53201;
(414) 278–0631; www.nrcsa.com (I–E)

The NRCSA is a consortium of 125 universities, language institutes, and specialized schools in thirty-eight countries of Latin America, Europe, and Asia that welcome North Americans of any age as well as participants from around the world. They offer hundreds of language and culture programs from a week to a year abroad with lodging options from apartments and pensions to local family stays. Through this organization, you can learn French in France, Monaco, Switzerland, or Canada; study Spanish in Mexico, Spain, Costa Rica, Honduras, or South America; and improve your Italian in Rome, Florence, Milan, Sicily, or Siena. Programs are also available in Japan, Greece, Russia, and other European and Asian countries. Many courses also include art, crafts, cooking, and local history. Contact NRCSA for a brochure detailing these opportunities.

LANGUAGES ABROAD

413 Ontario Street, Toronto, Ontario, M5A 2V9, Canada;
(800) 219–9924 or (416) 925–2112; www.languagesabroad.com

This group coordinates programs in thirty languages in fifty countries. You can learn French in Nice, or be more exotic and study Japanese in Tokyo or Spanish in Peru. The program, which began in 1996, places 500 to 600 participants each year. Lodgings vary, depending on the country, and may include homestays, dormitories, or self-catering apartments.

THE TALKING TRAVELER

620 Southwest Fifth Avenue, Suite 625, Portland, OR 97204;
(800) 274–6007; www.talkingtraveler.org

The Talking Traveler, founded in 1981, works with schools in France, Italy, Spain, Costa Rica, and Mexico, utilizing homestays with local families. About fifty participants are placed annually. The most popular stays are in Florence.

LEARNING DESTINATIONS
P.O. Box 640713, Oakland Gardens, NY 11364;
(718) 631–0096;
www.learningdestinations.com

This organization represents a large number of language programs as well as cooking schools and homestay programs. French is offered in several locations in France and in Switzerland, Quebec, Martinique, and Guadeloupe. Italian courses are available in a dozen locations in Italy; German is taught in Germany and Switzerland; and Spanish courses are held in a choice of cities in Spain as well as in Mexico and in South and Central America. Affiliations with language schools in Japan and China are also available.

AMERISPAN UNLIMITED
117 South Seventeenth Street, Philadelphia, PA 19103;
(800) 879–6640 or (215) 751–1100; www.amerispan.com (I–M)

Since 1993, this company has specialized in Spanish programs in Mexico, South America, Spain, and the Caribbean, with some 300 participants each year. They offer varied lodging, including homestays. The Web site has a useful feature detailing "what we like" and "what we don't like" about each program.

Annual listings of language school vacations abroad also appear in:

TRANSITIONS ABROAD MAGAZINE
P.O. Box 1300, Amherst, MA 01004; (413) 256–3415 or (800) 293–0373;
www.transitionsabroad.com.

Another excellent source is www.shawguides.com.

Cooking Schools

The opportunity to master the authentic cuisine of France or Italy with instruction from top regional chefs and teachers gives a special dimension to a foreign location and a view of the country most tourists miss. Cooking schools are also a rewarding option for solo travelers in scenic regions of the United States, giving focus to a trip and a chance to learn more about the area. All of these programs include time for sightseeing and opportunities to visit local markets and sample fine cuisine—including some that you will produce yourself. Some cooking programs are quite expensive, but participants say they are wonderful experiences worth saving for!

U.S. Cooking Schools

JANE BUTEL'S SOUTHWESTERN COOKING SCHOOL
125 2nd Street NW, Albuquerque, NM 87102;
(800) 472–8299 or (505) 243–2622;
www.janebutel.com (EE)

Years in business:	30+
Age range:	35–65
Most common age:	45–55
Percent alone:	50
Number of participants:	Maximum of 18
Male/female ratio:	40/60

For chefs who like their menus hot, Jane Butel, the queen of Tex-Mex cuisine and author of sixteen books on Southwestern cookery, shares her secrets in state-of-the-art kitchens with ample room for hands-on learning. The kitchens are located in La Posada, a lovely landmark inn near Old Town Albuquerque, where students are also lodged.

Recipes include regional favorites such as fajitas, tortillas, enchiladas, tacos, and tostados as well as chili stews, tamales, black bean soup, quesadillas, empanadas, and the classic dessert, flan. Students get a taste of Southwest history and food lore along with cooking tips.

Morning sessions are followed by the lunch or dinner that has been prepared in class. Two dinners in local restaurants are included in the weekly rates. Afternoons are free to explore the many shops, galleries, and museums of the city. One-week and weekend sessions are held January through early December.

COMMENTS **Male, 50s:** *I loved it. I went to the weekend course and enjoyed it so much, I went back for a week. There were sixteen in my week-long group, from late 20s to 50s, from all over the country and the world. Four of us were alone, and there was no problem at all. We stayed in the same bed-and-breakfast; I'm still in*

*touch with one lady from the Netherlands by e-mail. The day starts with Jane ex-
plaining things like different types of chiles. Then we paired off to make the dishes
of the day, with Jane and her assistants supervising, and we shared the food over
lunch. Afternoons were free to explore Albuquerque, which is a beautiful city with
lots to do. Old Town is fun just to wander through, and there are great museums
nearby. Some nights we got together for dinner. I had a ball and would definitely
recommend this to anyone.*

COOKING ARTS AT THE GREENBRIER

The Greenbrier, White Sulphur Springs, WV 24986;
(800) 228–5049 or (304) 536–7863;
www.greenbrier.com;
e-mail: cookingschool@greenbrier.com (EE)

Years in business:	20+
Age range:	20–80
Most common age:	46
Percent alone:	75
Number of participants:	60
Male/female ratio:	1/3

Located at a classic, very upscale resort, the Greenbrier Cooking School offers hands-on classes covering everything from how to entertain in style to the basics of cooking. The Culinary Arts Program also offers daily demonstrations.

For fans of barbeque, the Greenbrier offers BBQ University with Steven Raichlen, a well-known cookbook author, who teaches the basic techniques of barbeque while using a variety of state-of-the-art grills and smokers. The program includes morning demonstration classes, three meals daily, and a welcome reception and West Virginia Pig Pickin' dinner.

CULINARY INSTITUTE OF AMERICA

946 Campus Drive, Hyde Park, NY 12538; (800) 888–7850;
www.ciachef.edu (click on "enthusiasts") (EE)

America's most prestigious college for professional chefs offers five-day "Boot Camps" throughout the year for enthusiastic amateurs who want to don chef whites and learn from the renowned teaching pros in an intensive yet fun-filled environment featuring lectures, demonstrations, and hands-on production in the CIA kitchens. Students also dine in each of the CIA restaurants. Topics include "Basic Training I," "French Cuisine," "Techniques of Healthy Cooking," "Appetizers and Hors d'Oeuvres," "Baking," and "Pastry." In the basic course, recruits become well-versed in the fundamentals of cooking, including knife skills, kitchen terminology, dry-heat cooking methods (roasting, grilling, sautéing, pan-frying, and stir-frying), and moist-heat cooking methods (braising, shallow poaching, deep poaching, and steaming). Students make their own lodging arrangements.

Cooking Schools Abroad

COOKING WITH FRIENDS IN FRANCE

c/o 696 San Ramon Valley Boulevard, #102,
Danville, CA 94526; (800) 236–9067;
www.cookingwithfriends.com (EE)

Years in business:	Since 1993
Age range:	21–85
Most common age:	35–55
Percent alone:	Varies
Number of participants:	6
Male/female ratio:	1/6
Guaranteed shares	

The tile-roofed classic Provençal houses once occupied by the late Simone Beck and her coauthor, the late Julia Child, are shared by students at this six-day program in Provence taught by Kathie Alex, who studied with Beck and other French greats. Up to six students take part in the program, which offers morning lessons that culminate in lunch and two days of guided excursions exploring local culture and cuisine.

C O M M E N T S **Female, late 30s:** *It was excellent, interesting, fulfilling. There were two couples, two friends, and two single women in our group. Basically you travel and take meals with these people for six days straight—you can't help but get involved. The day is structured until 3:00 P.M. After that, everyone in the group was very inclusive—always invited everyone to go sightseeing or share a car to the beach. I was very nervous to get up in front of everyone and try a technique, but the staff made it extremely comfortable, and I felt I had support from the group. The teacher is wonderful, her recipes are great, and her teaching method makes it very easy to learn.*

ITALIAN COUNTRY COOKING

Diana Folonari, Via Pasitea, 246; 84017 Positano (sa),
Italy; 39 (0) 89 875–784; www.cookingschool
positano.it; e-mail: diana@starnet.it (E)

Years in business:	Since 1980
Age range:	20–60
Most common age:	25–45
Percent alone:	60
Number of participants:	12
Male/female ratio:	60/40

Diana Folonari, of a noted Italian wine family, conducts this four-day program at her home in Positano, a magnificent setting in the cliffs on the Amalfi Drive. The program begins with a reception and a talk on Italian food and wine. Mornings are spent in class, with students preparing lunches they share. Daily tastings of Italian wines are held as well. Participants stay in a local hotel and have afternoons and evenings free for sightseeing in nearby Amalfi, Ravello, Sorrento, Pompeii, and the Isle of Capri.

COMMENTS **Male, 40s:** *This is fantastic, one of the best trips I've ever made. I happened to be the only student who enrolled, and Diana and I became great friends. You stay at the best hotel in Positano, with wonderful accommodations. The area is beautiful, the wines delicious, the instruction fantastic. It's expensive but worth it.*

CUISINE INTERNATIONAL

P.O. Box 25228, Dallas, TX 75225;
(214) 373–1161; www.cuisineinternational.com (E–EE)

Years in business:	20+
Age range:	35–60
Most common age:	35–60
Percent alone:	50
Number of participants:	8–15
Male/female ratio:	Varies
Will try to arrange shares	

Cuisine International represents cooking schools and culinary tours in Italy and France in a variety of locations, including Venice, Rome, Florence, Sicily, the Tuscan countryside, and Provence, in France, as well as programs in England, Portugal, and Brazil. Each week-long program offers cooking demonstrations in the mornings and excursions to markets, wineries, and local historic sites in the afternoons. Dinners are in local restaurants and private homes. Accommodations range from converted farmhouses to ancient monasteries to five-star hotels, and are priced accordingly.

COMMENTS *Female, 40s: I did not think that cooking could be made to look so easy or be such fun . . . a most enjoyable week. It was like one long party.*

INTERNATIONAL COOKING SCHOOL
OF ITALIAN FOOD AND WINE

c/o Mary Beth Clark, 201 East 28th Street, Suite 15B, New York, NY 10016; (212) 779–1921;
www.internationalcookingschool.com (EE)

Years in business:	Since 1987
Age range:	20s–80s
Most common age:	40s–50s
Percent alone:	50
Number of participants:	10
	maximum
Male/female ratio:	1/3
May, June, September, October	
Will try to arrange shares	

Mary Beth Clark, an experienced American cooking instructor and author of the cookbook *Trattoria*, offers hands-on cooking classes, "The Basics of Great Italian Cooking," in Bologna, one of Italy's culinary centers. Classes are held in a modern kitchen in a stunning sixteenth-century palazzo in the center of the city, and cover dishes from antipasto to "dolce" (desserts). Participants enjoy the meals they have prepared paired with specially selected wines. Classes also cover the making of pasta and pizza. The week also includes shopping at local markets, visits to winemakers, and behind-the-scenes demonstration classes and dining in top restaurants. Clark has recently added a class that includes a stay in Tuscany, ending in Florence. A special October week includes travel and the White Truffle Festival in Alba, where participants go on their own truffle hunt. Participants can choose first-class or deluxe hotel accommodations.

COMMENTS Male, 40s: *I had a great time. The course was very well organized and everything promised in the brochure really happened. Besides learning to make wonderful dishes and how to pair them with the proper wines, we shopped in local markets and dined in two 2-star restaurants. One day was spent in a local pizzeria learning to make a pizza from scratch, and we then enjoyed our creations and wine with the chef. I was the only male in a class of five, ranging in age from 30s to 60s. When it was over, I felt I had made five new friends—my classmates and our teacher, Mary Beth, who was a delight.*

ECOLE DES TROIS PONTS
(see page 64)

Students here can spend six days learning French Provençal cooking or may combine cuisine with French lessons. The cooking course, offered in English, includes six nights' accommodations and all meals, four afternoon cooking classes, and shopping excursions to local markets. On Friday afternoon there is an excursion to see medieval villages in the countryside.

Classes are no more than ten people. Those who join the language course have five morning classes in French and four afternoons of cooking.

COMMENTS Female, 40s: *Enjoyed the whole week . . . it was a great experience. . . . What made the week so special was the way they made me feel at home, a part of the family.*

Additional programs worth considering are:

AT HOME WITH PATRICIA WELLS
Registration c/o Judith Jones, 708 Sandown Place, Raleigh, NC 27615; Fax: (919) 845–9031; www.patriciawells.com (EE, without lodging); e-mail: jj708@bellsouth.net

Patricia Wells, an American, is the restaurant critic of the *International Herald Tribune* and author of notable books on French dining and cuisine. Since 1995 she has offered cooking classes from May to September and one February session at Chanteduc, her restored eighteenth-century farmhouse in Provence on a hilltop outside Vaison-la-Romaine, about 30 miles northeast of Avignon. The five-day program in English is limited to eight participants and includes visits to markets, vineyards, shops, and local restaurants as well as hands-on cooking sessions. Wells also offers classes in her Saint-Germain home in Paris in April and October. Lodging is arranged individually and is not included in the fee.

TUSCAN WAY

2829 Bird Avenue, PMB 242, Coconut Grove, FL 33133; (800) 766–2390 or
(305) 598–8369 or (305) 281–6634; www.tuscanway.com (EE)

Tuscan Way is a four- or seven-day program begun in 1999 at Casa Innocenti, the hilltop medieval home of colorful chef/host Carlo Innocenti in the small village of Arcidosso, where guests are taught the flavorful cooking style of southern Tuscany. Additional locations include the Villa Castelleti, a Tuscan estate outside Florence; the Etruscan Valley with a regional chef; and the Villa Gaia near Siena, where Carlo and several guest chefs preside. Daughter Isabel conducts a one-week wine program, which includes visits to Tuscan vineyards, villas, and wine cellars. Rates include accommodations, daily lessons, food, wine, airport transfers, and excursions to markets and picturesque nearby villages. The single supplement is very small.

HANDS-ON COOKING WITH GIULIANO HAZAN

c/o The Educated Palate, 4471 South Shade Avenue, Sarasota, FL 34231;
(941) 923–1333; www.giulianohazan.com (EE)

This well-known Italian chef and cookbook author offers cooking classes in spring and fall at the Villa Giona, a restored sixteenth-century villa on twelve acres of parks, gardens, and vineyards in northern Italy. The location is near the charming town of Verona and scenic Lake Garda. A maximum of twelve students participate in four hands-on classes, learning to make homemade pasta, risotto, meats, local fish, vegetables, and desserts. Each five-hour class concludes with a dinner of the several courses prepared during the class. Dinners also feature wine and presentations on the major wine-producing regions of Italy. The program includes six nights at the villa, five outside restaurant meals, and trips into the countryside to see how local cheese, olive oil, ham, and special rice for risotto are produced.

LE CORDON BLEU, PARIS AND LONDON

40 Enterprise Avenue, Secaucus, NJ 07094;
(800) 457–CHEF; www.cordonbleu.net

While there is no residential program, this world-renowned school offers Paris visitors "Gourmet Sessions," demonstrations, and hands-on classes from a half-day to several days in length, as well as a morning tour of Paris markets with their chefs. A Saturday spent at a soufflé workshop or learning French regional cuisine will add a tasty dimension to a Paris visit. All demonstrations are translated into English. Gourmet sessions are also offered in English at the London Le Cordon Bleu school.

U.S. City Options

Cooking classes in cities in the United States also can provide a focus to a solo visit, and a way to make friends. In New York, the Institute of Culinary Education, established by the late Peter Kump, (800–522–4610; www.iceculinary.com) offers one-day, one-week, and weekend classes; in San Francisco, Tante Marie's Cooking School (415–788–6699; www.tantemarie.com) has similar programs. Both schools also train professional chefs. Check with the visitors bureau in the city you are visiting for local offerings.

For a comprehensive list of cooking schools around the world, order:

THE GUIDE TO COOKING SCHOOLS

ShawGuides, P.O. Box 1295, New York, NY 10023;
(212) 799–6464 or (800) 247–6553; www.shawguides.com

Learn about Wine

GERMAN WINE ACADEMY

c/o German Wine Information Bureau, 245 Park Avenue, 39th Floor, New York, NY 10167; (212) 792–4134; www.germanwineusa.org (E)

Six days of learning about German wines include lectures in English by local experts, travel to grape-growing regions for visits to wine estates and cellars, tastings with winemakers, seminars on wine, and a wide spectrum of tastings of some of the world's classic white wines. Several activities are based at the academy headquarters, a twelfth-century monastery called Kloster Eberbach. Among the activities is the festive last-night dinner, which includes a blind wine tasting and the presentation of "diplomas." Students are lodged at the charming Hotel Schwan in Oestrich/Rheingau and spend one day on a Rhine cruise with an overnight stop at the Alte Thorschenke at Cochem, one of Germany's oldest hotels. Areas usually visited include the Mosel Valley, Rheingau, Pfalz, Mittelrhein, and Rheinhessen regions, and the itinerary takes in many picturesque villages. Tours are usually offered in late September or early October.

COMMENTS **Female, 30s:** *Some come for business, some for personal interest, but everyone shares the basic interest in wines; several people came alone. Because groups are small and you travel and eat together every day, it's very congenial.* **Male, 40s:** *I came first with a companion, came back alone, returned a third time with my 21-year-old daughter, and always had a ball. About half are couples, the rest come alone, and there was plenty of company even for those in their 20s or 30s. I think this is one of the great bargains of the world—the food is great, and you taste more than 250 wines. As the wine flows, so does the fun. Even on the bus we sang songs and told jokes. It was a constant party.*

Other options:

Avalon Tours (888–499–WINE or 949–673–7376) offers a variety of wine-tasting tours to France, Italy, Chile, Australia, and New Zealand. Or, if you really want to be immersed in the wine-making process, sign up for Camp Schramsberg at the Schramsberg Winery, one of the oldest winemakers in California's Napa Valley (707–942–2414; www.schramsberg.com). The three-day fall sessions with this highly regarded maker of sparkling wines begin with a sunset dinner in the vineyard, followed the next day with picking and crushing grapes and ending with campers performing dosage for their own custom bottles to take home. In between, they get in-depth lessons in making wine, learn about tasting juices and base wines, tour the caves—and drink lots of bubbly. The last day is devoted to the "science" of food-and-wine pairing, which includes a five-course luncheon. The tab is steep, but half is tax-deductible as a donation for scholarships at the Culinary Institute of America.

Visitors to Paris can learn about French wines at the Centre d'information, de documentation, et de gustation (CIDD) (30, rue de la Sablière, 01–45–45–32–20) where courses are offered in English, ranging from "The Mechanics and Principles of Tasting" to "Champagne and Sparkling Wines," for beginning to advanced levels. The Centre also arranges wine country tours.

Photography

Sharpening your ability with a camera not only makes for a rewarding vacation but gives you skills that will enhance your travel pleasure forever after, guaranteeing wonderful personal souvenirs from any trip.

MAINE PHOTOGRAPHIC WORKSHOP

P.O. Box 200, 2 Central Street, Rockport, ME 04856; (207) 236–8581 or (877) 577–7700; www.theworkshops.com (M)

Years in business:	30+
Age range:	14–70
Most common age:	30
Percent alone:	90
Number of participants:	Class size, 10–18; total weekly, 100–200
Male/female ratio:	40/60

With the picture-perfect Maine coast village of Rockport as subject matter and inspiration, one of the nation's leading educational centers for photography offers more than 200 one-week workshops from June to September. The curriculum is designed for serious amateurs as well as professional filmmakers, photographers, digital artists, storytellers, actors, and writers.

Photography classes range from Photography I and beginning darkroom techniques to master classes in such aspects of the craft as portraits and landscapes, in black-and-white and color. Taught by some of the top people in the field, classes are intensive, all-day experiences aimed to stretch participants to new heights of personal expression, technical excellence, and creative achievement. Workshops also include creative storytelling, feature films, video, and television documentaries.

The home campus, located in the fishing village of Rockport, offers state-of-the-art studios, darkrooms, a theater and gallery, a digital media center, a production center, dining rooms, housing, and a campus store. The weekly schedule features exhibitions and lectures and screenings by leading photographers and directors. Meals are served in an old New England farmhouse where students dine with the faculty.

Additional workshops are offered in more distant destinations such as Oaxaca, Mexico; Tuscany; Paris; and Africa.

COMMENTS Letters from past students say:

"There was such an excitement in the air that I jumped out of bed each morning looking forward to being surrounded by such creative, loving, and interesting photographers."

"A high-energy, intensely inspirational experience. I have never worked such long hours and had so much fun. Not to mention the fact that I learned in quantum n."

More Options

The most comprehensive list of photography workshops is offered by ShawGuides on the World Wide Web at www.ShawGuides.com.

Many workshop advertisements are listed in other photography publications such as Popular Photography, *1633 Broadway, New York, NY 10036 (212–767–6000).*

ARIZONA HIGHWAYS PHOTO WORKSHOPS
P.O. Box 6106; Phoenix, AZ 85005;
(602) 712–2004 or (888) 790–7042;
www.friendsofazhighways.com (M)

Years in business:	15+
Age range:	20s–70s
Most common age:	Varies
Percent alone:	Majority
Number of participants:	5–15
Male/female ratio:	60/40
January to November; moderate single supplement	

The Friends of *Arizona Highways,* a nonprofit auxiliary of *Arizona Highways* magazine, conducts over two dozen workshops in scenic locales around the Southwest. Programs range from one to ten days and are led by the photographers whose works have appeared in the magazine, which is known for its high-quality photography. Both amateur and veteran photographers are welcome.

Every year trips are scheduled to Arizona favorites such as Monument Valley, Canyon de Chelly, and the Grand Canyon. Destinations introduced in recent years have included Colorado, Yosemite National Park, and the Grand Tetons in Wyoming. Workshops often include a moderate amount of walking and some hiking.

Many local photography centers in attractive resort communities offer one-day photo workshops as well as longer courses. Enrolling in one of these is an excellent way to give an added dimension to an already-planned vacation and to meet new people. A few of the many possibilities are:

CENTER FOR PHOTOGRAPHIC ARTS
San Carlos and 9th Streets, Box 1100, Carmel, CA 93921;
(831) 625–5181;
www.photography.org.

MENDOCINO ART CENTER

45200 Little Lake Street, P.O. Box 765, Mendocino, CA 95460;
(707) 937–5818;
www.mendocinoartcenter.org.

NANTUCKET ISLAND SCHOOL OF DESIGN AND
THE ARTS (N.I.S.D.A.)

Sea View Farm Barn Studios, 23 Wauwinet Road, Box 1848,
Nantucket, MA 02554; (508) 228–9248; www.nisda.org.

Photography workshops are also ideal ways to enjoy and fully appreciate national parks and wilderness areas that are sometimes difficult to visit on your own. For national park programs including photography, see nature listings beginning on page 116.

Art

An art-oriented vacation is more than a chance to develop a lifelong hobby; it means looking at a new locale from a different point of view—with the painter's eye—truly absorbing the details of the landscape and the architecture. The following are among hundreds of art workshops held around this country and abroad each year. For a comprehensive listing, look for the annual directory of art schools and workshops usually published in March in *American Artist* magazine, 1515 Broadway, New York, NY 10036; (212) 764–7300.

ART WORKSHOP INTERNATIONAL

463 West Street, Apartment 1028H,
New York, NY 10014;
(212) 691–1159 or (866) 341–2922;
www.artworkshopintl.com (M)

Years in business:	20+
Age range:	17–80
Most common age:	40–60
Percent alone:	50
Number of participants:	20–30
Male/female ratio:	Majority female
All are assigned roommates unless they specify singles; suitable for beginners	

Painting and writing are the focus of this long-established program. Beatrice Kroloff, the director, describes it as "a sublime merge of vacation (sunflower fields, Umbrian plains, like-minded travelers, dinners on the terrace) and creativity." Assisi, Italy, a twelfth-century Umbrian hill town, is the inspiring setting for classes in painting, drawing, and visual arts in a variety of media for both beginners and independent artists; courses are also offered in art history. The creative writing program draws top writers as instructors—names such as Michael Cunningham, Marilyn French, Vivian Gornick, Maxine Hong Kingston, Tony Kushner, Frank McCourt, and Grace Paley. Fees include hotel accommodations, most meals, studio space, critiques, and lectures. Supplementary trips are offered to the Venice Biennale, The Guggenheim Museum in Bilbao, Spain, and other locales.

C O M M E N T S **Female, 40s:** *This is an excellent program with no pressure. It was very easy to get to know everyone. My group was all women, ages 16 to 72, half of whom were single, and with all levels of art training. The food and the atmosphere were wonderful. We had painting instruction in the morning, afternoons free, and ate all meals together. A few times each week there were lectures and slide presentations. We went to local concerts or went swimming on our own.*
Female, 50s: *A group of very interesting people from all over the United States and Europe, mostly women and mostly single. Teachers provided a painting theme each day, but you could paint whatever you wanted if you preferred. There was a certain amount of time for peer criticism. Painters tended to stay together in the afternoon, and met with the whole group for dinner. It was excellent. I would recommend this to any single person.*

LA ROMITA SCHOOL OF ART
P.O. Box 58219, Washington, DC 20037
(202) 337-1599 or (800) 519-2297, pin 03;
www.laromita.org (M)

Years in business:	30+
Age range:	30–70
Most common age:	40–55
Percent alone:	60
Number of participants:	10–18
Male/female ratio:	1/8
Shares usually compulsory; suitable for beginners	

Two-week programs held in the glorious Italian Umbrian hill country between Rome and Florence give participants a chance to tour as well as paint. Studio days of sketching and painting in watercolor, oil, and multimedia are interspersed with visits to such towns as Spoleto, Assisi, Orvieto, and Perugia. The school is housed in a sixteenth-century monastery with modern facilities. The group includes a leader who is bilingual.

C O M M E N T S **Female, 40s:** *On my three-week trip to Italy, many people came on their own. The group was only twenty people, and we were together all the time. People tended to bond together and pair up, but everyone got along really well. It was a pretty diverse group from all over the United States, ages 40 to 70s, nineteen*

*women and one guy. It seemed that most people did know at least one other person.
It was a lovely location, and the side trips were great—we got to see things other
tourists would not. Plus, you don't have to worry about the language. It's a very safe
way to travel in a foreign country. It was a fabulous trip.*

Female, 60s: *I've gone three times alone. A lot of people come by themselves, and it
is easy to meet people, as you all have something in common. There are about sixteen to eighteen people in each group, set up by the type of painting you are working
on—watercolor, oils, et cetera. There's a mix of skill levels in each group, from
painting teachers to people who are just learning. It's a lovely place—I love the
owners and how it is run. But you have to want to be painting—it's not just a vacation—it's all about painting.*

Art, Crafts, Music, and More

ANDERSON RANCH ARTS CENTER
5263 Owl Creek Road, P.O. Box 5598,
Snowmass Village, CO 81615;
(970) 923-3181; www.andersonranch.org (M–E)

Years in business:	Since 1973
Age range:	20–80
Most common age:	30–50
Percent alone:	50–75
Number of participants:	150 per week; 12–15 per workshop
Male/female ratio:	30/70

It is a place where people change and grow and what they create is their own renewed lives." So says director Jim Baker of Anderson Ranch, one of the country's top summer programs for arts and crafts. Both novice and accomplished potters, photographers, painters, printmakers, woodworkers, and sculptors come each year to this inspiring setting in the Colorado Rockies for one- and two-week workshops taught by accomplished artists. The four-and-a-half-acre campus, a former working ranch, maintains its rustic look, but working facilities are state of the art and buildings are constantly being upgraded. Participants can live in the dorm on campus or opt to share a condominium, often within walking distance. Good cafeteria-style meals are served in a simple dining room with a pleasant outdoor terrace. The talented faculty gives talks and slide shows several evenings each week. Having the sophisticated restaurants and noted summer music festival of Aspen just 10 miles away is a big bonus for the location.

Anderson Ranch is one of the few arts centers with a children's program (see page 263) and also sponsors enriching field expeditions studying art and a variety of crafts, including photography, and absorbing new cultures and scenery in the American Southwest and in Jamaica, Thailand, France, Greece, Ireland, and Nepal.

COMMENTS E.B.: *This was a rewarding experience in every way. I came to Anderson Ranch alone, with no experience whatever in pottery, and found encouragement and aid not only from the instructor but from my more accomplished fellow students as well. I became so absorbed in the learning that, along with most of my classmates, I came back many nights after dinner to continue working. My lodging in a comfortable two-bedroom condo provided privacy as well as the chance to meet an interesting condo-mate, and mealtimes were a pleasant social experience with consistently good food. Having the beauty and activities of Aspen so near added a wonderful weekend to my stay.*

PENLAND SCHOOL OF CRAFTS

P.O. Box 37, Penland, NC 18765;
(828) 765–2359;
www.penland.org (M)

Years in business:	Since 1929
Age range:	19–80
Most common age:	Varies with courses
Percent alone:	50–70
Number of participants:	1,200 annually
Average class:	12–15
Male/female ratio:	40/60

Another center nationally recognized for top crafts instruction, Penland was founded by Lucy Morgan, a teacher at the Appalachian School, which once occupied several buildings that are still a part of the campus. In 1923, she organized the Penland Weavers, providing looms and materials to local women, and marketing their handwoven goods. She invited guest instructors to teach weaving, and when requests for instruction began to come from other parts of the country, Penland School was born. Soon after the first students arrived in 1929, other crafts were added and the school began to raise funds, acquire property, and construct buildings.

Today Penland encompasses about 400 acres in the Blue Ridge Mountains of western North Carolina, with forty-three structures. Instruction is offered in clay, glass, textiles, art, printmaking, woodworking, ironworking, and photography as well as weaving. One- and two-week classes are held in summer, and eight-week sessions in spring and fall. Students live in simple housing on the grounds and eat together in the Pines dining room. A stay at Penland also offers daily movement classes, evening slide shows, visits to nearby studios, a library, volleyball games, dances, walks in the beautiful countryside, or a swim in the Toe River.

JOHN C. CAMPBELL FOLK SCHOOL

One Folk School Road, Brasstown, NC 28902;
(828) 837–2775 or (800) 365–5724;
www.folkschool.org (I)

Years in business:	Since 1925
Age range:	20–75
Most common age:	40–60
Percent alone:	Many
Number of participants:	80–120 per week; most classes limited to 12
Male/female ratio:	50/50

After studying the folk schools that had been a major force in the rural life of Denmark, Sweden, and other countries, John C. Campbell and his wife, Olive Dame, brought this concept to a mountain valley in the Appalachians. The school has grown to twenty-seven buildings on 380 acres, with buildings ranging from romantic European style to typical Appalachian farmhouses. Two- to seven-day workshops explore some 450 traditional and contemporary crafts, including basketry, beadwork, broommaking, chair caning, clay, calligraphy, bookbinding, enameling, glassblowing, jewelry making, dyeing, cooking, dance, drawing, music, nature studies, painting, paper art, printmaking, quilting, weaving, soap making, spinning, and woodworking. The warm folk school ambience encourages friendly group activities and song. Days begin with a group walk through the woods and morning songs. After dinner, participants can sing, dance, visit, or spend extra time in the studio. Everyone lives on campus in dorms or simple rooms with a choice of shared or private baths, and dines together. The school is less than two and a half hours by car from Chattanooga and Knoxville, Tennessee; Asheville, North Carolina; Greenville, South Carolina; and Atlanta, Georgia. Airport pickup can be arranged from Atlanta.

HAYSTACK MOUNTAIN SCHOOL OF CRAFTS

P.O. Box 518, Deer Isle, ME 04627;
(207) 348–2306;
www.haystack-mtn.org (I)

Years in business:	50+
Age range:	18–80
Most common age:	Mid-30s
Percent alone:	About 50
Number of participants:	80 per season
Male/female ratio:	Varies

Located in a handsome complex in a spectacular setting on the coast of Maine, Haystack attracts many accomplished artisans as well as beginners who want to explore a new medium or begin seriously studying a particular art. Courses in clay, fibers, metals, wood, graphics, blacksmithing, and glassblowing are offered in two- and three-week sessions, June through August.

COMMENTS **Female, 40s:** *This is a working vacation . . . there's always something to do and you can go from area to area and learn several types of crafts. How structured or loose the course is depends on each instructor. The atmosphere is very* *warm and people come away extended creatively. Most students are female—some professional women, some retired.*

Female, 30s: *About half the students are single or come alone. There's a nice balance of public and private time. People come here to have an experience with others who are interested in crafts, and it's not just surface—they form lasting friendships. The food is terrific, very healthy and appetizing. There's something to do all day, and at night there is usually a slide show or a dance or some sort of program.*

ARROWMONT SCHOOL OF ARTS AND CRAFTS

556 Parkway, Gatlinburg, TN 37738;
(865) 436–5860; www.arrowmont.org (I)

Years in business:	50+
Age range:	18–80
Most common age:	30–65
Percent alone:	20
Number of participants:	40–100 per week
Male/female ratio:	1/3
Will try to arrange shares; suitable for beginners	

Arrowmont is a visual arts complex tucked away on a wooded hillside in the heart of Gatlinburg, and adjacent to the Great Smoky Mountain National Park. One- and two-week workshops in spring, summer, and fall draw men and women of all ages and levels of ability who wish to learn both traditional and contemporary crafts. Classes in ceramics, fiber, weaving, basketry, jewelry making, enameling, fused and stained glass, wood turning, and furniture making as well as painting and drawing and photography are conducted by more than 150 visiting faculty members. Students are housed in simply furnished dormitory rooms in cottage-type buildings. Home-cooked meals are served in a congenial dining room. Having everyone together makes for a warm atmosphere.

COMMENTS **Male, 40s:** *This is an intense learning experience, the best school of its type. It is fine to be here by yourself, as about half the students come alone. Most are women. People come from all over the world.*

Female, 30s: *I had a very pleasant experience. My group was mostly women, and many of the men who did come were with their wives, but it was a great mix of people. People here leave their lives behind. It's like summer camp—easy to become close quickly. The instructors are very well qualified. It's a good place to go alone.*

FLETCHER FARM SCHOOL FOR THE ARTS AND CRAFTS

611 Route 103 South, Ludlow, VT 05149; (802) 228-8770; www.fletcherfarm.com (I)

Years in business:	50+
Age range:	20–70
Most common age:	over 40
Percent alone:	80
Number of participants: 40–80 per week	
Male/female ratio:	3/10
Late June through early September; guaranteed shares; suitable for beginners	

The lovely setting in Vermont's Green Mountains adds to the enjoyment of students who come to this school operated by the Society of Vermont Craftsmen. A variety of classes, most two to five days in length, cover painting, photography, basketry, weaving, rug hooking, fiber arts, stained glass, quilting, wood carving, and folk arts such as stenciling and chair caning. Single and double rooms with shared bathroom facilities are available on campus in summer. Meals are family style. The Society sponsors two major crafts fairs on the grounds each year and also maintains a gallery and shop.

COMMENTS **Female, 20s:** *I had been quilting for about a year and wanted to learn new techniques. I researched a bunch of schools, and this is where I chose to go. The instructor was great; the accommodations and food were fine. My class of five was all women. It was open seating at meals so you get to meet people—there were always plenty of people to talk to. Many people do come by themselves.*
Male, 60s: *I always travel on my own. I've been going here every year since 1992. I go for wood carving. It's a beautiful spot. I stay in a motel, but I meet people at meals, plus they encourage you to look in on other classes and projects to see what everyone is doing. There are usually eight to ten people in the woodworking class; quite a few come alone. The people are from all over; they range in age from 30s to 80s, and there are usually more women than men. The instructors are very competent. There's always a group of nice outgoing people and a lot of camaraderie.*

AUGUSTA HERITAGE CENTER

Davis & Elkins College, Elkins, WV 26241–3996; (304) 637-1209; www.augustaheritage.com (I)

Years in business:	Since 1972
Age range:	10–75
Most common age:	25–45
Percent alone:	30–40
Number of participants: About 500 per week, divided into small groups	
Male/female ratio:	Varies; about 50/50
Singles matched in dorm rooms	

Appalachian arts—from fiddling, blacksmithing, and basketry to whittling and folk painting—are the focus of this excellent five-week summer program. Dance, storytelling, quilting, songwriting, folk carving, clogging, and music from bluegrass to Cajun are also included in the list of 200 workshops, highlighting folk cultures from around the country and around the world. Most workshops run five days, with classes running from morning until late afternoon. Evening brings concerts, informal jam sessions, and get-togethers. Inexpensive housing is available in twin-bed college dorms or in motels off campus. Rates for those staying on campus include most meals. The program ends with a three-day folk festival featuring a juried craft show with scores of artisans offering handmade items, plus home cooking and music and dancing that leaves toes tapping for weeks after.

C O M M E N T S **Female, 30s:** *It is very easy to meet people, and a great number are alone. It's fairly even male and female. I went for the dancing; the days were strenuous, the instruction very good. The dorm rooms and food are not good, but that's not why you go. It is creative time.*

SNOW FARM
The New England Craft Program, 5 Clary Road, Williamsburg, MA 01096; (413) 268-3101; www.snowfarm.org (M)

In January 2001, Snow Farm took over the fifty-acre farm and school that was the former site of Horizons, which has become a traveling program (see page 157). The executive director, Mary Colwell, and her husband, A. J. LaFleur, helped to found Horizons and had been involved in many capacities before taking charge. Much of the staff also has remained, so the most obvious changes are upgrading of the facilities. Glassblowing, welded sculpture, ceramics, metalsmithing, jewelry making, fiber arts, woodworking, photography, and painting are among the offerings in one- and two-week programs. The contemporary studio and living spaces blend well with the historic 1700s farm structures. Classes are kept small to launch beginners as well as to challenge the more advanced.

TOUCHSTONE CENTER FOR CRAFTS
1049 Wharton Furnace Road, Farmington, PA 15437; (724) 329-1370 or (800) 721-0177; www.touchstonecrafts.com (I)

Painting, drawing, photography, ceramics, weaving, quilting, basketry, pottery, pewter and ironworking, stained glass, bead making, and

Years in business:	30+
Age range:	35–65
Most common age:	40–50
Percent alone:	20
Number of participants:	35–65
Male/female ratio:	1/3
Guaranteed shares	

woodworking are all on the agenda for five-day workshops in summer and week-end sessions in May through October. Lodging is in rustic log cabins or newly built dorm buildings on a 150-acre wooded campus. Meals are served in a community dining hall. The center is located 60 miles southeast of Pittsburgh, a drive of about three and a half hours from Cleveland, and four and a half hours from Washington, D.C.

C O M M E N T S **Female, 50s:** *It's a wonderful place. I've been six times and every time, I never want to go home. Everyone has pretty much the same interests—that's why they are there. They made me feel at home the first time I came and still do.*

Try Adventure Travel

"ADVENTURE TRAVEL" IS A CATCHALL TERM FOR SCORES OF WAYS TO get into uncrowded, unspoiled countryside or untouched wilderness and to be actively involved with the environment and with your fellow travelers. It is an escape from the pressures of urban living as well as a welcome change from passive travel that shows you the world through the windows of a tour bus or a car. Since groups are small and camaraderie between participants is strong, the percentage of single vacationers who choose this kind of vacation is predictably high.

For years, travel labeled "adventure" was considered exotic, limited to hardy backpackers or thrill-seekers who delighted in climbing Mount Everest or careening over dangerous rapids in a rubber raft. But owing to their explosion in popularity over the last decades, adventure trips have become accessible and safe for almost everyone.

Statistics chronicle this boom. In 1949, eighty years after John Wesley Powell completed the first descent of the Colorado River, only one hundred people had ever rafted through the Grand Canyon. By 1972, the National Park Service was forced to limit traffic on the river to 17,000 people a year! By now, millions of people have experienced the thrill of exploring the bottom of the canyon by boat. Figures published in 1998 by the Travel Industry of America reported that ninety-eight million people had taken an adventure trip in the previous five years. In 2001, 17 percent of travelers included outdoor activities in their trips, a total of 173 million people.

With so many people signing on, the number of operators offering adventure outings has zoomed, and the variety of trips is truly amazing. Just a few of the choices include rafting, backpacking, backcountry skiing, horseback trekking, mountain climbing, and gentler pursuits such as sailing, biking, and walking. Tour operators grade their offerings to suit a wide range of abilities, making it easy for travelers to make a wise choice. A popular recent trend is to offer trips with a variety of activities—hiking and rafting, for example.

Trips are offered on the seven continents and almost every place on earth, from the subarctic ice floes to the jungles of the equator to the placid countryside of Europe or the United States. You can take your choice of camping out or staying in quarters that are positively plush.

The following pages offer a small sampling of the great selection available. The listing represents some of the longer-established operators or the more unusual adventure choices and runs the gamut from rustic to deluxe. Use the additional references given to find more operators in whatever area interests you most.

The majority of these outdoor trips are priced per person, with no single supplement. When necessary, operators try to arrange shares. Where single supplements do exist, they tend to be low. Luxury trips with a substantial supplement are so indicated.

A warning: More than any other type of trip, adventure travel depends for its success and safety on the experience and skill of the operator, so check references carefully before you make your choice.

There are a few sources for information. Groups operating in national parks must have a permit from the superintendent, so you can write or call to verify the credentials and ask park authorities about the reputation of the company. The American Mountain Guides Association (303–271–0984; www.amga.com) in Boulder, Colorado, offers accreditation for outfitters and certification for individual guides and will provide names of those who have qualified. The Professional Paddle Sports Association (703–451–3864 or 800–788–2202; www.propaddle .com) in Springfield, Virginia, a trade association for white-water rafting outfits, will provide information about choosing a trip, a list of accredited members, and any information on file on a particular company.

Choosing an Adventure Trip

There are no standardized requirements for operators of adventure trips or for guides, so choosing a reliable company is important. Here are some questions to ask before you sign on:

- *How long has the company been operating? How long have they run this particular trip?*
- *Does the operator belong to any professional association?*
- *Can you describe the day-by-day activity and the level of difficulty of this trip? Is there any training or preparation for participants?*
- *What kind of training is required for guides? How much experience have they had on the route in question?*
- *Are guides required to know first aid and CPR?*
- *What kind of insurance does the company carry? (Don't choose any company lacking coverage.)*
- *On a rafting trip, are life jackets and helmets supplied?*
- *What do you do in case of serious injury or illness in the wilderness?*
- *Can you provide names of recent participants on this trip?*

Operators with Trips in Multiple Categories

APPALACHIAN MOUNTAIN CLUB

5 Joy Street, Boston, MA 02108;
(617) 523–0636; www.outdoors.org
(I; E for some foreign excursions)

Years in business:	120+
Age range:	5–85
Most common age:	28–55
Percent alone:	35
Number of participants:	85,000 members; trip groups are small
Male/female ratio:	50/50

Hiking, biking, backpacking, climbing, skiing, camping, canoeing, kayaking, and snowshoeing are among the pursuits of this venerable, conservation-minded club with local chapters in the eastern United States, from Maine to Washington, D.C. In addition to the year-round workshops at its permanent lodges (see page 38), AMC sponsors hundreds of major excursions throughout North America and abroad. Organized and supervised by volunteer members, these trips range from cross-country skiing in Wyoming's Teton National Park to biking in Tuscany, from a Serengeti safari to backpacking in Patagonia.

SIERRA CLUB OUTINGS

85 Second Street, Second Floor,
San Francisco, CA 94105; (415) 977–5522;
www.sierraclub.org/outings/national (I)

Years in business:	100+
Age range:	1–97
Most common age:	Varies
Percent alone:	50
Number of participants:	3,800 total; 12 average per trip
Male/female ratio:	50/50

Another longtime leader in conserving and appreciating the wilderness, Sierra Club Outings offers over 350 trips to all seven continents. Trips range from four days to three weeks in length and include backpacking, hiking trips using a single base camp, biking, rafting, canoeing, sea kayaking, and sailing. All are cooperative ventures with volunteer leaders; on camping trips all pitch in with chores and cooking.

The trips require varying degrees of stamina and experience, but the trip guide clearly characterizes each outing. Additional brochures available for each trip spell out the details. Base-camp trips tend to be easy to moderate and are a good idea for beginners since they allow for taking the day off if you are weary. Highlight trips are usually moderate; they are designed for people who like to hike or walk with only a daypack. Service volunteer vacations often attract solo travelers and are a great way to explore wilderness areas while giving something back to the environment.

Special outings are available for seniors and women.

WILDLAND ADVENTURES

3516 Northeast 155th Street,
Seattle, WA 98155;
(206) 365–0686 or (800) 345–4453;
www.wildland.com (E–EE)

Years in business:	Since 1986
Age range:	35–80
Most common age:	40–60; 35–55 on hiking trips
Percent alone:	65
Number of participants:	Small groups
Male/female ratio:	45/55
Trips year-round; share rates guaranteed for advance reservations	

Off the beaten path cross-cultural experiences," says the literature for this company with interesting itineraries in Central and South America, the Galápagos, Turkey, Jordan, New Zealand, Africa, and Alaska. The trips combine active exploration with intellectual stimulation. You can choose lodge-based odysseys, yacht voyages, rafting, or hiking-camping trips. Guides provide local history and discussion of contemporary social issues to make the visit more meaningful.

COMMENTS **Female, 30s:** *It was a very busy itinerary, but we learned a lot and the guides were very knowledgeable. We went to remote places and saw things no tourist would ever see, like a village that can only be reached by boat or plane. There were about fifteen in the group, only three singles. It was about 50/50* *male/female and ages from 30 to 70. The people were pretty outgoing, and most were bird-watchers, so we all had something in common. Also most were world travelers, so they shared a lot of interests. The accommodations and food were wonderful. My only criticism was that the people were too old for me. It was great, and I'd recommend it, but to someone a little older.*

Male, 60s: *I went once by myself to Patagonia. It is hard to find a tour to Patagonia, so when I heard of this one, I signed up. There were only four in the group—one woman and two other men. They all worked at a university together. It was very comfortable being alone. We all got to know each other intimately. Everything worked right with this tour—they're very good at what they do, and the guides are very knowledgeable. I plan to go again, and I'd recommend it to anyone.*

OVERSEAS ADVENTURE TRAVEL

One Broadway, Suite 600,
Cambridge, MA 02142;
(800) 955-1925;
www.oattravel.com (M–E)

Years in business:	25+
Age range:	45–75
Most common age:	30–50
Percent alone:	60
Number of participants:	Total of 2,000 per year; no more than 16 per trip
Male/female ratio:	37/63
Year-round; will try to arrange shares	

This experienced outfitter, a division of Grand Circle Corporation (see page 201), is a longtime organizer of "soft adventure" trips, geared to somewhat older travelers who want to get off the beaten path. They have also expanded their offerings to include cultural tours. Tours are always limited to a maximum of sixteen people, and wherever possible, itineraries allow more than one night in each destination. Descriptions include a section called "Is this adventure right for me?" that describes the physical requirements of each trip. Adventure destinations include Peru, Thailand, Vietnam, Antarctica, Japan, Australia, safaris in Africa, and the "Route of the Maya" in Central America. Cultural tours visit Portugal, Spain, Tuscany, Sicily, Scotland, and England's Lake District. "Real Affordable" trips to Peru and Costa Rica offer a break for those on a budget.

COMMENTS **Female, 40s:** *I've been to Costa Rica and to Jordan with this company, and each time the trip was very well run. There were about twelve people in the group, probably 60/40 women to men on the first trip and 70/30 to Jordan. The trips seem to attract a lot of older women who like to travel both by themselves and with friends. There were a few singles on the trip; they were teamed with roommates. The trips attract very nice, outgoing people. You're with a small group for a fairly*

long time, so it is easy to get to know everyone. OAT is a great way to do this kind of trip—the itineraries are fairly complicated, and they take care of everything for you.
Male, 40s: *I've been to the Amazon and Galápagos. The trip was fairly demanding—a certain amount of walking and climbing, but not overly strenuous. We were informed of the type of physical activity before we left. The materials you receive beforehand are excellent—they really tell you what to expect in all aspects. It was an extremely diverse and interesting group—a woman from Alaska, a man who was the Canadian consul to Bolivia. It was mostly couples or friends, just two single women. The staff/tour leaders were top-notch—they really understood the people and culture of Peru. The food was excellent. They caught fresh fish for us each night on the boat. It's a great trip to take by yourself, but you have to be slightly adventurous.*

MOUNTAIN TRAVEL SOBEK

1266 66th Street, Suite 4,
Emeryville, CA 94608;
(510) 594–6000 or (888) 687–6235;
www.mtsobek.com (M–E)

Years in business:	35+
Age range:	30–70
Most common age:	35–45
Percent alone:	60
Number of participants:	4,500 annually; small individual groups
Male/female ratio:	45/55
Year-round	

The whole world is the territory for these adventure specialists, a merger between two of the oldest and largest outdoor trip operators. Trekking, hiking, rafting, sea kayaking—they cover all the adventure categories, plus cultural tours to exotic locales for the less athletic. Trips are listed in five categories from easy to strenuous and range from trekking to the base of Mount Everest to canoeing in New Guinea to African safaris to easy walks in Tuscany. In addition to the comment below, this group seems to get uniformly high marks from past participants.

COMMENTS **Female, 30s:** *I went on a rafting trip alone, but I never felt alone. The people were ages 20 to 60, half single, twice as many men, and a very interesting group. The food was great, and the leaders even brought hot coffee to each tent in the morning. We all got along and had a great time. The scenery was spectacular, and the instruction was also great. You could do as much or as little paddling as you wanted.*

More Sources for Adventure Travel

- REI Adventures (P.O. Box 1938, Sumner, WA 98390; 253–437–1100 or 800–622–2236; www.rei.com/travel) is part of Recreational Equipment Inc., the largest consumer cooperative selling outdoor gear in the United States. Their travel program, now past its seventeenth year, includes dozens of trips from easy to strenuous in Europe, North America, Latin America, Asia, the Pacific, Australia, Africa, and Antarctica.

- Wilderness Travel (1102 Ninth Street, Berkeley, CA 94710; 510–558–2488 or 800–368–2794; www.wildernesstravel.com) publishes a big color catalog listing this organization's dozens of trips in Africa, Antarctica, Latin America, the Middle East, Asia, Australia, New Zealand, the Pacific, Europe, North America, including the Galápagos Islands, and the Himalayas.

- Lindblad Expeditions (96 Morton Street, New York, NY 10014; 800–EXPEDI-TION; www.expeditions.com) has been a respected name in adventure travel for over twenty-five years. A wide range of programs explores North America from Alaska to Baja, as well as Central America; South America including the Galápagos, the Andes, and Patagonia; the Arctic and Antarctic; and European trips to Scotland, Scandinavia, and the Azores. A nineteen-day "European Odyssey" from Lisbon to Copenhagen travels the coasts of seven countries.

- Crow Canyon Cultural Explorations (see page 61). In addition to archaeo-logical programs at its headquarters in Colorado, Crow Canyon has a busy adventure travel program, taking small groups, never more than twenty peo-ple, to destinations with interesting archaeology and history. Trips range from remote sites to exclusive entrée into Native American communities. Activities may include hiking, horseback riding, and river trips. In the United States they have visited Utah's Desolation Canyon and backcountry, New Mexico Pueblo communities, and Navajo country. Peru, Guatemala, Syria, Jordan, Mexico's Chaco Canyon, and India are among recent foreign destinations.

- GorpTravel.com is an online resource linking to dozens of adventure tour op-erators.

- Some top operators of bicycle tours now offer multisport adventures. See the write-ups for Backroads (page 95), Butterfield & Robinson (page 99), and The World Outdoors (page 96).

ALASKA WILDLAND ADVENTURES
P.O. Box 389, Girdwood, AK 99587;
(907) 783-2928 or (800) 334-8730;
www.alaskawildland.com (E–EE)

Years in business:	25+
Age range:	8–80
Most common age:	Around 45
Percent alone:	35
Number of participants:	16 per trip
Male/female ratio:	35/65

June to September; some offerings in March, April, and October and special winter safaris in February and March; will try to arrange shares; very small single supplement

This group offers three- to ten-day adventures that include hiking, rafting, sea kayaking, marine wildlife cruises, and sportfishing, all in the national parks and refuges of the great Alaska wilderness. Part of the thrill is close-up views of wildlife such as bald eagles, moose, black and brown bears, caribou, puffins, and seals. Trips are led by trained naturalist guides. The operator uses comfortable backcountry lodges in or adjacent to federally protected Alaska wildlands. The five-day Alaska Backcountry Safari combines active days with a comfortable lodge. The Alaska Explorer Safari includes luxury camping in Denali National Park and is a bit more adventurous.

COMMENTS **Female, 60s:** *Fantastic! I've never been on a better trip. The guides and food were wonderful; there was something new and different to do every day. Most people were in their 40s and 50s, but the range was to 75. There were more women than men, more single than married, brought together by their spirit of adventure. Days were well organized, but there was no regimentation.*

Bicycle Tours

Bicycle touring offers an in-depth look at beautiful parts of the United States and the rest of the world with congenial company and plenty of time to explore off the beaten path. Tours are available for intermediate as well as for experienced riders, and all tour operators offer rental bikes, helmets, and other necessary equipment. The tour company maps out a choice of detailed bike routes of varying difficulty. Some bicycle tours camp overnight, but most are "inn-to-inn" with a different comfortable lodging destination each night. Depending on the pace and the choice of routes, you can vary your daily mileage. Everyone is together for breakfast and dinner. Many tours also offer the option of a lunch pool with everyone chipping in and sharing picnics assembled en route by the hosts. Or you may choose to try restaurants along the route. A van accompanies the tour, carrying all the luggage, equipment for repairs, and extra bikes for emergencies. Known as the "sag wagon," the van is also readily available if your legs are weary and you want a ride to the inn.

BACKROADS

801 Cedar Street, Berkeley, CA 94710;
(800) 462–2848 or (510) 527–1555;
www.backroads.com (M–E)

Years in business:	Since 1979
Age range:	25–65
Most common age:	35–55
Percent alone:	40
Number of participants:	26 maximum per tour; average group, 18
Male/female ratio:	42/58

Year-round; will try to arrange shares; guaranteed share rates for reservations sixty days in advance; trips for singles

Long known as a major operator of bicycle tours, Backroads has expanded to offer more than 150 active itineraries. Cooking classes are available in addition to biking, walking, and multisport adventures in different combinations that mix hiking, biking, kayaking, rafting, canoeing, snorkeling, and sailing.

A roster of some one hundred destinations includes Europe, the Mediterranean, Asia and the Pacific, Latin America, Canada, and the United States. Tours vary in their level of challenge and are clearly labeled in the catalog for their difficulty. Easy, moderate, or challenging options are usually offered. Itineraries range from five to thirteen days.

Backroads remains the largest bicycle tour company, with a thick catalog chock full of offerings in the United States and around the world. A few of their itineraries are camping trips, most offer comfortable inn accommodations, and some destinations give a choice of either. Beginners cycle two to four hours daily; advanced tours may cycle five to seven hours a day. Bikers can always choose to take it easy, enjoying the scenery and attractions and picnicking along the way. Many itineraries are scheduled for singles.

COMMENTS **Female, 30s:** *I've done a number of their programs, sometimes alone, sometimes with friends. It is very easy to be alone, as there are often more singles than couples. The people are from all over the world, with equal numbers of men and women from early 20s to 70. I've made many friends that I keep in touch with. The people are highly educated and health-conscious. The best thing about the program is the people who run it. They take care of everything, and you get pampered. The food is amazing, and the hotels are luxury. It's ideal for women alone because it is nonthreatening.*
Male, 30s: *I've taken eight tours. The average group is half singles. It is easy to*

meet people, and you quickly become like a family. About half the group is from California, the rest from all over the United States and the rest of the world. It is an upscale crowd. There are several routes to choose from each day, and you can bike as little or as much as you want. The food is very good, and the accommodations are fine, though not elegant.

THE WORLD OUTDOORS

2840 Wilderness Place, Suite F,
Boulder, CO 80301;
(800) 488–8483 or (303) 413–0938;
www.theworldoutdoors.com (I–M)

Years in business:	15+
Age range:	25–65
Most common age:	43
Percent alone:	60
Number of participants:	13 maximum per group
Male/female ratio:	Varies
Year-round; guaranteed shares	

Hiking, biking, and multisport activities that might combine hiking, mountain biking, horseback riding, and sea kayaking are on the agenda of this multifaceted company operating throughout the Americas and the South Pacific. Itineraries give a choice of comfortable inn-to-inn journeys, more rustic hut-to-hut lodgings, or camping trips.

Destinations include the Rockies, Southwest, and East and West Coasts of the United States, as well as Canada. Winter warm-weather escapes take place in Australia, New Zealand, Belize, the Caribbean, Peru, Chile, Costa Rica, Cuba, Ecuador, and Hawaii.

Skiing, snowshoeing, dogsledding, and snowmobiling adventures are available in winter in Colorado or the Grand Tetons. Singles are welcome on all trips and also have some thirty of their own special trips.

TREK TRAVEL

801 West Madison, Waterloo, WI 53594;
(920) 478–4672 or (866) 464–8735;
www.trektravel.com (M–EE)

Years in business:	Since 2002
Age range:	7–78
Most common age:	40–45
Percent alone:	Varies
Number of participants:	10–15 (20 maximum)
Male/female ratio:	50/50

This is a new and fast-growing program created by one of the largest bicycle manufacturers in the United States. The 2005 catalog lists nearly fifty guided trips in Europe, North America, and New Zealand. "Classic Luxury" trips use top-rated hotels and restaurants and offer easy-to-moderate itineraries from Washington's San Juan Islands to the Czech Republic. Economy-priced "Explorer" trips take place in Vermont, Utah, the Canadian Rockies, Spain's Costa Brava, and the Tour de France route in France. Some trips offer extra diversions such as golf or wine tastings. Several three- and four-day weekend escapes have scenic destinations, including California wine country, the Moab Desert of Utah, and fall foliage in Vermont. All trips include a social hour each evening and the complimentary use of Trek bicycles.

VBT BICYCLE VACATIONS

614 Monkton Road, Bristol, VT 05443;
(802) 453–4811 or (800) BIKETOUR;
www.vbt.com (M)

Years in business:	30+
Age range:	22–70
Most common age:	35–55
Percent alone:	50
Number of participants:	6,000 annually; groups average 14–20
Male/female ratio:	45/55
April to October, a few March and November dates; guaranteed shares	

This outfitter was the originator of the inn-to-inn idea in Vermont, but they have expanded way beyond their home state to cover the United States, Canada, Europe, and New Zealand. Along with the choicest New England sites, trips cover the North Carolina coast, Hawaii, and California wine country. One of the most popular tours is through the quaint fishing villages of Nova Scotia in the Canadian Maritimes. European destinations include France, Italy, England, Ireland, Holland, and Austria. A winter trip cycles New Zealand. Trips are clearly identified as easy, moderate, or challenging. They range from six to seventeen days and can cover anywhere from 25 to 40 miles per day. Lodging is in country inns.

COMMENTS **Female, 30s:** *It was really easy to meet everyone on the trip. The staff tried to make sure everyone would get along and pointed out similar interests. The age range was from mid-20s to 70s, pretty even male/female, and a great group, really interesting. There were a few friends, one couple, and four or five singles on my trip, and everyone had a great time. It is very well run; the staff really made the trip. They helped everyone get to know each other, designed excellent routes, and were very nice people.*
Female, 20s: *I was very comfortable on a trip to New Zealand alone. There were only two or three married couples. The group ranged in age from 27 to late 50s and came from all over the United States. We stayed in hotels and always had dinner together. You could do what you wanted each day, pick your routes, and go at your own pace. It was a great trip.*

BIKE VERMONT, INC.

P.O. Box 207, Woodstock, VT 05091;
(802) 457-3553 or (800) 257-2226;
www.bikevt.com; www.bikeireland.com (M)

Years in business:	25+
Age range:	18–65
Most common age:	30–50
Percent alone:	25–35
Number of participants:	15–20
Male/female ratio:	40/60
May to October; will try to arrange shares	

This operation arranges inn-to-inn bicycle tours in the lovely Vermont, Maine, and New Hampshire countryside with a new destination every night, as well as tours in Ireland and Scotland. Vermont is hilly, but this company's weekend trips and four- to six-day tours are within the ability of beginning cyclists, and the support van is available when you need a rest. Average runs are 25 to 35 miles a day. Some trips include a day of hiking. This is "a nonthreatening, relaxing vacation," say the organizers. "We don't bike as a group, so everyone is going at his or her own pace. It is easy to make new friends."

C O M M E N T S **Male, 40s:** *I've taken several tours. There is a good mix of singles and couples, plus children from about age 12. Backgrounds vary, but generally the adults are highly educated professionals. It is easy to make friends.*
Female, 20s: *I've done this for six years. When you share a sport, there's automatic camaraderie and all ages mix. You have breakfast together, then set out at your own pace, alone or with others. You meet people along the way, stop together for hot chocolate or a cold drink, and you make friends. I always come home with names and addresses, and often you plan to come back on another trip with these people.*

BICYCLE ADVENTURES

P.O. Box 11219, Olympia, WA 98508;
(360) 786-0989 or (800) 443-6060;
www.bicycleadventures.com (M)

Years in business:	Since 1984
Age range:	20s–60s
Most common age:	30–40
Percent alone:	40–50
Number of participants:	13–18
Male/female ratio:	40/60
June to November; winter trips to Hawaii; no single supplement	

The glorious scenery of the Pacific Northwest is the home territory for this outfitter. Their signature trip is an eight-day tour of Puget Sound, using ferries to cover five different islands and staying in delightful inns. Two-day stays on Orcas Island and Vancouver Island in Canada allow for extra sightseeing. On Vancouver Island, there is the chance to visit world-famous Butchart Gardens and the city of Victoria. Shorter versions of this trip are also available. Other popular destinations are the Olympic Peninsula, the Cascade Mountains, the Oregon coast and the Columbia

River Gorge, British Columbia, the Canadian Rockies, California wine country, Bryce and Zion National Parks, Santa Fe-Taos, and Hawaii. Winter trips cycle in New Zealand. Beginner trips can range from 15 to 40 miles daily on easier terrain; intermediate trips cover 30 to 70 miles each day.

Like so many bicycle tour operators, Bicycle Adventures has expanded to a multisport roster that includes many bike-hike itineraries and trips that offer horseback riding, rafting, or canoeing. Winter brings the opportunity to bike, hike, and snorkel in Hawaii or cross-country ski in Washington's Methow Valley, with spectacular views of the Cascade Mountains.

COMMENTS **Female, 30s:** *I would encourage anyone going solo to be adventurous and just do it. The weather, people, food, inns, and scenery were all super. It was the best money I've ever spent on myself.*
Male, 30s: *This group is superb—the routes were well planned, the food and inns were wonderful, everything was done professionally. The group was small, one couple and the rest singles in their 30s, all successful professionals, more men than women. Everyone got along well. I've been on more expensive bicycle trips that were nowhere near as good. I also like going with a smaller specialized company; the groups are smaller, and they really know this area.*

BUTTERFIELD & ROBINSON

70 Bond Street, Toronto,
Ontario, M5B 1X3 Canada;
(416) 864–1354;
in U.S., (800) 678–1147;
www.butterfield.com (EE)

Years in business:	Since 1966
Age range:	30–70
Most common age:	45–55
Percent alone:	30
Number of participants:	18–24 per small group; 5,500 annually
Male/female ratio:	40/60
Year-round; will try to arrange shares	

This long-established company has a full roster of luxury biking tours through France, Italy, Ireland, Austria, the Czech Republic, and Holland. Recently offerings have expanded to include walking tours and combination walking and biking trips in Canada, the United States, and Europe. More adventurous biking/walking expeditions have gone to Bhutan, China, Costa Rica, Cuba, India, Japan, Morocco, Nepal, New Zealand, Patagonia, Peru, South Africa, Spain, Turkey, and Vietnam. Kayak and rafting adventures have also been added in Mexico's Baja peninsula, Belize, Botswana, and British Columbia. The most recent additions to the roster are urban and rural experiences, combining visits to Barcelona, Florence, and Paris with a few days of biking or walking in the countryside nearby. These are top-of-the-line trips, using the best accommodations available. On biking trips this means elegant country accommodations (usually two nights at each stop) and top restaurants, including some Michelin all-stars. There are stops for tastings at regional wineries as well. Routes are rated for difficulty, but cyclists should be able to ride at least three to five hours a day. B&R adds new itineraries every year. See the Web site or write for a catalog for current offerings.

COMMENTS **Female, 40s:** *This is expensive, but it's the best vacation I ever had and I am going again. About half the group was unattached, equal numbers of men and women, and everyone quickly formed a close-knit group. The couples usually split up at meals and ate with different people. Ages were 25 to 63, interesting folks from the United States and Canada. Days were flexible, at your own pace. They take very good care of you, and there are a lot of repeat customers.*
Female, 30s: *I've been several times. There were a lot of people from the East Coast, more couples than singles, usually more women than men. Sometimes we met for activities like wine tasting; sometimes you cycled at your own pace all day. The lodging and food are tops, and most meals are eaten as a group. I'd recommend it to all singles as long as they don't go expecting to meet someone special.*

INTERNATIONAL BICYCLE TOURS

P.O. Box 754, Essex, CT 06426; (860) 767-7005;
www.internationalbicycletours.com (M)

Years in business:	25+
Age range:	7–85
Most common age:	50+
Percent alone:	50
Number of participants:	23 maximum
Male/female ratio:	1/2
April to September; will try to arrange shares	

Older and novice cyclists are attracted to these leisurely excursions through scenic countryside in the United States and abroad. Trips begin at a gentle pace, then gradually increase in daily mileage as everyone becomes more comfortable with cycling. There are periodic stops to relax, share snacks, or take pictures. Destinations include Holland, Sweden, Austria, France, Italy, England, Germany, and the Czech Republic. Closer to home, shorter trips are available to Cape Cod and Nantucket.

COMMENTS **Male, 70s:** *I've been on six international trips and four domestic. Every trip has been excellent. I always go alone; there are always a number of singles on the trip. They attract an older crowd—about half are over 50. The staff is*

> # More Sources for Biking
>
> *There are many other tour operators offering biking vacations.* Almanac:
> Tourfinder and Ride Guide *(1612 K Street NW, Suite 800, Washington, DC 20006;*
> *(202) 822–1333; www.bikeleague.org) is a comprehensive directory of more than*
> *150 bicycle tour operators in the United States and abroad, published by the*
> *League of American Bicyclists. It can be ordered by mail; check for current prices.*

fabulous; I've been with other companies and they're not even close. The routes and mileage varies by the trip. Unlike other companies that give you a map and you're on your own, you ride as a group so you can't get lost. You have a real sense of security. The trips are paced for someone who doesn't want anything too strenuous. The food is excellent, and the value can't be beat.

Female, 60s: *I've been on a dozen trips with IBT, and I'm leaving again in a few weeks. I started out going alone, but I met people on the trips and now we plan to go together. There's always a number of people who go alone. The group is always very congenial and friendly—all very outgoing people. It's a well-run program. They have a unique system with a leader, a corner, and a sweep. The corner stops at an intersection and waves everyone along, and the sweep brings up the rear to make sure no one gets lost or left behind. There are usually a few more women than men, but it varies with the trip. The age range is really 30s to 70s, but I'm bringing my thirteen-year-old granddaughter on the next trip. The mix of young and old makes it really interesting. You get to know everyone because you ride together all day and sit together for meals. These are great trips.*

Hiking/Walking

Walking trips with comfortable lodgings awaiting each night are a lovely way to linger through some of America's and Europe's most beautiful areas, far from tourist crowds. There are trips for every ability, from rugged mountain hiking to a relaxed pace in the gentle countryside. A van carries all the gear; walkers need only a light day pack for an extra sweater, a slicker, or snacks. These trips are increasingly popular, and many bicycle touring companies have added walking tours to their offerings.

BUTTERFIELD & ROBINSON
(see page 99)

This is a top-of-the-line organization for walking as well as biking tours with luxury accommodations and food. High recommendations are common from past participants. Each person goes at his or her own pace, and a van is posted at several points so that walks can be shortened if necessary. Many tours combine biking and walking. See page 99 for the long list of destinations. Reservationists try to steer solo walkers to trips where they will find company.

C O M M E N T S **Female, 50s:** *The Morocco trip was one of the most wonderful experiences I've ever had. They took us to places ordinary tours never get to. We camped out in the desert, rode camels, had fabulous experiences. My group happened to include six married women who had come together, but my most compatible companions were couples. Everyone was friendly, and being alone was perfectly comfortable.*

THE WAYFARERS
172 Bellevue Avenue, Newport, RI 02840;
(800) 249–4620 or (401) 849–5087;
www.thewayfarers.com (E)

Years in business:	Since 1984
Age range:	26–72
Most common age:	50
Percent alone:	20
Number of participants:	15 maximum
Male/female ratio:	40/60
Will try to arrange shares	

This British-based company has expanded their original English itineraries to cover Ireland, Scotland, Wales, Italy, France, Spain, the Czech Republic, the United States, Switzerland, and New Zealand, always choosing fine country inns as lodgings. Their interesting trips include a garden tour of Devon, Dorset, the hills of Tuscany, Ireland's Ring of

Kerry, the Scottish highlands and islands, and, for hardy walkers, a coast-to-coast route across England. New itineraries include Andalusia in Spain and Croatia and the Dalmatian coast. An average day's walk covers 10 miles, with stops for lunch and morning and afternoon coffee or tea breaks. The van is always close by for those who tire or want to take a day off. The group eats all meals together, allowing plenty of time for socializing. The company reports a large number of repeat travelers.

COMMENTS **Female, 50s:** *I've tried other groups, but I keep coming back to this one because the trips are so well put together and you get so much for your money. Everything is excellent—the leaders, the itineraries, the places we stayed. They are very flexible and go out of their way to see that every single person has a good time. There are mostly couples and single women, not very many single men, but very comfortable for all. I've made friends from Australia and England and planned future trips with people I've walked with in the past. It's a very good choice for singles and the very best way to see a country.*

COUNTRY WALKERS

P.O. Box 180, Waterbury, VT 05676;
(802) 244–1387 or (800) 464–9255;
www.countrywalkers.com (I–E)

Years in business:	25+
Age range:	30s–70s
Most common age:	40–60
Percent alone:	60
Male/female ratio:	1/2
Number of participants:	Average 15 per group
Year-round; will try to arrange shares; share rate guaranteed on bookings made 91 days in advance	

The coast of Maine, the valleys of Vermont, the West, beautiful areas in England, Ireland, France, Greece, Italy, and Spain, and exquisite scenery in Ecuador, New Zealand, Peru, Chile, Bhutan, Morocco, Puerto Rico, and Costa Rica are among the far-flung itineraries this company covers on foot. Tours focus on the natural history and culture of the area and are led by knowledgeable local guides. Lodgings are first-class throughout. Hiking options range from 4 to 12 miles a day, and there is always the option to stroll a few miles to a local village, enjoy a cafe lunch, and relax for the afternoon. Everyone gathers for dinner. In winter, snowshoeing is offered in the Canadian Rockies.

COMMENTS *Male, 50s: I've been to Peru and Chile, alone both times. There were nine people on the last trip—two couples, two single women traveling together, and three people traveling alone. I was very impressed with how they ran both programs. The staff that traveled with us and the local guides were excellent and very knowledgeable. They were also there to help if you need a "leg up." We had no problems because everything was so well planned. The people were from all over the United States, and all had traveled fairly extensively so we had experiences to share and there was never a struggle for conversation. People got along really well and were very helpful to each other. The room and food were fine. The Peruvian food was interesting—including eating guinea pig! The commonality of interests—liking the outdoors, traveling, and being active—brought the group together.*

BACKROADS
(See page 95)

Backroads has gone into walking in a big way, with year-round trips for all abilities in scenic locales around the world. Beginner routes cover 3 to 5 miles daily, averaging a gentle two to four hours of walking. Advanced hikers may cover 8 to 12 miles in a day, averaging five to six hours. Several trips are scheduled for singles.

SMITHSONIAN JOURNEYS
(see page 160)

Taking advantage of the current interest in active vacations, the Smithsonian program has added international walking and hiking adventures in scenic locales such as Poland, the Galápagos Islands, Hawaii, and the American Southwest. In many cases naturalists or local experts accompany the walks.

THE ITALIAN CONNECTION
11 Fairway Drive, Suite 210, Edmonton, Alberta T6J 2W4, Canada; (780) 438–5712 or (800) 462–7911; www.italian-connection.com (E)

This organization offers nine walking itineraries in Italy with special emphasis on regional food, often dining in local homes. Some tours include cooking lessons. Itineraries include Tuscan Hill Towns, the Cinque Terre along the coast, Piedmont vineyards and lakes, Umbria, and Sicily.

Sailing

Take to the sea for a windswept adventure like no other, with lazy days of snorkeling and swimming in solitary coves, convivial shipboard fun at night, and stops in picturesque ports where the big ships can't follow.

WINDJAMMER BAREFOOT CRUISES

P.O. Box 190120, 1759 Bay Road,
Miami Beach, FL 33139;
(800) 327-2601; www.windjammer.com (M)

Years in business:	50+
Age range:	25–55
Most common age:	30–40
Percent alone:	60
Number of participants:	66–122
Male/female ratio:	Varies; about equal
Year-round; will try to arrange shares	

"The thought of a tall-ship cruise to a small remote island turns people on," says the captain and founder of this Caribbean fleet that offers sailing vacations on five classic sailing ships. The fleet sails from several ports, including Tortola, St. Martin, Grenada, Antigua, St. Thomas, St. Lucia, Panama, Costa Rica, Nassau, Freeport, Trinidad, and Aruba. Each week more than sixty islands are visited on six- and thirteen-day outings around the Caribbean.

These are not luxury cruises but chances to experience the exhilaration of sailing and to get to isolated islands. The cabins are small, but they are air-conditioned and have private toilets and showers. Meals are served buffet style on ship or on picnics ashore. Drinks and wine are plentiful. Dress is always informal, and entertainment can be wacky—toga parties, crab races, steel-drum bands on board. Shore excursions include snorkeling, scuba diving, mountain biking, hiking, and kayaking. Several cruises are designated for singles.

COMMENTS **Female, 30s:** *I took this trip with my twelve-year-old son—it is great for both singles and single parents. About half the adults were single, ranging in age from 20s to 50s and 60s, a few more women than men. We were from many parts of the country and with very different backgrounds, but everyone had a wonderful time. The food was fantastic, the cabins comfortable and air-conditioned. We sailed mostly at night and spent days on the islands. The crew is great and tells you the ins and outs of each new port. At night there was always an activity. I made a lot of friends—and I can't wait to go on another trip. It's the best vacation I've ever had.*

Male, 40s: *I'm getting ready for my third trip. I've gone with friends and once by myself and I always had a fantastic time. You can let your hair down and relax. There's no pretense, you wear a T-shirt and shorts even for dinner. Everyone is* *friendly and outgoing, so it's easy to find a group of people you enjoy and go off in port together. The ages were from 20 to 70, but most are 30 or 40, and the 70s are very young at heart. Everyone has fun. You can be alone if you want to, but it's hard not to meet people. The food is very good, but not gourmet. There's only a choice of two entrees at dinner—this is not a luxury liner. But the staff is great and the captain is really accessible. One night he gave an impromptu stargazing class on deck. The itinerary is very special—you meet the local people and see places you can't on a big ship.*

MAINE WINDJAMMER ASSOCIATION

P.O. Box 1144, Blue Hill, ME 04614;
(207) 374-2993 or (800) 807-WIND;
www.sailmainecoast.com (I–M)

Years in business:	60+
Age range:	16–80
Most common age:	30–50
Percent alone:	25–30
Number of participants:	20–40
Male/female ratio:	Varies; fairly equal
June to October	

This fleet of fourteen nostalgic nineteenth-century two- and three-masted "tall ships," originals and replicas, sets sail each summer from Camden, Rockland, or Rockport for Penobscot Bay to explore the evergreen coast and the islands of Maine and to rest in quiet anchorages of unblemished beauty. Ships range from 46 to 132 feet and take six to forty passengers. There are single cabins, or singles may share. The rates are a real bargain. Passengers can help with the halyards and lines, keep a lookout for seals and ospreys, watch the lobstermen setting out traps, or just lie back and soak up the sun. Family-style meals featuring New England chowder, "Down East" lobster bakes, and Maine blueberry pie are not the least of the attractions! Three- to six-day cruises are offered.

COMMENTS **Male, 30s:** *I've been twice, and it was great. I was looking for something I could do without pressure to find a partner, and this was it. There were a few other singles, but it hardly mattered because with such a small group sharing meals and bath facilities, it was informal and comfortable for everyone. The sailing was terrific, and the food was fantastic.*
Female, 40s: *I really enjoyed it and am thinking of going again. There were people from age 30 to one man in his 70s, and nine out of twenty-three of us were single. Everyone got along and enjoyed each other's company.*

ECHO: THE WILDERNESS CO., INC.

6529 Telegraph Avenue, Oakland, CA 94609;
(510) 652–1600 or (800) 652–ECHO; www.echotrips.com (EE)
Singles are paired in cabins

Best known for rafting trips (see page 108), ECHO also runs intimate sailing adventures to Turkey.

The seventeen-day trips are aboard a sailing yacht with up to twelve guests plus a Turkish guide and crew. The sailing is along Turkey's beautiful Turquoise Coast. The trips include two days in Cappadocia, two days in Istanbul, and tours of several archaeological sites. If you are willing to share a cabin, these are grand excursions.

REMOTE ODYSSEYS WORLDWIDE (ROW)

P.O. Box 579, Coeur d'Alene, ID 83816;
(800) 451–6034 or (208) 765–0841; www.rowinternational.com (EE)
Singles are paired in cabins

This long-established rafting company pioneered guided yachting trips along the southwest coast of Turkey in 1984, and has expanded with similar ten- to sixteen-day programs in Croatia and Greece. Small groups of ten to eighteen guests travel on wooden motor/sail yachts ranging from 75 to 120 feet, discovering hidden coves with Greek and Roman ruins and idyllic swimming spots. On some nights the yachts anchor in small fishing villages. ROW also offers similar yachting adventures in Alaska and British Columbia, featuring whale watching, wildlife viewing, and sea kayaking.

COMMENTS **Male, 40s:** *What a fabulous trip to Turkey. I've traveled around the world, and this was the best trip I've ever taken. There were ten of us from mid-30s to early 70s, and we saw things we couldn't see any other way. The crew was excellent and open to suggestions—if we wanted to take a break in a pretty cove to swim, they said fine. There was no problem whatsoever being alone. I was always included as part of the group. I highly recommend it and am going on another cruise with this group next year.*

Rafting

W hat's so great about running a river? Those who love it call it "River Magic." One longtime operator says he has found that the cooperation required to meet the challenge of the river facilitates relationships, opens lines of communication, enhances personal growth, and helps participants develop lasting friendships more than any other form of outdoor recreation he has ever experienced—which may explain why so many river trips are available and why so many people sign up for them. Maybe Mark Twain said it best: "You feel mighty free and easy and comfortable on a raft."

SHERI GRIFFITH EXPEDITIONS, INC.

P.O. Box 1324, 2231 South Highway 191,
Moab, UT 84532; (800) 332–2439 or
(435) 259–8229; www.griffithexp.com (I–M)

Years in business:	30+
Age range:	23–60
Most common age:	25–40
Percent alone:	50
Number of participants:	25
Male/female ratio:	50/50
May to September	

T his classy operator prides herself on service of top food on two- to six-day river-running adventures through the majestic canyons along the Green, Colorado, and San Juan Rivers. There are runs for beginners to experts, plus some interesting specialty trips, such as trips featuring yoga and massage and an "Expedition in Luxury," a luxurious outing in Canyonlands National Park. Some river trips are combined with mountain biking, scenic flights, horseback riding, sea kayaking, or hiking on land.

C O M M E N T S   **Male, 30s:** *To a man, every person on the trip would have jumped at the chance to go again . . . tomorrow, if not sooner.*
Female, 30s: *A well-organized, smooth-running operation with a courteous, knowledgeable, and fun staff. Their ability in the kitchen was unmatched. The trip was a bargain.*

ECHO: THE WILDERNESS CO., INC.

6529 Telegraph Avenue, Oakland, CA 94609;
(510) 652–1600 or (800) 652–ECHO;
www.echotrips.com (M)

Years in business:	Since 1971
Age range:	7–70
Most common age:	30s–50s
Percent alone:	Varies
Number of participants:	1,500 per year
Male/female ratio:	50/50
Late May to mid-September	

R iver-rafting excitement with this group includes special outings with entertainment such as wine tasting, music, and yoga workshops. U.S. rafting trips are held on the Middle Fork and Main Salmon River in Idaho, the Rogue River in Oregon, and the Tuolumne river in California. Yachting trips to Turkey are a recent addition to their offerings.

COMMENTS **Female, 20s:** *I've gone alone twice and been very comfortable. I was really impressed because I went with a very large group and they handled it beautifully. They were very sensitive about pairing the guides with the different groups of people and skill levels. And evenings are congenial, so everyone gets to know each other. You have to work together in the boats. There is a comfortable mix of men and women (a few more women), and an age range of 15 to 65. The groups are diverse and interesting, and there are plenty of single people.*
Female, 40s: *I've been going on Echo's trips for fifteen years; I think they are the premier rafting company. I admit that if you go alone you have to be more outgoing—a lot of people do come as a group of friends, and you don't want to intrude. But there are usually one or two singles on each trip and the leaders organize group activities like nature walks and soaking in hot tubs so everyone gets involved. I would definitely recommend these trips to solo travelers. It's a great way to meet people, and I've formed lasting friendships. In fact, I'm planning my next trip with some people I met on an Echo trip.*

OUTDOOR ADVENTURE RIVER SPECIALISTS (O.A.R.S.), INC.
P.O. Box 67, Angels Camp, CA 95222;
(209) 736–4677 or (800) 346–6277;
www.oars.com (I–M)

Years in business:	30+
Age range:	18–54+
Most common age:	25–45
Percent alone:	25
Number of participants:	16–25
Male/female ratio:	50/50
April to October; will try to arrange shares	

One of the largest and most diverse outfitters in the West, O.A.R.S. offers over fifty trips on twenty rivers, from Class V rapids to gentle floats. Main destinations include California, Utah, Oregon, Wyoming, and Colorado, plus Canada, Mexico, and such far-flung locales as Chile, Costa Rica, the Galápagos Islands, and Tibet. The catalog ranks each trip for the difficulty of the rapids and describes the scenery. Recent specialty trips have included a "Wine on the River" series and spa trips with yoga and massage. Several trips are planned for solo travelers.

COMMENTS **Female, 30s:** *I've gone on two trips alone. You can have time to yourself if you want it, but you never have to be alone. My groups ranged from ages 20 to mid-60s; about half were single and two-thirds were male, and they were from all over the country. The people were great, very congenial. You switch boats each day so you get to meet everyone. The food was terrific and we slept under the stars. If you have a spirit of adventure, this is a great experience.* **Male, 30s:** *I've gone on five trips, alone and with my wife. Many of the people are married but come alone. We were up at sunrise, did everything from running rapids to hiking. You get to know everyone as you switch boats. You can do as much or as little work as you want. There is good food and lots of it. It's a good introduction to rafting—easy, relaxed, and everyone can do it.*

DVORAK'S KAYAK & RAFTING EXPEDITIONS
17921 U.S. Highway 285, Nathrop, CO 81236; (800) 824-3795 or (719) 539-6851; www.dvorakexpeditions.com (I)

Years in business:	Since 1969
Age range:	25–65
Most common age:	25–35
Percent alone:	60
Number of participants:	5,000+ annually; 12–25 per trip
Male/female ratio:	50/50
Late May to September in U.S.; November to February abroad	

Dvorak's was the first licensed operator in Colorado. It has grown to offer trips through scenic canyons on eleven U.S. rivers and on rivers in Nepal and New Zealand. Among the states covered are Colorado, Utah, New Mexico, Arizona, and Idaho, where rivers used include the Salt, Dolores, Colorado, Green, Arkansas, and others. Along with rafting, they offer fishing and multisport trips, and instructional paddling clinics.

COMMENTS **Female, 30s:** *A wonderful experience, the finest thing I've ever done. There were seven of us, all single, age 30s to 50s, about equal numbers of men and women. We stayed in tents, had wonderful, healthful food. The instruction was great—but even less physical people can enjoy this trip, as you don't have to paddle if you don't want to.* **Female, 30s:** *This was a great thing to do. I went with my ten-year-old son, and although he was the only child, it was no problem—the guides took care of him and were wonderful helping him fish when we hit calm water. We slept in tents, had great food. There was just one couple—from New Zealand—the rest were future guides on their first trip.*

RIVER ODYSSEYS WEST (ROW)

(Also Remote Odysseys Worldwide)
P.O. Box 579, Coeur d'Alene, ID 83816;
(800) 451–6034 or (208) 765–0841;
www.rowinc.com (E)

Years in business:	Since 1979
Age range of participants:	5–86
Most common age:	40
Percent alone:	18
Number of participants:	16
Male/female ratio:	47/53

Idaho is home base for this interesting company, which features rafting on the Snake, Lochsa, Moyie, Owyhee, Bruneau, St. Joe, and Clark Fork Rivers and the Middle Fork of the Salmon River. Several trips offer added activities such as hiking or fishing, or special features such as a drive along the Lewis and Clark trail, a stay at a guest ranch or a night at a resort with warm beds and hot tubs. Special trips are planned for families, men and women only, and rafters over age 55. A "River Soul Journey" combines rafting with hiking, yoga, and meditation.

In winter, ROW also stands for Remote Odysseys Worldwide, which offers adventure cruising (see page 107), rafting through the mountains and jungles of Ecuador, and travel by barge in France.

COMMENTS **Female, 60s:** *I've gone on two trips, Hells Canyon and the Middle Fork of the Salmon, and loved both. The crew is very professional. The guides are knowledgeable about the nature and history of the area as well as the rivers, and they do a great presentation of food. The group was about sixteen people, a mix of sexes and ages from 20s to 60s. I was the oldest on the last trip, but we all got along and the younger people went out of their way to be friendly and helpful. They make sure everyone gets acquainted the first night. I can't say enough good things about this company.*

NANTAHALA OUTDOOR CENTER ADVENTURE TRAVEL

13077 Highway 19 West, Box 41, Bryson City, NC 28713;
(828) 488–2176 or (888) 905–7238; www.noc.com (I–M)

This top Eastern teaching center (see page 35) also offers a variety of guided white-water and sea kayaking adventures. Rafting locales include not only North Carolina, the southern Appalachians, and the Florida Everglades but exotic destinations such as Costa Rica, Chile, Jamaica, and Panama.

Nepal: The Supreme Adventure

There are many mighty mountains in the world, but the trip to the Himalayas is unique. Since it remains on my dream list, I asked Ben Wallace, who helps organize trips and who has lived in Nepal, to explain why.

The lure of Nepal is the people as much as the mountains, he says. The trails you follow are the only roads in this remote region, the lifeline of the villagers who live here. Every day you are seeing intimately a fascinating and totally different way of life. You can linger, visit homes, and observe how people live, cook, farm, and work. Staying in local homes is an option. Most people come to Nepal thinking the thrill is going to be the big mountains and the views but find instead it is the local life that is the indelible memory.

Ben says that most people once were drawn to Nepal for the physical challenge, but that a higher percentage today are looking for something else, a total change from their life-style and environment. The least strenuous treks usually mean four to eight days on the trail, walking four to six hours a day, with a maximum ascent of about 1,500 feet—within the ability of anyone who does any exercising at home.

Everything is taken care of for you. Someone else puts up and takes down the camp, carries all gear, does all the cooking and cleaning up. You are free to simply soak in the experience. Many people today sign up for the shorter one-week treks, then spend another week sightseeing or rafting. Ben believes, however, that the longer trips deeper into the mountains are the most rewarding. People who spend the time to really immerse themselves in the culture are hooked—they almost always return.

Ben explains that the degree of difficulty has three components: the duration of time on the trail, how much altitude is gained or lost, and the living conditions. "Someone who is very fit but not used to living in a tent—a jogger, for example—may be able to stand up to the physical challenge but not be happy about spending three weeks in a tent.

"Altitude affects people differently—and the same people differently on different days. Above ten or eleven thousand feet, almost everyone feels discomfort, perhaps headaches. A good operator knows this and allows plenty of time for acclimatization."

The food on a trek is a pleasant surprise. A sample menu might include onion soup topped with melted yak cheese, sweet and sour chicken over vegetable fried rice, and cake baked over the campfire. As in any third world country, there may be an occasional stomach bug to contend with. All treks include a medical kit and someone who knows how to use it.

When to come? The trekking season is from late September to May.

More Adventuring Ideas

- Specialty Travel Index (P.O. Box 458, San Anselmo, CA 94979; 415–455–1643 or 800–442–4922; www.specialtytravel.com) is a semi-annual listing of ads from hundreds of operators of adventure and specialty trips of all kinds. It is the source used by many travel agents. Sample index listings: Environmental Education, Festival Tours, Film History, Fishing, Foliage Tours, Windjamming, Windsurfing, Winery Tours, Women's Tours. An annual subscription is $10.
- Adventure Center (1311 63rd Street, Suite 200, Emeryville, CA 94608; 510–654–1879 or 800–228–8747; www.adventurecenter.com) is an agency specializing in adventure travel, offering more than 1,000 annual departures to nearly one hundred countries.

Get Back to Nature

YOU DON'T HAVE TO HIKE OR RAFT YOUR WAY INTO THE WILDERNESS in order to enjoy the outdoors. Nature-oriented workshops are available in beautiful and remote settings, and there are wonderful tours and cruises geared to appreciating places where plant, animal, and bird life are abundant.

Many nature-oriented tour operators also offer "soft adventures," such as expedition cruises and safaris to remote places that require no camping or strenuous activity. The choice is rich, from watching penguins and polar bears in Antarctica to viewing moose and elk in Wyoming, from seeing brilliantly colored birds in the jungle to close encounters with giraffes and lions on the African plains.

Vacations that emphasize nature these days often come with a catchy label—"ecotourism." Ecotourism at its best means simply respecting nature. Many operators talk about ecotourism but do not practice it. Careless, commercial tour operators can drive animals from their habitats and destroy the natural wonders that have drawn visitors. If you choose a vacation emphasizing nature, by all means choose responsible operators and organizations who practice and promote conservation.

One way to do this is by choosing members of the International Ecotourism Society, a nonprofit organization with members working in more than seventy countries to create low-impact travel experiences. The group includes members of the travel industry and international and local conservation organizations as well as analysts from many fields, including biology, park management, community development, and environmental education. While tour operators who belong to the society are not certified, they have shown their support for conservation. For a roster of members, contact the International Ecotourism Society, 733 Fifteenth Street, NW, Suite 1000, Washington, DC 20005; (202) 347–9203. A list of tour operator members also can be found on their Web site, www.ecotourism.org.

Nature Workshops

The nicest thing about nature-oriented workshops is their magnificent settings, where recreation is as appealing as the learning opportunities. These programs aim not only to teach about nature but to inspire appreciation that will carry over into support for conservation when you return home. In that endeavor, the operators often include painting, photography, and writing workshops along with bird and nature walks.

AUDUBON ECOLOGY CAMPS
AND WORKSHOPS

National Audubon Society,
613 Riversville Road, Greenwich, CT 06831;
(203) 869–2017; www.audubon.org/educate/cw (I)

Years in business:	60+
Age range:	19–80
Most common age:	30s–40s
Percent alone:	High
Number of participants:	55 maximum; divided into smaller field groups
Male/female ratio:	40/60
July and early August	

Adults from across the country come to the one- and two-week summer sessions held in the society's sanctuaries in Connecticut, off the coast of Maine, in Vermont, Maryland, South Carolina, California, Wisconsin, and Minnesota.

In these beautiful outdoor settings, adults are able to learn, relax, and forge new friendships. Programs focus on field ecology, marine life, and birding as well as drawing and nature photography. The aim is to reintroduce you to nature, to show how all wildlife is interdependent, and to teach what you can do to protect it. Rustic lodgings are mostly dorm style; meals are buffet. Participants are all ages and backgrounds, from college students and retired senior citizens to teachers and firefighters. Links to individual camps can be found on the Audubon Web site.

COMMENTS **Female, 30s:** *A typical day means getting up for an early breakfast and then walking from about 8:30 to 11:30 A.M. with a naturalist who is usually a teacher. The leaders are excellent and really know their stuff. There's time to rest or relax before and after lunch, then there is another program from 2:00 to 5:00 P.M. Depending on the weather and the topic, you might go out by boat instead of on foot. The idea is always hands-on learning. If it rains, classroom talks are held. At night there might be a guest lecturer, square dancing, a slide show, or an evening* *astronomy walk. The big group is divided into four small groups, and you stay with that group every day for programs, so there's plenty of chance to get to know people. Everyone has an interest in nature, and it's really nice to share that with others. There's a lot of bonding within the group.*

NATIONAL WILDLIFE FEDERATION FAMILY SUMMIT PROGRAM
11100 Wildlife Center Drive, Reston, VA 20190; (800) 606–9563; www.nwf.org/summits (I)

Years in business:	30+
Age range:	Infants to 80s
Most common age:	30–50
Percent alone:	33
Number of participants:	500–600 annually
Male/female ratio:	Varies
July and early August	

Family Summits offer a week of nature education and recreation in beautiful locations that rotate annually. The cost is moderate, and the program is excellent. Depending on the site, activities might include boat excursions to observe whales and sea lions, hikes, or a field trip to a national park or forest. Nature hikes and outdoor photography are usually featured in all programs, and participants may learn about orienteering, bird-watching, geology, and astronomy. Activities are planned to suit all levels of fitness. Lodging options can vary from rustic lodges to apartment-style suites. All programs serve meals in a central location, either cafeteria or family style. The ambience is relaxed and friendly. Recent sites have included Estes Park, Colorado, the Pacific Northwest, and Big Sky, Montana.

COMMENTS **Female, 40s:** *The age range is literally infants to senior citizens. You're up early. There are lectures and field trips, yet also plenty of free time. The hiking isn't too strenuous, so anyone can do it. After dinner, there are slide presentations, music, stargazing, or evening wildlife viewing field trips. Accommodations and food vary from fair to excellent depending on location, but the lodgings are always clean and adequate.*
Female, 50s: *Summits have been the reason that I've seen most of the United States . . . and also a way to make lasting friendships. I still keep in touch with and visit friends I met at my first Summit fifteen years ago. But most of all, Summits instill in us a love for the earth and each other.*

THE NATURE CONSERVANCY

4245 North Fairfax Drive, Suite 100, Arlington, VA 22203;
(703) 841–5300; Pine Butte information, (406) 466–2158; www.nature.org (I)
April to September

Another highly respected conservation group, The Nature Conservancy offers weekend and week-long field trips in several scenic locations. Changing activities are set up by local field offices from Virginia's Eastern Shore to the Nebraska sandhills to the coast of Oregon. Other programs take place at permanent Conservancy properties such as Homestead at Hart Prairie in Arizona, where participants are housed in historic cabins beneath the San Francisco Mountains for explorations of peaks and canyons and a chance to work with ecologists on plant surveys or to watch for Arizona's jewel-hued hummingbirds.

Natural History workshops are held at the Pine Butte Guest Ranch in Montana, with lodgings in cozy private cabins at the foot of the Rockies. Home-cooked meals are served in the rustic lodge. There are planned programs for some weeks on topics such as wildflowers, birds, Montana geology, grizzly bears, a dinosaur dig, or naturalist tours of the Rockies, with daily treks into Montana mountains and prairies. This is also a wonderful spot just for the serenity and the chance to hike mountain trails, ride a horse, observe wildlife, or read a good book beside the heated pool. The Tensleep Preserve also offers weeks of adventures and birding in the Bighorn Mountains in Wyoming.

FOUR CORNERS SCHOOL OF OUTDOOR EDUCATION

P.O. Box 1029, Monticello, UT 84535;
(435) 587–2156 or (800) 525–4456;
www.sw-adventures.org (I–M)

Years in business:	20+
Age range:	7–90
Most common age:	45–65
Percent alone:	50
Number of participants:	375 per year, divided into small groups
Male/female ratio:	40/60
April to October, plus special winter national park programs from mid-January to mid-March; guaranteed shares	

This exceptional program offers a variety of backcountry explorations in the beautiful Southwest that include the chance to learn about archaeology or rock art, document archaeology sites, learn primitive skills, or learn Navajo weaving. Some programs include moderate hiking, backpacking, or rafting. Special workshops concentrate on photography and writing. Lodging varies with the program; camping, motels, ranch accommodations, and houseboating on Lake Powell are among the possibilities. Winter programs take place in Zion, Bryce, and Yellowstone National Parks.

COMMENTS **Female, 40s:** *I've been on seven trips with them by myself. They're actually responsible for my going back to school and getting my master's in anthropology. I've gone in all four seasons. The groups are small, eight to fifteen, so it's easy to hook up with people and you always get lots of personal attention. Besides the leaders there is always an intern or two who can answer questions or provide extra help if you need it. It's usually 50/50 men and women and ages from 20s to 80s. Many people are by themselves—I always feel comfortable. The food on their river trips is marvelous—I don't know how they do it! The staff are very tuned into the land and the culture of people. They take a very holistic approach to education. I heartily recommend it to anyone and can't wait to go again myself!*
Female, 50s: *I've gone on a number of trips, alone and with friends. There are about fourteen in the group, and you're with them all the time so it's easy to get to know everyone. The age range is 20 to 65, slightly more men than women. Most people are by themselves. The program is very well run. The staff are knowledgeable and very helpful about getting people to open up. The guides are chosen very carefully, and they really know their stuff.*

CAMP DENALI AND NORTH FACE LODGE
P.O. Box 67, Denali National Park, AK 99755;
(907) 683–2290; www.campdenali.com (EE)
June to September; will try to arrange shares

Camp Denali and North Face Lodge are small, family-owned and -operated lodges accommodating thirty-five to forty guests. Located deep within the heart of Denali National Park, they are the only accommodations offering a view of the snow-clad peaks of the Alaska Range and Mount McKinley. Stays are on a fixed arrival and departure schedule, three, four, or seven nights. Rates include bus transportation from the Denali Park Rail Station (90 miles each way); all meals; guided hikes and field trips each day with naturalist guides; use of canoes, mountain bikes, and fishing gear; and evening natural history programs. Guests may take advantage of the Denali Institute–sponsored Special Emphasis Series with visiting resource leaders sharing their expertise in the natural sciences, Alaska's cultural history, natural resource policy, and the arts.

OLYMPIC FIELD SEMINARS
OLYMPIC PARK INSTITUTE
111 Barnes Point Road, Port Angeles, WA 98363;
(360) 928–3720 or (800) 775–3720;
www.olympicparkinstitute.org (I)

Years in business:	13
Age range:	30–60
Most common age:	40–50
Percent alone:	70
Number of participants:	10–15 per class
Male/female ratio:	50/50
May to October	

The lovely setting on majestic Lake Crescent in the mountains of Olympic National Park adds to the pleasure of these weekend courses covering many aspects of the nature, art, and culture of the region. Nature classes look at birds, butterflies, plants, and marine life. Cultural offerings include Northwest Native American art, traditional plant uses, and hands-on wood carving in the Northwest Coast tradition. Other possibilities explore painting, storytelling, and photography. Participants stay in cabins nestled in a grove of fir trees; each one has a small common area with four adjacent sleeping rooms. Guests are automatically paired, though single rooms are often available for an extra fee. Everyone shares meals at the historic Rosemary Inn, a rustic lodge built by craftsmen at the turn of the twentieth century.

COMMENTS **Male, 50s:** *I've been there many times and I always go alone—it's a very warm and friendly place. Most people are from the Pacific Northwest, but there are always some from all over the country, with diverse backgrounds and a big age range. There are usually eight to twelve in a group, about 25 percent male, and only a third are traveling with someone else, so you never feel like you're the only person there alone. The staff are excellent hosts, making sure everyone feels a part of things. They're also very knowledgeable about the park. The professors who teach the courses are all experts in their fields. I'd definitely recommend this to people traveling alone because you bond with the group almost immediately and become unified. All the people I've encountered are very warm and outgoing.*

Female, 60s: *I've gone there seven times, alone all but once, and I always have an excellent experience. I've done programs that are more seminars, and I've done purely travel trips, too. The instructors are experts and have a real interest in the ecology of the area. I feel very safe with all these instructors. I've been on outdoor trips with other operators, and they're not as well run. You feel at home here immediately. The food is [almost] all organic and natural and extremely fresh. Everyone cares about the ecosystem of Olympic Park and wants to study and preserve it. I've formed lasting friendships.*

Other national parks offer classes similar to the Olympic Park workshops. Among these are:

THE GLACIER INSTITUTE

P.O. Box 1887, Kalispell, MT 59903;
(406) 755–1211; www.glacierinstitute.org (I)
Year-round

Field seminars covering everything from grizzly bears to global climate change take place in this magnificent national park known as the "Crown of the Continent." Wildflowers and mushrooms, wild medicinal herbs, animal tracks, geology, wildlife, birds of prey, river ecology, painting, and photography are among the one- to three-day offerings, many including hiking with naturalists. Most of the summer adult programs take place at the Glacier Park Field Camp just inside the west entrance of the park, where beds in six comfortable rustic cabins can be reserved by enrollees; a modern kitchen and bathroom facilities are located nearby. Participants can also choose to stay in park lodges. Either way, this is an opportunity to explore one of the most beautiful national parks with good company while you learn more about nature.

THE YELLOWSTONE ASSOCIATION INSTITUTE

P.O. Box 117, Yellowstone National Park, WY 82190;
(307) 344–2294; www.yellowstoneassociation.org (I)

Workshops emphasizing the wilderness areas of the park are offered year-round. Classes are small (ten to fifteen students) and can run from one to five days. Classrooms are headquartered at many locations in the park, including the historic Buffalo Ranch in the quiet, unpopulated Lamar Valley in the northeast part of the park, where roaming herds of wildlife are so abundant that the area has been nicknamed the "Serengeti of North America." Many programs include guided walks with naturalists. Wolf watching programs are among the most popular choices. "Lodging and Learning" packages provide accommodations and meals at park hotels. For courses at the Lamar Ranch, lodging is available in heated log sleeping cabins at a nominal fee. The ranch has a fully equipped central kitchen, bath, and classroom building.

YOSEMITE OUTDOOR ADVENTURES

Yosemite Association, P.O. Box 230, El Portal, CA 95318;
(209) 379–2321; www.yosemite.org. (I)

Over 800 participants each year attend these programs, taking in many aspects of the park's ecology and beauty, from studying the stars to tracking wildlife to photography and painting. Backpacking and hiking are also offered. Besides the superb surroundings, directors say people come to meet people, have fun, and to feel safe in a wilderness environment. They add that many people come alone. High-country programs require camping; some programs include reserved lodging in the park at an additional fee.

ROCKY MOUNTAIN FIELD SEMINARS

Rocky Mountain Nature Association, Rocky Mountain National Park, Estes Park, CO 80517; (970) 586–3262 or (800) 748–7002; www.rmna.org (I)

Over one hundred one- to six-day workshops include photography, art, geology, tracking mammals, butterflies, and moths, Rocky Mountain flora, mushrooms, herbs, grasses, and other natural and cultural history topics relating to the park. Students make their own lodging and meal arrangements.

Nature Tours

Nature tours offer advantages you could not enjoy on your own. They go to remote areas where getting around can be difficult and where required arrangements often are not easily made from home. The trips have been researched to take advantage of the seasons and make the best use of limited time. They provide the benefit of a knowledgeable guide to answer questions and enrich your experience. And you will also learn from other members of the group, who tend to be interested in and knowledgeable about the natural world. While these tours come with a high price tag, they are often less expensive than trying to duplicate the trip yourself.

Selecting a nature tour involves some of the same issues that you must consider with any tour—the reliability of the company and good references from past participants. But when you choose a tour operator, also remember the issues of ecotourism. Find an operator who has been working for a long time in the country you will be visiting, who knows and cares about the local culture, and who uses local guides and services whenever possible. Find out how guides are trained. Ask about conservation issues and what the company does to minimize its impact on the environment. The background material participants receive often provides a good test of the operator's attitude and sense of responsibility. The best operators send information on cultural traditions and the environment as well as clothing tips and reading lists. Companies listed here have shown their commitment to the environment.

VICTOR EMANUEL NATURE TOURS, INC.

2525 Wallingwood Drive, Suite 1003, Austin, TX 78746; (512) 328–5221 or (800) 328–8368; www.ventbird.com (M–E for domestic trips; EE for foreign trips)

This is the largest company specializing in birding tours, with more than twenty-five years of experience, and their trips guarantee compatible company for birders. They cover the globe from Alaska and Australia to Africa and the Amazon, moving with the seasons to find good weather. Trips labeled "introductory" are ideal for beginners. "Birding and History" tours include sightseeing and cultural excursions. Rates vary according to destination, with U.S. trips the least expensive.

WORLD WILDLIFE FUND (WWF) TRAVEL PROGRAM

1250 24th Street NW, Washington, DC 20037; (202) 778–9683 or (888) 993–8687; www.worldwildlife.org/travel (M–E for domestic trips; EE for foreign trips)

Saving wildlife and wild places is the prime aim of this respected organization, and to engage people in their mission, WWF sponsors trips to prime wildlife-watching destinations on all seven continents. Guides are top-notch, and many trips visit important conservation areas. Some recent trips have visited national parks in India; some of Africa's prime marine sanctuaries—from Zanzibar to the Seychelle Islands; and the rain forests and other wild places of South America. They cover the United States from the Florida Everglades to Alaska. Trips are for members; only a $15 annual fee is needed to join.

THE NATURE CONSERVANCY

(See page 118)

To further their mission of preserving the world's "last great places" and to foster responsible ecotourism, the Conservancy organizes trips to see some of its conservation policies at work. Recent destinations included the northern coast of Honduras and the protected areas of the Dominican Republic. They promise trips offering education, adventure, and time to reflect on the beauty and wonder of our natural world.

AMERICAN MUSEUM OF NATURAL HISTORY DISCOVERY TOURS
Central Park West at 79th Street, New York, NY 10024; (800) 462–8687 or
(212) 769–5700; www.discoverytours.org (M–E for domestic trips; EE for foreign trips)

Some sixty-five tours are offered each year by this great museum to explore the
natural wonders and cultures of the world, with the finest teams of scientists
and educators as leaders. The choices range from Mexico to Mongolia, including
cruises and safaris; gorilla tracking in Uganda; and traveling the ancient Silk Road
through China and central Asia. While the cost is high, so is the quality of these
tours.

CHEESEMAN'S ECOLOGY SAFARIS
20800 Kittredge Road, Saratoga, CA 95070; (408) 867–1371 or (800) 527–5330;
www.cheesemans.com (M–E for domestic trips; EE for foreign trips)

A nature-loving family has run this operation since 1980, planning trips that are
all about nature and wildlife, with most of the day spent in the field. The destinations cover three A-list nature locales—Antarctica, Africa, and Australia—plus
South and Central America, the United States and Baja, Mexico. Check the listings
well in advance. Some of the trips are sold out a year ahead of time.

INTERNATIONAL EXPEDITIONS
One Environs Park, Helena, AL 35080; (205) 428–1700 or (800) 633–4734;
www.ietravel.com (M–E for domestic trips; EE for foreign trips)

Two major travel magazines in 2004 named International Expeditions among
the top nature travel companies. In business since 1980, their aim is to foster
appreciation of the natural wonders in the world, and their trip roster includes almost all the great places: Belize, Tikal, India, Egypt, Iceland, Patagonia, Africa, the
Amazon, the Galápagos, Costa Rica, and Machu Picchu, to name a few.

GEO EXPEDITIONS
P.O. Box 3656, Sonora, CA 95370; (209) 532–0152 or (800) 351–5041;
www.geoexpeditions.com (M–E for domestic trips; EE for foreign trips)

Since 1982 this group has led tours around the world, including India, Nepal,
Indonesia, Australia, polar expeditions, and South America, including the
Galápagos Islands. They promise groups small enough to provide for a rich
experience.

QUARK EXPEDITIONS

980 Post Road, Darien, CT 06820; (203) 656–0499 or (800) 356–5699;
www.quark-expeditions.com (M–E for domestic trips; EE for foreign trips)

One of the innovators in expeditions to view the wildlife and birds of the polar regions, Quark uses small boats, including former Russian ice-cutters, to visit regions once inaccessible. Highlights are the penguins in Antarctica in winter and polar bears in Alaska in summer.

SOUTHWIND ADVENTURES

P.O. Box 621057, Littleton, CO 80162; (303) 972–0701 or (800) 377–9463;
www.southwindadventures.com (EE)

The Andes, the Amazon, Patagonia, and the Galápagos are the territory of this operator specializing in tours to South America since 1990. Itineraries range from tours and cruises to active adventures for mountain bikers and hikers.

Voyage to the End of the Earth: Cruising Antarctica

The penguins were everywhere, dozens of them, dapper in formal black and white, paying no mind to the visitors just landed in their midst. Some were two-stepping downhill to dive into the water for a swim, others sitting perfectly still, guarding eggs or downy chicks in their nests. A few show-offs almost seemed to pose for the cameras clicking in all directions. Every one of us was grinning ear to ear at the fun of being close-up to these irresistible little creatures.

Playful penguins are the stars of a cruise to Antarctica, but they share the spotlight with some of the most glorious scenery on earth. On this pristine continent, mighty snow-covered mountain peaks are punctuated with the icy-blue sheen of glaciers. Enormous icebergs in the sea were sculpted almost like fellow ships floating beside us. A cry of "Whales!" rushed everyone to the decks to spy the spumes and arcs of these giant swimmers.

Antarctica, the southernmost point in the world, is an increasingly popular cruise destination in December, January, and February, the summer months in South America, when ice caps melt, temperatures thaw, and the waters become navigable. Despite the remoteness of the destination, these are not hardship cruises. Each destination can be reached either on small, nimble ships holding ninety to one hundred passengers, which allow for more stops, or via comfortable ocean liners. Either way, passengers board small, sturdy Zodiac rubber rafts to reach the shore for exploring.

All of the ships bound for Antarctica leave from the town of Ushuaia (*U-shwhy-a*) at the tip of Argentina, the town that calls itself the "Port at the End of the World." It is the capital of Tierra del Fuego, a large triangular island with a well-known forested national park. It turns out to be a quaint little frontier town, terraced up a hillside surrounded by scenic mountains. In the short summer season, when temperatures rise into the sixties, Ushuaia is abloom with flowers, a surprisingly colorful sight. Along its narrow streets are shops selling items such as wood carvings, leather goods, and penguin souvenirs in every possible shape, from penguin-shaped salad utensils to cuddly stuffed penguins for the kiddies.

I chose to sail on one of the larger ships, the *Discovery*, designed for travelers who want their adventure travel with the amenities of a cruise ship. On Antarctic cruises, the passenger total is kept to around 400 to ensure that everyone has at least an hour on shore at each landing. We were divided into four groups, taking turns being first to board the Zodiacs that brought us to three different penguin colonies.

Port Lockroy, one of the largest colonies of gentoo penguins, was a joyful introduction. More gentoos awaited at the aptly named Paradise Harbor, a scenic setting ringed by ice cliffs and dotted with floating icebergs. My favorite was the last landing at Half Moon Island, a rocky volcanic island where we met chinstrap penguins, named for the narrow band of black feathers that extend from ear to ear just below their chins. One group that was perched in tiers along a steep crag almost seemed to be croaking a serenade, led by a conductor flapping his fins at the bottom.

One evening we were treated to floats in the Zodiacs for close-up views of the scenery. Visibility was no problem, since it stays light until almost midnight in the summer months in Antarctica. The temperature was always above freezing, often in the forties. We were quite comfortable in the bright red insulated parkas given to each passenger.

Excellent talks by one of a dozen experts on polar exploration on board filled us in on the birds, whales, seals, glaciers, and geology we would be seeing. They stressed the importance of guarding the fragile ecosystem we were privileged to visit, explaining that we would be kept at a safe distance from nesting penguins and would intrude as little as possible on their world.

Most of the passengers were older and well traveled, with Antarctica the seventh continent visited for many people. They hailed from Britain, Scotland, Australia, and Japan as well as the United States. Because the *Discovery* charges no single supplement on most Antarctic trips, a large number of passengers were traveling alone.

The one possible downside to this cruise is sailing through the Drake Passage, the notoriously turbulent waters where the Pacific and Atlantic Oceans meet at the tip of South America. It can be as smooth as a lake or as scary as "the Perfect Storm." There were times during the cruise when some of us had wondered whether the trip might have been even more rewarding on a smaller vessel with more stops. But with waves as high as 50 feet crashing over the decks, everyone was grateful to have chosen the security of our larger ship.

Almost every adventure outfitter listed in this book now includes Antarctica in its winter trips. Quark Expeditions, page 125, is highly recommended for those who prefer a smaller ship. For the current schedule and rates for *Discovery*, phone (866) 623–2689 or see www.discoveryworldcruises.com.

Darwin's World: Cruising the Enchanted Galápagos Islands

None of the photographs and none of the shipboard briefings can prepare you for the fantastic reality of the Galápagos, an extraordinary configuration of islands formed by the peaks of million-year-old volcanoes. Isolated some 600 miles off the coast of Ecuador, the Galápagos are unusual in their lava-scarred landscapes as well as their tame wildlife. This is an enchanted world where rare birds and animals that have never been hunted by predators accept human visitors as just one more of nature's species—no more to be feared than a passing bird.

Who lives here? Birds like none you've ever seen. Blue-footed boobies stand a foot and a half high, with feet and legs the color of a clear summer sky. Masked boobies, eyes framed in black, cluck over their tall, fuzzy chicks. Flapping albatrosses, graceful oystercatchers, and exotic lava herons all but pose for the photographers who furiously snap camera shutters in their midst.

In the Galápagos, you'll go swimming with sea lions, step around two-foot-long iguanas, examine bright-red sea crabs, and exclaim at the giant turtles that give the islands their name. Still present are the finches that fascinated Charles Darwin—evolved into thirteen distinct species, each with a beak shaped for most efficiently obtaining its food. Forty-five percent of the plants here are found nowhere else, including the amazing Opuntia cactus that has evolved into a strange and sturdy tree. No matter how much film you bring, it won't be enough.

To visit the Galápagos, you must travel to Guayaquil, Ecuador, and board a cruise ship or a sailing yacht. The most comfortable way is to go on one of several ships, including the ninety-passenger *Santa Cruz* or the newer 110-passenger *Galápagos Legend*. Excursions to the islands are in small boats, each holding only about twenty people, so you will soon be friends with your fellow passengers, marveling together at what you have seen.

Many excellent ecotourism companies schedule cruises to the Galápagos Islands, but the largest and one of the oldest handling this destination (and all of Ecuador) is Metropolitan Touring, c/o Adventure Associates, 13150 Coit Road, Suite 110, Dallas, TX 75240; (800) 527–2500 or (972) 907–0414; www.metro politantouring.com. They run the *Santa Cruz* as well as the *Isabella II,* a deluxe forty-passenger yacht. The *Galápagos Legend* can be booked through many agencies, including Galápagos Holidays (800–661–2512).

Sources for Expedition Cruises

Excellent sources for a number of expedition cruises are the Smithsonian Study Tours (see page 160), and the DISCOVERY Tours program run by the American Museum of Natural History (see page 124). The Nature Conservancy also includes cruises on its travel agenda (see page 118).

Other top operators who run some of the cruises described above as well as a host of others from the Arctic to the Amazon include:

EXPEDITION TRIPS
6553 California Avenue, Seattle, WA 98136;
(206) 547–0700 or (877) 412–8527; www.expeditiontrips.com.

OCEANIC SOCIETY EXPEDITIONS
Fort Mason Center, Building E, San Francisco, CA 94123;
(415) 441–1106 or (800) 326–7491; www.oceanic-society.org.

ABERCROMBIE & KENT, INC.
1520 Kensington Road, Oak Brook, IL 60523;
(800) 323–7308 or (630) 954–2944; www.abercrombiekent.com.

SWAN HELLENIC CRUISES
631 Commack Road, Suite 1A, Commack, NY 11725; (631) 858–1263 or
(877) 219–4239; www.swanhellenic.com.

CLIPPER CRUISE LINE AND INTRAV
(See page 171)
Also have nature tours among their offerings.

Safari!

Joining a safari to see the big game in East Africa was a longtime dream come true for me—but the reality outdid even my fondest fantasies.

Nothing you've read or seen in picture books can prepare you for the deep emotion that wells up on viewing these magnificent creatures at close range, living in their own environment. It is a jolt of joy and wonder that fills the senses and goes straight to the heart.

Strangers soon become close friends on safari because of this shared emotion and the excitement of the trip. It makes no difference whether you are on your own or with a companion. You are all fellow hunters, intent on prowling the national parks and game preserves, ready to aim your binoculars and shoot on sight with your camera.

The targets are ever-changing. Lightning-swift cheetahs stalk graceful gazelles. A pride of lions sleeps in the sun. Hordes of dizzily striped zebras, big and small, graze in the grasses. Giraffes bat their eyelashes and nibble daintily at the treetops. Thousands of wildebeest stand around like a congregation of bearded old men. Herds of elephants trumpet and splash in a water hole. A family of rhinos stares out like giant, nearsighted Mr. Magoos. Every day, every park holds a new discovery.

The trip is easy for a single traveler because every detail is handled for you. From the moment you are met by a tour representative in your arrival city, you are part of a carefully attended group. There seemed no common denominator for the people who chose this trip, except that they all could afford the high price. The majority of those I met at the lodges were over age 50, but there were younger people as well, and even an occasional family who had brought young children to share the adventure.

While no physical exertion or danger is involved, safaris do mean tiring and difficult travel. The distances between parks are great. Rutted roads are often unpaved, sending up dust or mud, depending on the weather. We were out by 6:30 A.M. many mornings, since the animals are most active just after daybreak, and we often drove for hours searching for the bigger game. No one could stay awake much past 10:00 P.M. The thrill is worth it all.

In Kenya, the best-known park is the Masai Mara Game Preserve at the northern tip of the Serengeti Plains, where literally millions of animals graze and hunt. In two days in this park, we spotted more than thirty species of animals and untold numbers of exotic birds.

Other parks have their own specialties. Lake Nakuru is known for huge flocks of pink flamingoes, Amboseli for its large herds of elephants. Samburu Game Reserve, in northern Kenya, has its own species of zebras and giraffes, with markings different from those to the south. At Treetops, you stay up late to watch animals congregating outside at a softly lit water hole. At the Mount Kenya Safari Club, the place made famous by the late actor William Holden, you'll have a break—a day spent relaxing in luxury, dining sumptuously, and coming back to find that the logs in the fireplace in your room have been lit for you.

After a fabulous week in Kenya, we were unsure as to what more could possibly be waiting for us in Tanzania. The answer was simply the most spectacular animal watching in the world.

Ngorongoro Crater, an inverted volcano, is one of the wonders of the world, a veritable Noah's ark. In Kenya, we had driven long stretches searching for the elusive big animals. Here, the naturalist guide who drove us down by Jeep had only to say, "Now we'll look for the lions," and there they were. Then, "Here's where the rhinos stay"—and there they were.

Serengeti National Park, with its huge numbers of animals, is overwhelming in its beauty and richness. A recent census counted a quarter of a million gazelles, an equal number of zebras, another quarter million of other species including cheetahs, lions, and other predators, and well over a million wildebeests.

Even the smallest of the national parks, Lake Manyara, was rewarding, with its amazing variety of animals owing to the topography that ranges from lush jungle to flat plains. One sight here fills you with amazement—lions that climb the trees in order to nap undisturbed by the park's large herds of elephants.

We were worried about lodging when we crossed the border into Tanzania. Kenya is relatively prosperous and, with over a million visitors a year, has learned how to provide safari guests with creature comforts. Accommodations were not so

Important Questions to Ask Before You Choose a Safari

- How long has the company been in the business?
- Is Africa its main destination or just one of many?
- Are departure dates guaranteed regardless of how many people sign up?
- How large is the total group? (More than twenty-five is unwieldy; fewer than fifteen is ideal.)
- Will you be guaranteed a window seat in your van? Will you have a naturalist along in addition to the driver-guide?
- Does the company employ local people?
- Are its guides and drivers trained by environmental experts?
- What airline will you fly and where will you stop en route? (All airlines make a stop in Europe. Changing planes in Amsterdam is an advantage because Schiphol Airport is easy to navigate and it is a quick and inexpensive train ride into town if you have several hours to spend.)
- Will you have day rooms during the stopover between Europe and Africa, or simply wait around at the airport?
- Where will you stay when you land in Nairobi? (The Norfolk is the great old hotel.)
- Is the operator a member of the U.S. Tour Operators Association?
- Most important—can it furnish firsthand references from travel agents and recent former passengers?

different from rustic park lodges in the United States. But Tanzania is poor and undeveloped, and we had been warned to expect difficult living conditions.

"Difficult" meant that we lacked hot water at times and the electricity might be turned off from midnight to 6:00 A.M. Still, the beds were comfortable, and every room had a private bath. I've had worse accommodations in Yosemite Park. The striking architecture and scenic locations of the lodges were a wonderful surprise. True, the food left much to be desired, but when the main course did not please, there were plenty of fresh vegetables and rolls to fill in.

For me, the extraordinary animals made a few inconveniences more than worthwhile. In fact, if I could return to only one country, Tanzania is where I would choose to go.

My experiences were in only two countries; safaris are also available in South Africa and several other African nations. Safaris are expensive, but they are a once-in-a-lifetime experience. Start saving.

Choosing a Safari

There are many operators offering safaris that vary in price, from budget trips via open trucks with nights spent in sleeping bags to trips that include comfortable vans and accommodations and the services of skilled guides. Deluxe tours such as those sponsored by the Smithsonian Institution add the services of a naturalist. Some of the most luxurious trips are the tented safaris, where the cooks pride themselves on turning out remarkable fare over the campfire.

Wildlife is abundant and weather is mild year-round in East Africa, but the "long rains" period from late March through May is not a good time for animal viewing. The big herds of the Serengeti are in Tanzania in the winter months and in Kenya from mid-July to September.

To compare trip costs, look at the actual days spent on safari. Tours that spend extra days in Nairobi may sound like more time for your money, but bed-and-breakfast accommodations in a city are not the point of an African trip. The most important consideration is a guaranteed window seat in your van.

Among the better-known operators specializing in safaris are:

ABERCROMBIE & KENT, INC.
1520 Kensington Road, Suite 111, Oak Brook, IL 60523;
(800) 323–7308 or (630) 954–2944; www.abercrombiekent.com.(EE)
Years in business: 30+
A & K maintains its own offices and staff in Kenya and Tanzania.

UNITED TOURING INTERNATIONAL, INC.
1 Bala Plaza, Suite 414, Bala Cynwyd, PA 19004;
(610) 617–3300 or (800) 223–6486; www.unitedtour.com. (M–EE)
Years in business: 50+
This Nairobi-based company is the largest tour operation in Africa, with offices throughout the continent and a wide variety of offerings.

PARK EAST TOURS

100 Environs Park, Helena, AL 35080; (800) 223–6078;
www.parkeast.com. (EE)
Years in business: 40+
This tour company has done trips for the ASPCA, an excellent recommendation for their emphasis on conservation. Offerings include moderate and luxury itineraries.

BORN FREE SAFARIS AND TOURS

5555 DTC Parkway, Suite D2002, Greenwood Village, CO 80111;
(800) 4SAFARI; www.bornfreesafaris.com. (E–EE)
Years in business: 28+
A range of prices, a guarantee of no more than six passengers per vehicle, and some guided walks and village visits make this operator well worth considering.

MICATO SAFARIS

15 West 26th Street, New York, NY 10010; (212) 545–7111 or (800) 642–2861;
www.micato.com.
This long-established family-run company has won an award and many kudos for its ecotourism efforts.

Get into Shape:
The Spa Vacation

The Spa Philosophy

IMAGINE A VACATION THAT SENDS YOU HOME FREE OF STRESS, FULL of energy, and maybe a bit slimmer, as well. That's just what you can expect from a visit to a spa, a healthy vacation experience that is gaining a growing group of advocates from both sexes. Because spas provide a *you*-centered vacation that is dedicated to making you look and feel better, they are perfect for solo travelers, and a large number of guests choose to come alone.

Don't confuse a spa facility at a hotel with a destination spa. These spas are really health resorts, geared as much to the over-stressed as the overweight. While some guests do arrive determined to work hard and diet away some pounds, many spa-goers today come for relaxation, and spas have changed to accommodate them. A wide choice of activities means that exercise may include hiking or tennis as well as aerobics, or you can choose to do nothing at all if you like. While the meals are low calorie and healthy, second helpings are available so that no one feels deprived.

Spa vacationers pay premium prices, yet advocates declare it is a worthwhile investment. For along with a week or two of healthy living, a good spa aims to give a lifetime bonus—education and inspiration for a healthier lifestyle when you return home.

At a good spa, guests can learn, often for the first time, exactly how their bodies function—how they react to stress, inactivity, different types of exercise, and different types of food. One of the most important benefits is finding out how to eat well without gaining weight. Cooking demonstrations are a popular feature at many spas. For those who have talked about exercising without doing anything about it, a spa can be a motivation center, reinforcing good intentions and generating lasting new attitudes and behaviors.

For men who fear that spas are still mainly for overweight women, a pleasant awakening may be in store, since the opposite is often true today. People who come to spas tend to be those who are fit or want to be. They are usually people who take care of their bodies.

Along with relaxing massages, many spas offer stress-control techniques to keep you calm, collected, and better able to stick with your good intentions back home. Many have a holistic slant, including meditation, yoga, t'ai chi, and similar techniques. You can take part or not, as you wish.

Most spas will try to match you with a roommate to help hold down the cost.

The Spa Routine

A typical spa day begins with a brisk walk before breakfast. There is a choice of exercise classes, which are spaced throughout the day. The exercises include a balanced mix of aerobics, workouts for body conditioning, and stretching and yoga for both strength and relaxation. Aquatic workouts frequently are part of the routine, turning exercise into fun and games in the pool. Many spas have weight machines, and some schedule special muscle-building and stretching sessions just for men, accommodating the increasing number of male guests.

Between the workouts come the rewards: soothing massages, relaxing whirlpools, saunas, and steam baths that erase tension and aches. A variety of treatments is offered. Facials, hydrotherapy massage (done in a tub using soothing streams of water), and herbal wraps (mummy-like wrappings of scented moist sheets designed to draw out body impurities, soften the skin, and relax the muscles) are among the choices. Attendants report that many men whose macho upbringing made them reluctant to try these treatments discover they have been missing out on some of life's nicer luxuries and immediately sign up for repeats.

There is also plenty of time for a leisurely lunch—and a dip in the pool or an hour in the sun with a good book.

Although strong alcohol and fattening hors d'oeuvres are definitely not part of the regimen, some spas do allow a glass of wine at dinner, and many have pleasant pre-dinner "mocktail parties" that offer sociability along with sparkling water, carrot sticks, and surprisingly tasty low-calorie dip. All the food, in fact, is a pleasant surprise. The menus are sophisticated and cleverly served so that every meal has an appetizer, a salad, a main course, and a dessert. While portions are small, wily spa nutritionists know that after four courses most people do not feel deprived.

Evenings include speakers, how-to hints for stress reduction, tips on establishing good health habits at home, or talks and movies just for entertainment. A number of spas now offer workshops in biofeedback and other behavior-modification techniques.

A week's stay is recommended to get the full benefit of a spa. Some warn you when you arrive that day three can be a day of muscle soreness and doubts for those unaccustomed to exercise. Each day following, however, finds you feeling better—about your body and yourself.

Choosing a Spa

Although the basic programs at spas are similar, the ambience can vary as much as the price range, which runs the gamut from a few-frills $2,000 to a luxury $7,000 or more a week.

At the top of the scale, and the ultimate spa experience, according to many people, is the Golden Door in Escondido, California, with serene Oriental decor and a staff that outnumbers the guests by 3 to 1. Reflecting current trends, the former all-female spa now offers special weeks for men. Cal-a-Vie is another super-luxury retreat limited to twenty-four guests, each lodged in his or her own villa-style cottage. Most weeks are coed.

At the other end of the spa spectrum is the coed Ashram, also in California, described by one recent guest as "a boot camp without food." The raw-food diet and rigorous regimen designed to test guests to the limit of their physical endurance may not be everyone's cup of herbal tea, but those who survive declare it almost an existential experience, and many do return.

Locations of spas vary. Some are in the middle of a city; others are in the middle of nowhere. Some are part of a larger resort; others are independent operations. And there are still traditional spas that are for women only.

When you compare costs of spas, be sure to note how many massages and beauty treatments are included; some fees sound inexpensive because you must pay extra for these services.

Spa guest references weren't too helpful, since all were raves. After visits to a number of spas, however, I do have recommendations for best bets for single guests.

The first suggestion is a reminder: Choose a destination spa rather than a resort, where many guests are not part of the spa program and you may be eating spa fare in a dining room where others are enjoying steak and lobster.

Pick-of-the-List Spas

At the top of the list of the best spas for single guests are two coed "fitness re-sorts"—Rancho la Puerta and Canyon Ranch. Both are well known, and each attracts an active, generally fit, and interesting mix of guests. On a more modest scale, the New Age Health Spa offers good value in a beautiful setting. Here is what each has to offer:

RANCHO LA PUERTA

Tecate, Baja California, Mexico (about an hour south of San Diego; guests are met at no charge at San Diego airport); P.O. Box 463057, Escondido, CA 92046; reservations (800) 443–7565; www.rancholapuerta.com (E–EE)
Coed; 150 guests; 30 percent male

This rates my first-place vote for tranquility and beauty, and value. The 3,000-acre complex, filled with flowers and fountains and ringed with boulder-strewn mountains, was born in 1940, long before the fitness boom. It remains a find for any world-weary traveler who wants a rejuvenating getaway in lovely surroundings. Guests stay in Mexican casitas decorated with hand-painted tiles and folk art. Accommodations have no distracting television; many have fireplaces, stacked with wood and ready to be lit each night, and each has its own garden.

You do as much or as little as you please here and eat as much as you want—not as hedonistic as it sounds, since the diet is modified vegetarian. Eighty percent of the vegetables are grown in the ranch's own organic gardens, and you've never tasted fresher or better. Fish is served two or three times a week; otherwise main dishes are pastas, lasagnas, Mexican tortillas and beans, and other dishes that belie their low calorie count.

The guests are professionals from all over the United States and Canada. The age range is 25 to 75, but because the Mexican location makes this spa a better buy than many of its American competitors, the average age tends to be younger than at more costly spas. Everyone arrives on Saturday, making for a cohesive group. By the time you have hiked, exercised, done your yoga, and dined together for a couple of days, you all feel like old friends. The relaxed, friendly, and low-key atmosphere extends to the health and beauty services. You come here for renewal, not expert pampering.

There are tennis courts, lit for night play, and four separate pools. The lodgings also offer private decks for sunbathing or stargazing. This is one spa I could imagine coming to for sheer enjoyment, even if I never went near an exercise class.

The Right Spa
for You

Before you decide on a spa, check current magazines for the latest write-ups or browse through a bookstore or library for more comprehensive coverage. Some good book choices are:

- SPA FINDER (91 Fifth Avenue, Suite #301, New York, NY 10003; 212–924–6800 or 800–255–7727; www.spafinder.com). A bimonthly magazine is published by this travel company that specializes in spa vacations worldwide.
- FODOR'S HEALTHY ESCAPES (Fodor's Travel Publications) includes more than 280 spas, resorts, and retreats.
- 100 BEST SPAS OF THE WORLD, Bernard Burt and Pamela Price (The Globe Pequot Press).
- DESTINATION SPA VACATIONS, a useful annual magazine-format guide featuring over twenty destination spas across the United States, Canada, and Mexico, can be ordered for $5.95 (including postage) from the Destination Spa Group, 8600 East Rockcliff Road, Tucson, AZ 85750; (888) 772–4363, or free ($3.00 shipping charge) on the Web at www.destinationspas.com.

Pick several spas whose approach, location, and rates seem to meet your needs. Write for brochures, which will tell you a lot about the philosophy of the spa and its facilities, schedules, and accommodations. It should also tell you whether massages and other services are included in the fee or are extra. It should describe the menu, the number of calories served, whether larger portions are available if you want them, and whether the emphasis is on a balanced diet or a vegetarian menu.

If you still have questions, phone the spa's fitness director. Ask about the number of single guests or male guests if it is a concern to you. Find out whether someone seats you at meals to be sure you have company when you want it. Spa vacations are expensive, so be sure you make the right choice for your needs.

CANYON RANCH HEALTH RESORT

8600 East Rockcliff Road, Tucson, AZ 85750; (800) 742–9000 or (520) 749–9000; www.canyonranch.com (EE) Coed; 250 guests; 35 percent male.

The ambience at this first-class facility is charged with energy, even though higher rates are reflected in a slightly older (and often celebrity-studded) clientele. The gyms and the health center are state of the art; the staff is crackerjack; the menu is varied and delicious; and the beauty treatments are first rate. Single guests have the daily option of joining a group table or dining alone. People who come here love it, but while they may recharge, they don't really escape from the real world. Dress can be a fashion parade of designer leotards and sweat suits. Televisions and telephones are very much part of the hotel-ish guest rooms, and there is a fax machine in the office that gets a lot of use from guests keeping up with business.

Canyon Ranch is blessed with wonderful desert and mountain surroundings, but you must board a van to reach the starting points of the hikes. Some people prefer this because it allows for more variety and is more challenging. Hiking is a big part of the program, and special weeks are devoted to it for those who want a more rigorous schedule.

A Life Enhancement Center is a self-contained part of the spa that focuses on helping participants overcome such habits as smoking or overeating. Special theme weeks focus on aging, spirutality, and midlife. The Behavioral Health Department of the Center uses all the latest techniques, including private counseling, biofeedback, and hypnotherapy.

CANYON RANCH IN THE BERKSHIRES

Bellefontaine, 165 Kemble Street, Lenox, MA 01240; (413) 637–4100 or (800) 742–9000; www.canyonranch.com (EE) Coed; 240 guests; 35 percent male.

The location of this outpost opened in 1990 is 120-acre Bellefontaine, one of the great old Berkshire estates. Although not much of the original complex remains, one of the three buildings in the U-shaped complex is the old mansion house, which retains the original library but is otherwise completely changed. It now houses the dining room, health and healing, and medical consultation areas. Exercise facilities are in the new, state-of-the-art fitness complex, which includes tennis, squash, and racquetball courts, an indoor running track, indoor pool, all manner of fitness equipment, and exercise rooms as well as treatment and salon facilities. Another pool and other tennis courts are outdoors. Guests stay in the third area. The rooms, like the dining room, are much like what you'd find in an upscale hotel.

Morning walks may be excursions into the village of Lenox, and hikes, biking, canoeing, kayaking, and other outdoor activities take advantage of the lovely Berkshire countryside. Summertime guests can take advantage of the wonderful seasonal cultural facilities of the Berkshires, including Boston Symphony concerts at Tanglewood. In winter, cross-country skiing and snowshoeing are added to the agenda. The services here are first rate, but given a choice, I still find the Arizona Canyon Ranch and its exquisite desert surroundings a more satisfying experience.

NEW AGE HEALTH SPA

P.O. Box 658, Route 55, Neversink, NY 12765; (845) 985–7600 or (800) 682–4348; www.newagehealthspa.com (I–M) Coed; seventy-two guests; year-round.

This moderately priced, low-key spa greatly exceeded my expectations. It is set on 280 wooded acres in the hills of the Catskill Mountain region and surrounded by scenic views with five miles of hiking trails right on the property. The feeling is more country inn than spa, with thirty-seven guest rooms in five country cottages and an old farmhouse, converted to house a cozy sitting room with a stone fireplace and a spacious dining room with an outdoor deck. The facilities are fine, offering both indoor and outdoor pools; two tennis courts; a sauna, steam room, and solarium; a gym with workout equipment and ample space for massages, facials, and other spa services.

As the name suggests, the emphasis at New Age is definitely holistic, with frequent sessions of yoga, t'ai chi, and meditation held in a handsome new building with arched picture windows overlooking the surrounding countryside. But classes in body conditioning, aerobics, and aqua-aerobics are available for those who want more traditional activities. A 50-foot Alpine climbing tower on the grounds offers an ultimate challenge. Morning and afternoon walks take place daily, and from May to October, half- and full-day hikes are scheduled each week in the scenic Catskills. Evening activities while I was there included a nightly movie in the upstairs lounge and talks on "Intuitive Imagery," "Acupuncture," and "Drumming Away Stress."

Meals at New Age are healthful and low calorie but ample. Vegetarian lunches include soup, a salad buffet, and a hot entree. Dinners give a choice of entrees— poultry or fish or a vegetarian selection. Many of the vegetables served come from the spa's own garden and greenhouse, which are open for touring. Supervised juice fasts are available for those who want to detoxify and purify the system.

Being alone here is easy. With a maximum of seventy-two guests, you quickly get to know people on walks or in the dining room.

The sizes of guest rooms vary; some have hot tubs and seating areas, but all have private baths. Even the most expensive rooms are about half the price of those at more luxurious spas. If you want phones or a TV lounge, you'll have to come to the office building.

The lack of distractions contributes to the wonderful sense of tranquility. Lying in a hammock under a giant tree, gazing out at the surrounding hills, it's hard to imagine a nicer escape.

New Age is located about two and a quarter hours from New York. Limousine service can be arranged from New York airports.

Luxury Spas

When you have the wherewithal ($300 to $700 per night and up), you might want to choose these ultimate spa experiences:

THE GOLDEN DOOR
P.O. Box 463077, Escondido, CA 92046; (760) 744–5777 or (800) 424–0777; www.goldendoor.com; forty guests (EE)

Dating back to 1958, the Golden Door's Oriental ambience and tranquil setting on 377 acres are still considered by many to provide the ultimate serene retreat. A staff of 160 caters to the forty "treasured guests." Most weeks are for women only, but several are scheduled for men and for coed sessions.

CAL–A–VIE
29402 Spa Havens Way, Vista, CA 92084; (760) 945–2055 or (866) 772–4283; www.cal-a-vie.com; twenty-four guests (EE)

Think of a small village in Provence, and you'll have the picture of this retreat shared by two dozen fortunate guests. Located on 150 acres in a secluded valley north of San Diego, the spa houses guests in Mediterranean-style tile-roofed cottages filled with hand-carved furniture and pastel floral chintz. Women's and coed sessions are offered.

GREEN VALLEY SPA AND RESORT

1871 West Canyon View Drive, St. George, UT 84770; (435) 628–8060 or
(800) 237–1068; www.greenvalleyspa.com (EE)

A beautifully appointed spa with a holistic bent, Green Valley's special bonus is the surrounding Utah red rock country, where hiking in locales such as Zion National Park is a joy. The spa offers relaxation, meditation, and nutrition education along with exercise. Golf and tennis lessons are also available.

LAKE AUSTIN SPA RESORT

1705 South Quinlan Park Road, Austin, TX 78732; (512) 372–7300 or (800) 847–5637;
www.lakeaustin.com; Coed; eighty guests (EE)

A multimillion-dollar expansion completed in 2004 has moved this spa into the top echelon, with additions that include a grand spa building, an outdoor pool and open-air indoor pool, and foliage and aquatic gardens. The spa is situated on nineteen lakefront acres in Texas hill country, half an hour from Austin. The new facilities offer outdoor treatment porches and private garden courtyards with tented treatment areas for men and women. Some twenty fitness activities are offered daily including yoga, Pilates, hiking, and activities on 23-mile-long Lake Austin, such as hydro-bikes, canoeing, and kayaking. Much of the food comes from the on-site organic gardens. Guest cottages overlook the gardens and the lake.

Good-Value Spas

Finding spas is no problem. They are mushrooming all over the country—so much so that several books are devoted to describing them. What is not easy is finding reasonable prices. Here are a few suggestions:

THE OAKS AT OJAI

122 East Ojai Avenue, Ojai, CA 93023; (805) 646–5573 or (800) 753–6257;
www.oaksspa.com; Coed; eighty guests (M–E)

Fitness and exercise is the forte of director Sheila Cuff, whose California spas in Ojai and Palm Springs represent good value. With plenty of Cuff's vigorous exercise classes and spa cuisine, guests soon feel healthy and relaxed. The spa opened in 1977 in the center of a quaint arts-oriented town about ninety minutes north of Los Angeles. It attracts many young career women, including starlets from the Los Angeles area. About 20 percent of the guests are male. Some 75 percent of the guests come alone.

Spa Traveling Specialists

The popularity of spas has spawned specialized travel agencies that promise to keep up with the field and suggest the right places for varying tastes and budgets. There is no extra charge for their services; in fact, they often can get you a discount because they are favorite sources of guests. They are:

- Spa-Finder Travel Arrangements Ltd., *91 Fifth Avenue, New York, NY 10003; (212) 924–6800 or (800) 255–7727; www.spafinder.com.*
- Spa Trek International, Inc., *475 Park Avenue South, New York, NY 10016; (212) 779–3480 or (800) 272–3480; www.spatrek.com.*

Two Web sites also offering good information on spas are www.spaindex.com and www.about.com/travel/spas.

THE PALMS AT PALM SPRINGS

572 North Indian Canyon Drive, Palm Springs, CA 92262; (760) 325–1111 or (800) 753–7256; www.palmsspa.com; Coed; eighty-three guests (M–E)

This sister to the Oaks has a similar program and a similar clientele. It is equally well priced.

JIMMY LESAGE'S NEW LIFE HIKING SPA

P.O. Box 395, Killington, VT 05751; (802) 422–4302 or (866) 288–5433; www.newlifehikingspa.com; Coed; thirty guests (M)
Runs mid-May to late October. Very small single supplement.

Set in an attractive hotel, the Inn of the Six Mountains on the slopes of Killington mountain, this active program emphasizes mountain hikes, one of the most pleasant ways to exercise. The program also includes aqua exercise classes, body toning, yoga, and meditation, as well as a healthful low-fat, high-fiber, high-carbohydrate diet. Massages and facials are available. The small size of the group makes for a highly personal program monitored to each guest's needs.

RED MOUNTAIN SPA

1275 East Red Mountain Circle, P.O Box 2149, St. George, UT 84771;
(800) 407–3002 or (435) 673–4905; www.redmountainspa.com;
Coed; 202 guests (I–M)

Set in the beautiful red rock country of southern Utah, this spa takes advantage of its location with hiking and mountain biking from the property, day trips to nearby state and national parks, and kayaking in local mountain reservoirs. Also offered are fitness classes, rock climbing, cooking classes, yoga, Pilates, and a full range of spa services. Four- to thirty-day programs offer a choice of lodging in standard or deluxe or villa suite rooms.

THE SPA AT GRAND LAKE

Route 207, 1667 Exeter Road, Lebanon, CT 06249; (860) 642–4306; outside Connecticut, (800) 843–7721; www.thespaatgrandlake.com (I–M); April through December; will try to arrange shares.

The nicest thing about this well-priced, few-frills spa is the daily half-hour massage included in the rates. Set on seventy-five acres of Connecticut countryside, the facilities include indoor and outdoor pools, tennis courts, a sauna and Jacuzzi, and a fully equipped gym. Free pickups are available from Hartford train, bus, or plane terminals. Classes ranging from aerobics to t'ai chi and daily walks and hikes in nearby state parks make for a well-rounded program. Dinner by candlelight is a restful end to the day.

Mexican Spas

Though nowhere near the class of Rancho la Puerta, two additional Mexican spa resorts deserve mention because their rates are so attractive for Americans.

RIO CALIENTE HOT SPRINGS SPA AND NATURE RESORT

Guadalajara, Mexico; P.O. Box 897, Millbrae, CA 94030;
(650) 615–9543 or (800) 200–2927; www.riocaliente.com; Coed; eighty guests; no shares arranged; small single supplement (I)

Located in the Primavera Forest about forty-five minutes from Guadalajara, this small, informal hot springs resort is a bargain. Guests enjoy hot mineral-water pools and a sauna, guided hikes, pool exercise and yoga classes, and evening programs as well as three buffet-style vegetarian meals daily. Spa treatments include massages and facials, reflexology, clay foot baths, and mud wraps. Cable TV and Internet service are on-site. One wrap, two treatments, and one shopping excursion outside the spa are included in weekly package rates.

IXTAPAN HOTEL AND SPA

Ixtapan de la Sal, Mexico; c/o 13750 San Pedro, Suite 860, San Antonio, TX 78232; (800) 638–7950 or (210) 495–2477; www.spamexico.com; Coed; 220 rooms; no shares arranged (M)

The 104º natural thermal waters of Ixtapan have drawn visitors for many years to this resort in the Sierra Madre Mountains, 65 miles southwest of Mexico City. The weekly package includes six massages, three facials, one manicure, one pedicure, two hair treatments, and a hair styling. Activities include walks, four aerobics classes, five aquatic exercise classes, three yoga sessions, and three golf or tennis lessons. Guests can use the spa dining room, where meals equal 900 calories a day, or the regular resort dining room. Everyone dresses up at night. Concerts and movies provide after-dinner entertainment. Prices are far below similar offerings in the United States, even after you add on airfare. Cars can be arranged to meet guests in Mexico City for the two-hour drive to the hotel.

More options:

Two additional Mexican spas worth knowing about, both located in lovely historic Mexican colonial towns, are Hosteria Las Quintas (Cuernavaca, 877–784–6827, www.spalasquintas.com) and the new El Santuario Spa, (Valle de Bravo, 866–896–7727).

The best source for additional information on Mexican spas is Spa Getaway, 381 Park Avenue South, Suite 1202, New York, NY 10016; (212) 251–0877 or (800) 321–4622; www.spagetaway.com. They represent over twenty spas. For a Caribbean option, see Le Sport on page 188.

Join a Tour

I F YOU'RE DREAMING OF SEEING THE WORLD, YOU'LL FIND THAT TOUR companies are in the dream-fulfillment business. They print up shiny brochures showing the world's wonders, which they will gladly wrap up for you in neat packages.

The Up Side

Tour packages offer many advantages. On a prepaid tour, you can sit back and let somebody else take care of all the details of travel. A tour relieves you of the chores of getting around on your own in unfamiliar cities, choosing hotels, deciding where to eat, making restaurant reservations, or planning every day's sightseeing. You'll never have to worry about transporting luggage or finding your way to a hotel. And if your luggage does not arrive, it's the tour manager, not you, whose job it is to follow through.

Tour buses generally offer comfortable seats and big windows that give you the best views as you travel. Not the least of the appeal of a tour is the cost. Because of the economies of group buying, tours almost always save money over trying to duplicate the same trip on your own. In peak season, the clout of a tour company often ensures room reservations that an individual cannot wangle.

Some tours also offer roommate-matching services to avoid the single supplement, allowing a big saving for solo travelers. Single sojourners also enjoy the advantage of companionship, especially important at mealtime. Most often, a block of tables is reserved for tour members, and a single person would naturally join the other members of the group.

Tours are a natural for a first trip to Europe or for travel in the Orient or the South Pacific, where getting along and getting around may seem more complicated than in the Western world. Tours with a special focus such as art or cuisine may appeal to those who have traveled more widely and done the basic sightseeing.

The Down Side

Despite the many pros of group travel, however, you should not sign on for a tour without understanding the negative points. In exchange for the advantages, you give up the right to set your own schedule. There's a set time that you must leave your bags outside your hotel room door each morning, as well as a designated hour for breakfast and departure—and those times are likely to be early! The average tour is geared to covering as much ground as possible, so you have little opportunity for browsing or lingering. On a typical "Continental Introduction" grand tour, for example, the highlights in one three-day area might include a canal cruise and a chance to see the Rembrandts at the Rijksmuseum in Amsterdam, Cologne cathedrals, a Rhine cruise, Heidelberg, Nymphenburg Palace in Munich, the Bavarian Alps, and a walking tour of Innsbruck—a lot to take in over a short period of time. You get a sampling, never an in-depth view. And sometimes you get more than you can absorb. You know the old joke—"If this is Tuesday, this must be Belgium." It's easy for everything to become a blur on a whirlwind tour.

And while motor coach travel may sound restful, most tours take a lot of stamina. Besides those early departures, there is a lot of walking. Buses are often prohibited from parking in the center of town and are restricted to coach parks. You will get a good bit of exercise just getting to attractions, climbing hills to castles, and following the guides.

Of course, just because you've paid for the full tour doesn't mean that you must climb every hill or see every sight on the itinerary. It's perfectly okay to decline and meet the group afterward. But when the bus is ready to roll, you'd better be on board.

The size of the group also limits your choice of lodgings and restaurants. Intimate inns and cafes cannot accommodate a busload of tourists. So you'll be staying in larger commercial hotels chosen for their ability to handle a group well, and you will frequently be offered fixed menus in large restaurants, unless you want to pay extra to venture out on your own. Gourmet fare is not the rule, except on deluxe tours. Some hotels and restaurants may be better than you expect; the majority will be quite ordinary. Many tours do not include lunch in order to allow you the chance to visit some local places on your own.

You should also be aware that most motor coach tours tend to attract older travelers. According to the National Tour Association, approximately 70 percent of U.S. motor coach tourists are 50 and older. And the number of travelers by themselves is small, seldom more than four or five per busload. That doesn't mean that couples are not good company, simply that it is not realistic to expect a lot of fellow singles. Budget tours tend to attract more singles as well as a larger number of younger passengers; companies that guarantee shares are also more likely to attract people on their own.

Despite these warnings, the makeup of any one tour is unpredictable, and sometimes you can luck out. One single woman I know reported, "I took a Globus two-week tour of the Orient by myself and to my delight had about eight single people between 30 and 55 for companionship, including a few bachelors and widowers—which the brochure definitely did not guarantee."

What about tours designed exclusively for singles? By all means consider them—many people do (see pages 178–82). But sign on with the advance knowledge that the greater proportion of the travelers is likely to be female. Not only do single women outnumber single men, but men seem more hesitant about striking out without a companion. Choose a singles tour as you would any other—because the destination or itinerary intrigues. And don't be surprised or dismayed at the scarcity of male company.

The one element that makes or breaks a tour is the tour director or escort. It is up to the tour director to see that everyone shows up on time, to appease the inevitable grumblers, and to set a tone of goodwill and fun for the group. Ideally, this person should be all things to all people—friendly, outgoing, humane, intelligent, articulate, witty, well informed, and ever tactful. Directors are usually college educated, and those conducting European tours may speak two to four languages. The better established the tour company, the better the chances that you will have an expert tour director.

Choosing a Tour

Knowing both the good and not-so-good points of group tours, a little homework in choosing your tour will ensure a more successful trip.

The first consideration is strictly a monetary one. Tours come in three classifications: budget, first class, and deluxe, based on the type of hotels used. Decide on your price range and compare the offerings within it.

Tours that spend more than one night in most of the stops are more restful and give the option of time on your own.

You'll also need to choose between general sightseeing or special-interest tours. Many varieties of specialized tours concentrate on everything from castles to gardens, Mozart to mushroom hunting. These tours most often are deluxe, but if the itinerary is really exciting to you, it may be worth the splurge. A shared interest helps ensure you will find compatible company.

Most group tours are all-inclusive, meaning that they take care of both air and land arrangements, most meals, and an escort. Local guides may be used in each destination, since it is difficult for a tour escort to be an expert on everything. However, the better operators do have one person who stays with the group throughout even if someone else gives the specialized talks. On trips for special-interest groups, particularly those sponsored by museums and universities, the escort is usually also a well-qualified specialist whose knowledge can add a lot to your trip.

Many escorted tours are available also as land packages only, in case you want to combine them with independent travel. Sometimes you can use the group air arrangements from a package and plan your own itinerary.

Consumer Protection

To protect your investment, be sure your tour operator is a member of the United States Tour Operators Association (212–599–6599; www.ustoa.com). Their Travelers Assistance Policy requires members to post a bond or letter of credit of $1,000,000, ensuring that consumers will be reimbursed if the company goes out of business or into bankruptcy. Members are listed on the Web site, which also offers consumer tips and information.

General Tours

There are dozens of tour operators, and since each tour may vary in the number of participants and the expertise of the guides, travel agents who use the companies frequently are your best references. Listed here, as a starting point, are a few reliable, long-established tour operators.

GLOBUS & COSMOS

5301 South Federal Circle, Littleton, CO 80123;
Globus: (866) 755–8581; Cosmos: (800) 276–1241;
www.globusandcosmos.com

This long-established company offers tours on every continent except Antarctica in a choice of price ranges. Globus is first class;

Years in business:	70+
Age range:	20s–80s
Most common age:	62
Percent alone:	30
Number of participants:	Averages 36–46
Male/female ratio:	More females
Guaranteed shares on Cosmos	

Comparing Tours

To evaluate what makes one general tour more desirable than another, gather a number of brochures covering the areas you want to visit and do a bit of comparison shopping. A good travel agent can supply you with plenty of material to get you started, and can tell you which companies have pleased their clients in the past.

Compare the following areas, then consult your travel agent or the tour operator if you have further questions.

- **Cost:** *Figure out the cost of each trip on a daily basis by dividing the total price by the number of nights offered. Days are not a safe guide, because many tours start at noon or dinnertime and end with breakfast. Generally, you get what you pay for—higher prices mean better hotels and restaurants.*

- **Food:** *How many meals are offered? Do you have a choice of selections or are you limited to a pre-selected menu? Are there dine-around options?*

- **Accommodations:** *The hotels used by the tour should be noted in the brochure. Look them up in a guidebook or on the Internet to find out how they are rated. If the brochure makes up a name for categories, such as "tourist class," find out what that means. Do all rooms have private baths? Are the hotels centrally located? It's nice to be able to take a walk or visit the shops on your own, not so nice to be stuck miles outside the city.*

- **Airline:** *Will you travel on a regularly scheduled plane or a special charter flight? If a charter, who runs it? Is departure guaranteed or will your flight be canceled if a sufficient number do not sign up?*

- **Pace:** *How hectic is the program? Do you have time to rest up from jet lag when you arrive at your destination? Look for tours that spend more than one night in a location. Time to catch your breath during the day and free time for shopping or a bit of sightseeing on your own will be welcome.*

- **Group size:** *Will there be one, two, or three buses? How many passengers per bus? When tour groups are too large, there are delays getting into hotels and jams at tourist attractions.*

- **Reputation:** *There are scores of tour operators—a number of whom cancel unfilled trips—or, worse yet, go bankrupt with your money in the till. You should know how long the company has been in business and whether it belongs to the United States Tour Operators Association. That membership means the company has operated for at least three years and has solid references. The association sets stringent requirements on insurance, liability, and financial responsibility.*

- **Guaranteed rates:** *This can be a big advantage on trips abroad in case of extreme fluctuations in the value of the dollar.*

(continued next page)

> - **Guaranteed departures:** *This is the operator's pledge to run the tour as promised regardless of how many sign up.*
> - **Fine print:** *Read carefully both tour descriptions and the page at the back of the brochure—the one without the pretty pictures—to find out exactly what is and is not included. There are many kinds of limitations. The brochure should be explicit as to exactly what your tour price covers. Membership fees needed to qualify for the trip, refund regulations, trip cancellation and trip interruption insurance, departure taxes, travel accident insurance, and medical payments are among the items that may or may not be covered.*

Cosmos is more budget-minded and has a slightly younger clientele. Single supplements are low on many trips.

MAYFLOWER TOURS

1225 Warren Avenue, Downers Grove, IL 60615; (800) 323–7604; in Illinois, (630) 435–8500; www.mayflowertours.com

Moderately priced tours around the United States and Canada, plus Europe, India, Australia, and New Zealand.

Years in business:	Since 1979
Age range:	50–75
Most common age:	50–60
Percent alone:	20–40
Number of participants: 35	
Male/female ratio:	Varies
Guaranteed shares	

MAUPINTOUR

10650 West Charleston Boulevard, Summerlin, NV 89135; (800) 255–4266; www.maupintour.com

Luxury tours to Europe, Asia, Africa, Australia, New Zealand, South America, the Orient, and the United States, Canada, and Mexico. The choices include river cruises in Europe and Galápagos cruises.

Years in business:	Since 1951
Age range:	Varies
Most common age:	50+
Percent alone:	25–30
Number of participants: Averages 25	
Male/female ratio:	1/1
Will try to arrange shares	

TRAFALGAR TOURS

29–76 Northern Boulevard, Long Island City, NY 11101; (800) 854–0103; www.trafalgartours.com

Europe is the specialty of this large tour company, which also has trips in the United States and Canada, Australia, New Zealand, South America, and Asia. Both first-class and budget trips are offered.

Years in business:	Since 1947
Age range:	45–70
Most common age:	51
Percent alone:	10–15
Number of participants:	35–48
Male/female ratio:	38/62
Guaranteed room shares	

TAUCK WORLD DISCOVERY

10 Norden Place, Norwalk, CT 06855
(203) 899–6500 or (800) 788–7885
www.tauck.com

A family-owned business now in its third generation, Tauk's expanded upscale itineraries now cover seven continents, including rail tours, small-ship cruises, and African safaris. National park adventures in the United States and Canada include rafting, horseback riding, and heli-hiking (helicopter transport to remote areas).

Years in business:	Since 1925
Age range:	55–70
Most common age:	55–70
Percent alone:	15–20
Number of participants:	40
Male/female ratio:	Entire group, 40/60; solo passengers, 1/9
Will try to arrange shares	

ABERCROMBIE & KENT INTERNATIONAL, INC.

1520 Kensington Road, Oak Brook, IL 60523;
(630) 954–2944 or (800) 323–7308;
www.abercrombiekent.com (EE)

Probably America's best-known operator of luxury tours worldwide, this firm offers top-of-the-line tours including a wide choice of land tours, plus safaris and expedition cruises.

Years in business:	35+
Age range:	Wide
Most common age:	45–60
Percent alone:	40 in U.S.; 33 abroad
Number of participants:	12–20
Male/female ratio:	48/52 U.S.; 38/62 abroad

Special-Interest Tours

There is truly a tour for every interest, whether your love is food, wine, sports, cave art, dollhouses, bird-watching, or golfing. Because each of these itineraries is unique, references from past participants are the best way to judge whether you want to sign on. Assume that most special-interest tours will fall into the "very expensive" category, unless otherwise indicated. Here are some of the possibilities:

ARCHAEOLOGICAL TOURS

271 Madison Avenue, Suite 904, New York, NY 10016;
(212) 986–3054 or (866) 740–5130;
www.archaeologicaltrs.com (EE)

Years in business:	25+
Age range:	30–75
Most common age:	50+
Percent alone:	Average 30
Number of participants:	24–30
Male/female ratio:	40/60
Will try to arrange shares	

These luxury tour groups are accompanied by expert scholars who stress the anthropological, archaeological, and historical aspects of a host of destinations, including Italy, Greece, Turkey, Cyprus, Libya, Jordan, Tunisia, Egypt, Georgia, Portugal, Chile, Peru, Bolivia, France, Spain, Guatemala, Mali, Romania, and Ethiopia. Asian trips take in India, Sri Lanka, Vietnam, Japan, China, Myanmar, Thailand, Laos and Cambodia, and stops on the ancient Silk Road.

C O M M E N T S **Female, 30s:** *I've been on trips to Turkey, Sicily and Italy, Cyprus, and Crete. There were many people traveling alone on all. Most were in their late 40s and 50s, and there were more women than men. The program is excellent and very structured, with most of the time spent at dig sites. The accommodations and food were the best available, considering where we were.*
Male, 50s: *I've been to Sicily, China, and Yugoslavia alone; all were very good experiences. Though the trips are expensive, the group is not just rich people. Many are the people who save up and take a trip every other year. Most were interesting professionals. The destinations are interesting, the itineraries are meticulously planned, and the days are active. I highly recommend it.*

ANNEMARIE VICTORY'S DELUXE GOURMET TOURS

136 East 64th Street, New York, NY 10021;
(212) 486–0353;
www.annemarievictory.com (EE)

Years in business:	Since 1983
Age range:	45–70
Most common age:	55–70
Percent alone:	50
Number of participants:	10
Male/female ratio:	40/60
Will try to arrange shares	

Victory's luxury tours allow special access to the finest hotels, restaurants, and events the world over. Her annual New Year's tour to Vienna features the New Year's Eve Ball at the Imperial Palace, and dining in private palaces. Exclusive culinary and art tours in Europe, music festivals, and gourmet cruises on the legendary sailing yacht *Sea Cloud* are among her very special offerings.

COMMENTS **Female, 50s:** *The best of everything—fine small hotels, wonderful food, flowers in your room, the best guides, plenty of free time, never rushed or hectic. On three trips, the average age was 40s to 65; the biggest number of participants was eight. I was often the only person alone, but you eat together and quickly get to know everyone. I can't say enough good things about these trips.*

Male, 40s: *We had just four people, ages 46 to 72. Everything was deluxe, the days were varied, the food was superb. It was a wonderful experience.*

AMERICAN JEWISH CONGRESS
WORLDWIDE TOURS

15 East 84th Street, New York, NY 10028;
(800) 221-4694 or (212) 879-4588
www.ajcongresstravel.com (E–EE)

Years in business:	40+
Age range:	Wide
Most common age:	50+
Percent alone:	20
Number of participants:	25 average per tour
Male/female ratio:	60/40
Will try to arrange shares	

Tours run by the AJC go to Israel and thirty other countries on six continents. Mediterranean and Scandinavian cruises, the Orient, Latin America, Western and Eastern Europe, Australia, and New Zealand are among the many choices. Tour members have a heritage and an interest in Jewish affairs in common. They often meet Jewish residents in other countries and see sights of special cultural or religious interest. Singles tours for ages 29 to 49 are scheduled.

COMMENTS **Female, late 20s:** *I've been on two trips alone, to Morocco and on safari in Africa, and to Egypt and Israel. I chose a singles trip, so most people were in their 30s and 40s, though all ages were represented. Women outnumbered men, but everyone seemed to be from similar backgrounds and were fairly successful professionals. Everything was great in Egypt and Israel—guides, food, accommodations. In Africa, the guide left something to be desired and the trip was less structured, meaning you had to do a lot more on your own. I highly recommend the Israel trip but have reservations about Africa.*

Male, 30s: *I've been on three trips: singles tours to Israel and to Spain and an "adventure tour" with mostly couples. The singles trips average 130 people, so you can't get to know everybody, but you are divided into tour buses, and you do* *become very friendly with the people on your bus. Two-thirds of each group was from New York, and women always outnumbered men. I enjoyed the adventure trip because it was less structured than a guided bus tour. These trips aren't like the "love boat"—people are there to travel with others their own ages and with similar interests, not to look for a partner. The group leaders are very good, and I would recommend the tour to anyone.*

Following is a sampling of other special-interest tours:

AHI INTERNATIONAL ALUMNI CAMPUS ABROAD

6400 Shafer Court, Rosemont, IL 60018; (800) 323-7373;
www.ahitravel.com (E–EE)

Best known for planning college alumni group trips for more than forty years, AHI also runs educational trips. These one-week trips to appealing locations throughout Europe range from Sicily to the Swiss Alps. Groups usually are based in one place and make day trips to see the sights. These reasonably priced programs include lectures and meet-the-people sessions to help participants become knowledgeable and involved in local history and culture.

ARTS SEMINARS ABROAD
UNIVERSITY OF WISCONSIN–MADISON

729 Lowell Center, 610 Langdon Street, Madison, WI 53703;
(608) 263-6320 or 263-7787 or (877) 336-7836;
www.dcs.wisc.edu/lsa/travel; will try to arrange shares (E)

Offered by UW–Madison Department of Liberal Studies and the Arts in cooperation with UW–Extension, this varied program combines travel abroad with arts-oriented events such as the Edinburgh Festival or theater in London.

The program is expanding its range to focus on visual as well as performing arts in Paris and Amsterdam, as well as trips to learn about history, archaeology, and anthropology in destinations such as Egypt, Vietnam, Cambodia, Peru/Bolivia, the Amazon, and the Mayan route in Central America. The programs are more reasonably priced than many university-connected programs, but there can be a hefty single supplement.

ROAD SCHOLAR

11 Avenue De Lafayette, Boston, MA 02111; (800) 466-7762; www.roadscholar.org (EE)

A new program from Elderhostel that is open to anyone over age 21, Road Scholar offers more upscale and less structured travel while keeping an educational component. Programs are kept to a maximum of twenty-three as opposed to fifty for many Elderhostel programs, and lodgings are in three- and four-star hotels. While trips include a daily group lecture or presentation, there is ample time for exploring on your own, and field trips and excursions are optional. The topics are geared to contemporary culture and recent events. In Vietnam, Cambodia, and Laos, groups examine the complex transitions from traditional cultures to modern economies and the impact of the Vietnam War. In New Orleans, they experience the vibrant European, Cajun, and Creole customs, festivals, cuisine, and music of the city. Physical adventure might include an exploration of the Alaskan wilderness or a rafting adventure in West Virginia, in which participants navigate white water while studying geology and natural history. Elderhostel says they expect the core of the group will be travelers in their 50s and 60s who prefer a more flexible itinerary.

THEATRE DEVELOPMENT FUND (TDF)
1501 Broadway, New York, NY 10036; (212) 221–0885; www.tdf.org/travel (M–E)

TDF, an organization devoted to promoting theater (they run the half-price theater ticket booth in Times Square in New York) has a long roster of cultural tours that focus on theater and the arts. They get high marks from past passengers. The wide-ranging recent itineraries have covered Vietnam and Cambodia, London theater, arts of India, Brazil, Sicily, Ghana, St. Petersburg in Russia, and the Amalfi coast in Italy. Visits to U.S. cities have included New Orleans; Washington, D.C.; Charleston and Savannah; and Chicago and Minneapolis. A popular feature is trips over New Year's Eve to cities such as Prague, Berlin, London, and Rio.

HORIZONS
P.O. Box 634, Leverett, MA 01054; (413) 367–9200; www.horizons-art.com (M–E)

Horizons sponsors what they term "artistic travel" tours to inspiring and widespread locales such as Italy, France, Ireland, Sweden, Belize, Guatemala, Mexico, Thailand, Vietnam, and the American Southwest. Trips often include "mini-workshops" in painting, ceramics, photography, and glass with local artists and artisans. Groups are small and structured to include all skill levels.

HISTORY AMERICA TOURS
P.O. Box 26097, Plano, TX 75026; (972) 769–1865 or (800) 628–8542; www.historyamerica.com (EE)

A history buff's dream, this group visits the sites of the greatest moments of American history—from the ancient Anasazis of the Southwest to the

American Revolution, the Civil War to Pearl Harbor. In recent years the scope of the trips has expanded to cover the Canadian Rockies, the Battle of Britain, the battlefields of western Europe, and the War in the Pacific. "Reliving the Indian Past" and "Civil War on the Western Rivers" tours are covered by steamboat cruises on the *Delta* and *Mississippi Queens.* Knowledgeable historian-guides help bring the events to life.

CULINARY INSTITUTE OF AMERICA
WORLDS OF FLAVOR TRAVEL PROGRAMS
2555 Main Street, St. Helena, CA 94574, (707) 967–2312 or (866) 242–2433; www.ciaprochef.com (click on "educational programs," then on "travel") or www.worldsofflavor.com (EE)

America's leading college for professional chefs schedules cuisine- and wine-oriented trips to many parts of the world, conducted by recognized experts and augmented with the best local chefs and writers. Many participants are themselves chefs and cookbook writers, but the program is open to anyone with a serious interest in food, and the itineraries are delicious, ranging from Sicily to Spain, Mexico to the American South, India to Vietnam.

COOPERSMITH'S
P.O. Box 900, Inverness, CA 94937; (415) 669–1914; www.coopersmiths.com

This longtime specialist in garden tours also features country walks, theater and art visits, and visits to sites such as castles on their trips to England, Europe, New Zealand, and California. Some recent destinations have included Malta, Sicily, Spain, Belgium, Holland, and North Country gardens and the Chelsea Flower Show in England. Groups are small—anywhere from six to twenty-two—and, depending on the location, lodging is in country inns, manor houses, or city hotels. Participants range from early 30s to late 70s, but most are around age 50, and anywhere from one-third to one-half of the group usually comes alone.

EXPO GARDEN TOURS
33 Fox Crossing, Litchfield, CT 06759; (860) 567–0322 or (800) 448–2695; www.expogardentours.com

Another group for lovers of gardens and flowers, Expo trips have explored the gardens of Charleston, New Orleans, and the Pacific Northwest, as well as the flora and fauna of Costa Rica, England and Wales, and city gardens in Dublin, Rome, London, and Paris.

Photography Tours

Tours oriented to photography provide plenty of time and opportunity for bringing home great pictures. Inexperienced photographers setting out on a tour that promises instruction and critiques should be sure that other novices are along. It is also useful to know the ratio of participants to tour leaders to be sure you will receive personal attention. You should also get references from people who have traveled with your particular leader. Great photographers may or may not be great travel guides.

CLOSE-UP EXPEDITIONS
858 56th Street, Oakland, CA 94608;
(510) 654–1548 or (800) 457–9553;
www.cuephoto.com (EE)

Years in business:	25+
Age range:	35–75
Most common age:	60s
Percent alone:	65
Number of participants:	6–7
Male/female ratio:	1/1
Will try to arrange shares; suitable for all levels	

These small-group photographic adventures range from seven to twenty-one days and are paced for good photography. Itineraries are planned to take advantage of best light; early morning and late-day shootings sometimes alter mealtimes or call for picnics in a field. Recent foreign destinations have included Burma (Myanmar), Turkey, Italy, France, Spain, Mexico, the Galápagos, Bhutan, Vietnam, India, and South Africa. In the United States, trips have covered the Southwest, the Everglades, Sanibel Island, Yosemite, Minnesota's Back Woods, and the Pacific Northwest.

COMMENTS Male, 30s: *The age range of my group to Costa Rica was from 35 to late 60s and 70s, and about half were single. The program is well run and good for a beginner wanting to learn something new on vacation. The food and accommodations were fine. You have the freedom to do what you want, though it is generally a group situation because of the locale—you can't go off by yourself at night in the Costa Rican rain forest!*
Female, 50s: *I've traveled with several other companies and on my own, but Close-Up Expeditions is the best. As a photographer it is a real luxury to be traveling with just five or six like-minded folks, all sharing techniques and perspectives. Every trip with them has been good. I'm even repeating Greece this year. We do not stay in high-end hotels but rather in small, charming, comfortable inns. We eat well, usually where the locals frequent, so we experience the true cuisine of the area and not just American food provided for American tourists. It may be a bit more money*

than a larger tour company, but it is really worth the difference. You come home with knowledge, cultural appreciation, new friends, and great images.

> *There are many photo tour advertisements in photography publications such as* Popular Photography, *and extensive listings can be found on the Internet under www.shawguides.com.*

Museum- and University-Sponsored Tours

Some of the best special-interest tours are organized by museums, universities, and college alumni groups. Although generally quite expensive, they are also usually superior and may provide exceptionally knowledgeable escorts. Part of the cost often is considered a tax-deductible contribution.

To find such trips, start with the groups either in your own city or nearby large cities. You may also want to contact some of the following large institutions:

SMITHSONIAN JOURNEYS
c/o Smithsonian Study Tours, 1100 Jefferson Drive SW, Washington, DC 20560; (202) 357-4700 or (877) 338-8687; www.smithsonianjourneys.org (EE)

The Smithsonian has a long roster of both U.S. and foreign tours each year, accompanied by experts on nature, folklore, architecture, gardens, wildlife, culture, and many other special interests. The choices also include cruises.

AMERICAN MUSEUM OF NATURAL HISTORY DISCOVERY TOURS
Central Park West at 79th Street, New York, NY 10024–5192; (800) 462-8687 or (212) 769-5700; www.amnh.org/welcome/discotours (EE)

The museum offers tours and cruises to the world's greatest wildlife regions, cultural centers, and archaeological sites, with museum scientists and expert lecturers. (Also listed under nature, page 124.)

NEW YORK BOTANICAL GARDEN ECOTOURS
c/o Institute of Systematic Botany, 200th Street & Kazimiroff Boulevard, Bronx, NY 10458–5126; (718) 817-8647 or (800) 448-2655; www.nybg.org/bsci/nybg_excursions.html (EE)

Natural history tours led by members of the science staff visit destinations such as the Amazon, Costa Rica, the Galápagos, Mexico, Trinidad, and Peru. Members also enjoy exceptional garden tours.

Avoiding Travel Scams

Beware of dishonest tour operators. Here are some tips on playing it safe.

- *If you work with a tour operator, make sure that the company offers a consumer protection plan. Membership in the U.S. Tour Operators Association (www.ustoa.com) is a valuable safeguard.*
- *Use a credit card to purchase tickets, and if cash must be used, always get a receipt—everything must be in writing.*
- *Verify that the tour company has professional liability insurance—all professional tour companies should have this coverage.*
- *Ask for a reference from a client with whom you are familiar.*
- *Avoid high-pressure sales tactics with a limited time to evaluate the offer.*
- *Beware of companies sending a courier for a check, requesting a direct bank deposit, or demanding a certified check.*
- *Decline offers requiring a property sales presentation.*
- *Prior to payment, review complete details about any trip in writing.*
- *Request specific hotel and airline names, addresses, and phone numbers—broad terms such as "all major hotels" and "all major airlines" are a warning flag.*
- *Insist on a local phone number if given a toll-free number—this will establish that the tour company or travel agency has a central office from which it operates.*
- *Never use 900 numbers.*
- *If you receive a vacation certificate in the mail, take it to a respectable tour operator or travel agent who can evaluate it.*
- *Call the National Fraud Information Center (800–876–7060) or local and state consumer protection agencies to report all incidences of travel-related fraud.*

NATIONAL TRUST STUDY TOURS

1785 Massachusetts Avenue NW, Washington, DC 20036; (800) 944–6847 or (202) 588–6300; www.nationaltrust.org/study_tours (EE)

Tours are to areas around the world known for their architecture, culture, and scenery. Recent choices have included Mexico, the Amazon, Hawaii, India, and Paris. Send for their Study Tours Tour Guide for listings of some seventy-five trips.

Go to Sea

AYBE YOU DON'T WANT AN ACTIVE VACATION AT ALL. MAYBE WHAT you'd really like to do is lie back and soak up some sun. Or maybe you can't decide. You'd like to relax, but you'd also like the excitement of seeing new places.

Cruises offer the best of two worlds—the chance to travel while you enjoy the pleasures of resort life at sea. The new superliners really are floating resorts, with a lineup of activities ranging from exercise classes and trapshooting to lectures, dance lessons, contests, and the chance to strike it rich in the casino. And few resorts can match the menus on a cruise ship, where something is being served almost nonstop from 7:00 A.M. until that fabled midnight buffet.

Best of all, these are resorts where you will never lack for company at dinner.

Ship travel is also safe, easy, and convenient. Accommodations, activities, entertainment, and lavish meals are all part of one package price, often even including transportation to the port of departure. And you can travel to a number of new places on one vacation without the hassles of making plane connections or dealing with luggage. No matter how many ports you visit, once you unpack, you need never face a suitcase again until you head home.

Recent changes in the cruise industry offer more good news for single people. No longer catering only to the wealthy or to older travelers, many cruise lines have updated their facilities and programs, shortened their itineraries, widened their offerings, and whittled their costs to appeal to a much wider audience—including singles. According to statistics from a study by Cruise Lines International Association, as many as 15 percent more singles sailed in 2003–2004 than the year before.

Many cruise lines welcome singles with receptions to meet other solo passengers and have dance hosts on board to be sure women traveling alone do not feel like wallflowers when the band strikes up. Singles gatherings usually are held early in the cruise on board ships of Carnival, Costa, Crystal, Discovery, Holland America, Radisson, Royal Caribbean, Silversea, and Cunard's *QEII*.

A Singular Dilemma

But there are still challenges to cruising on your own, especially where cost is concerned. The single supplement can raise the cost of a cabin anywhere from 110 to 200 percent above the double occupancy rate, and many of the major cruise lines are not easing this burden.

Even with growing numbers, solo passengers remain a small minority on board, and women almost always greatly outnumber the unattached men. In a recent survey some lines reported as few as 5 percent of their passengers were traveling alone, and no line reported more than 15 percent. Evenings on shipboard can be romantic, and couples do tend to couple up, particularly on the nights when everyone dresses up for dinner. If you are a female who will feel like a wallflower without a dancing partner, don't cruise by yourself. If, however, you can enjoy the pleasures of days at sea and be content to watch the evening's entertainment, and then maybe chat with other women or read a good book at night, cruising is for you.

Meeting and Mingling

With all those couples around, cruising is a situation where you really want to find compatible single company, even just a good buddy of your own sex. The new cruise liners keep getting bigger and bigger, and it is harder to meet people on an enormous ship. On a large ship, it takes a little luck and a lot of effort because it is easy to feel lost on ships with more than 1,000 passengers.

The only people you see regularly each day are those at your dinner table, so your seating assignment is crucial. Ask to be placed at one of the largest tables, which usually seats eight, to increase your chances of meeting people you'll want to spend time with. And request the second, or later, seating. The first seating tends to attract those who are early to bed, and because the dining room must be cleared ahead for the next sitting, there is little time for lingering over conversation.

If you are not happy with your table, ask to have it changed—and do it right away.

Persistence and an outgoing attitude are needed to search out the other unattached passengers on board a big ship. Even on ships that hold a singles mixer, if you don't connect at that early gathering, there are no set places afterward to meet the other single passengers on board. To better your odds of meeting people, sign up for lots of daytime activities. Women should not be afraid to try the bar, which is easy and comfortable to do on a ship. A piano bar is often a particularly pleasant gathering place.

Florence Lemkowitz, a veteran cruise writer, suggests that it is a mistake to go to bed early the first night at sea if you want to meet people, since that's just when other solo travelers are probably checking the scene with the same thought in mind. The first night is the best night to visit the ship's lounges and bars, she says, before people give up on them because nobody seems to be around. She also recommends telling the social director that you want to make friends, putting him or her to work on your behalf.

One regular cruiser I know makes up little cards with her name and cabin number. These are not meant to serve as invitations to drop in. Ships' cabins have telephones, and, on a large ship, a card ensures that the new acquaintances will know where to call if they want to get together. You can't just assume you will run into one another again.

Recognizing the lack of dance partners, several lines have gone out of their way to make things pleasanter for single women at night. "Gentleman hosts" are now provided by a growing number of cruise lines, including Discovery, the *QEII,* Orient's *Marco Polo,* Radisson and Silversea ships, and longer cruises of Holland America and NCL. Congenial single men in their 50s and 60s are invited to come along as hosts to dance with unaccompanied women, attend cocktail parties, act as a fourth for bridge or a partner in dance class, or sometimes just serve as someone to talk to. These men, mostly retired, are carefully screened for both sociability and dancing ability. Forget about romance, however; they receive explicit instructions to mingle, with no favoritism allowed to any one passenger or group.

If you are a male who would like to apply, contact the employment office of the cruise line that interests you. Just remember this isn't a restful vacation; dancing every dance takes a lot of energy.

One solution to the cruising dilemma is to go with a group. Several companies organize cruises for singles each year, booking blocks of space aboard regularly scheduled sailings on popular ships. Each group has its own tour director, dines together, enjoys separate activities as well as participating in the ship's recreation, and does its own shore excursions. Group members are paired to avoid the single supplement. This solves the problem of single company, but not the male/female ratio, since women make up the majority of these groups.

Among the many organizations offering group cruises for solo passengers are:

www.singlescruise.com (800–393–5000)
www.singlestravelintl.com (877–765–6874
www.allsinglestravel.com (800) 717–3231
www.aimhighertravel.com (877–752–1858
www.singlescruises-tours.com (888) 775–0288, ext. 241
www.singlesdreamcruises.com (800) 676–1499

www.osolomio.com (800) 959–8568
www.allchristiancruises.com (888–43JESUS; Christian singles)
www.amazingjourneys.com (800–734–0493; Jewish singles)
www.binnacletravel.com (800) 936–2250
www.traveltimeforsingles.com (800) 469–0091

For an additional current listing, see www.cruisemates.com under "single cruising."

Boarding the Right Ship

If the lack of romance does not deter you, you can concentrate on the other pleasures of being at sea. And these are plentiful. There's nothing quite like the sense of freedom you feel standing on a breezy deck and gazing at the limitless horizon—or the excitement of watching a new port loom ever closer into view.

With a group or on your own, your first decision when planning a cruise should be based on which ports you most want to visit, and that depends a lot on the season. In winter, the Caribbean is by far the most popular destination. The eastern ports of the Bahamas, Puerto Rico, St. Thomas, and St. Martin are the most frequently chosen because they are easily reached on seven-day cruises from Florida. Close seconds are Jamaica, Cozumel, and Grand Cayman. Cruises out of San Juan go farther afield to western Caribbean islands such as Barbados, Guadeloupe, Martinique, St. Lucia, or Antigua. These harbors are less crowded with cruise ships and for that very reason are more appealing to many people. These itineraries are particularly appealing when the fare to San Juan is included in the price. Hawaiian cruises are also popular with single cruisers.

In summer, Bermuda is a convenient port of call in the east, while Alaska's Inside Passage, with its ice-blue glaciers and some of the continent's greatest scenery, makes for an unforgettable and increasingly popular cruise in the West. Unlike many trips where you see very little from port to port, the views of Alaska from shipboard are often so engrossing that many passengers need no other daytime entertainment than watching the show from their deck chairs.

If you have the time and the fare, there are also wonderful itineraries to South America, the Mediterranean, the Greek Islands and Turkey, the Baltic, the South Seas, and Asia, and a number of exciting and exotic expeditions to remote regions of the world, including Antarctica. In fact, there's almost no place on earth you cannot happily explore on a cruise.

One problem you rarely have to consider any longer is seasickness. Today's giant ships are remarkably stable, and there are plenty of over-the-counter remedies such as Dramamine available as an extra safeguard. Choose a cabin close to midships and near the waterline for the least amount of motion. And relax, knowing that if all else fails, the ship's doctor is ready with an injection that will quickly put you back on an even keel.

Getting the Best Deal

Once you have decided where you want to go, your next dilemma is choosing among the many companies offering similar itineraries. The makeup of passengers will vary from week to week, but here are a few general guidelines.

Your age may narrow your choices. Generally, longer and more luxurious cruises attract older passengers and many retired people. Three- and four-day cruises to the Bahamas and Freeport from the East Coast and to Baja California from the West Coast tend to attract younger passengers. Seven-day Caribbean trips are perfect winter vacations for all, and they get a good mix of people.

If you are worried about gaining weight from the nonstop meals on a cruise ship, you can choose from many ships with extensive fitness centers and daily exercise classes. Some even offer spa cuisine.

Theme cruises are a boon for single passengers because they have a focus. These are regular sailings with the customary itinerary of ports, but with special guests and entertainment on board to provide a drawing card. The singles percentages on these cruises may be no higher, but the chances of meeting people who share your interests probably will be.

Knowledgeable travel agents and cruise specialists will know about these offerings, which vary each year. Some of the specialty choices in the past have included jazz festivals, guest Cordon Bleu chefs, photography instructors, spas at sea, and themes from natural history to soap operas to sports. There are now cruises aimed at golfers, bridge players, wine and art connoisseurs, antiquers, opera and film lovers, and Civil War buffs.

Ambience is a less measurable aspect of a ship. It depends on the decor, the quality of service, the attitude of the crew and staff, the caliber of the food, and the general feeling created on board. Individual ships in a company's fleet may differ in size as well as personality. The best current information on ships is found on two Web sites featuring extensive ship reviews as well as comments from past passengers. Each has information especially for single passengers, as well as bulletin boards where singles may communicate. They may also act as booking agents or provide links to agents or directly to cruise lines, but their prime function is to provide guidance. The sites are:

www.cruisecritic.com
www.cruisemates.com

The best cruise guidebook I've seen is Kay Showker's *Unofficial Guide to Cruises*. She not only describes the good and bad points of each cruise line but tells you the kind of passengers you are likely to find aboard. And she gives in-depth descriptions of accommodations and amenities on each ship in the line.

For singles, Showker recommends smaller ships: "It is easier to mix, and the staff takes greater care to ensure that you are part of the ship's social life," she says. Among smaller ships, she advises that expedition and educational cruises are the best choices. "A camaraderie develops quickly among passengers who share common interests and a certain sense of adventure," she points out. "For single women, the number of unattached men is likely to be higher than on traditional cruises."

The Single Supplement

One of the big deterrents to cruise travel for singles is cost. Cruise lines may impose surcharges anywhere from 110 to 200 percent of the double rate if you want to occupy a cabin alone. The policy for singles is always stated in the ship's brochure, but pricing varies considerably on each line according to the season.

Some lines are more welcoming to solo passengers than others. Although policies change frequently and need to be checked before you book, at press time Crystal, Norwegian Coastal Voyages, Radisson Seven Seas, Riverbarge, Royal Caribbean, and Seabourn were adding only 25 percent to the per-person rate for singles occupying a double cabin for certain cruises. Silversea, Seabourn, and Swan Hellenic had only a 10-percent surcharge on their higher-category cabins. Since some of the upscale lines are those offering price breaks to solo cruisers, you may be able to afford a luxury ship rather than an economy ship with a heavy supplement.

When cabins are not filled, many other ships may offer discounts close to the sailing date. You can learn about the latest savings by checking often with the cruise specialists listed on pages 167 and 169–170. Even better, sign up for the free weekly e-mail newsletter at www.singlescruiseresource.com. Operated by Amber Blecker, an agent at Cruises, Inc. who specializes in singles travel, it lists often-unadvertised special discount rates for solo travelers on lines such as Celebrity, Holland America, Royal Caribbean, Radisson, and Carnival.

Comparing Rates

To compare prices of similar cruises, divide the total cost by the number of full days on board. Arriving in home port at 8:00 A.M. hardly counts as a day at sea. In calculating the cost of any cruise, remember that you must figure as much as

$10.00 per day for tips. The recommended sums are $4.00 per day each for room stewards and waiters, $2.00 for busboys. If you order drinks or use the barber shop or beauty salon, figure a 15 percent tip on each tab. Tips for shipboard personnel who provide special services are at your own discretion.

On all cruises, port charges and government fees add about $125 per passenger on a typical seven-day Caribbean cruise, more on longer trips. If you plan to take group tours ashore, be sure to include that cost in your calculations, as it can be considerable. The more ports, the more added expense.

To save money booking a cruise, you are better off reserving very early or very late. Early birds get advance booking discounts. Since the advent of so many new mega-ships with huge capacities, some lines are offering better pricing for single passengers who are willing to wait until thirty to sixty days before the sailing date for confirmation. And some offer standby fares for those who will take unfilled space close to the sailing date.

For this reason, once again, passengers are wise to deal with a travel agent who specializes in cruises and is up to date on all the current possibilities. Larger cruise specialists also can frequently offer their own discounts, passing along the reductions they get from the cruise lines for being favored customers who buy space in bulk.

Dealing with someone who is familiar with the industry will also give you an edge in choosing a ship where you will be happy, regardless of the price. Single passengers come in all demographics and tastes, as do any other cruise passengers.

Among the knowledgeable agencies that specialize in cruise travel and also offer discounts are:

CRUISES INC.
(800) 854–0500; www.cruisesinc.com
Features ship reviews and photo tours.

WORLD WIDE CRUISES INC.
(954) 720–9000 or (800) 882–9000; www.wwcruises.com.

CRUISES ONLY
(800) 278–4737; www.cruisesonly.com.

ICRUISE
www.icruise.com.
Includes picks of best choices for solo passengers.

GALAXSEA
(800) 662–5450; www.cruisestar.com.

FOREVER CRUISING
(800) 338–8005; www.forevercruising.com.

For discounts on late bookings:

SPUR OF THE MOMENT CRUISES
(800) 343–1991; www.spurof.com.

Insurance and payment advice:

Whichever cruise you choose, you are putting out a sizable sum, so don't fail to protect yourself with travel insurance. Read the regulations carefully: The two important things to cover are the cost of your fare if you must cancel or the cruise is interrupted, and the potentially large cost of major medical expenses away from home, especially in an emergency that would require evacuation from the ship. Almost all cruise lines offer insurance, as do travel agencies and independent insurance companies, so compare prices.

If you are traveling to an area that your own health insurance does not cover, you may need supplemental medical insurance as well. You will find more on travel insurance on page 285.

Kay Showker offers another word of warning: Always pay for a cruise with a credit card. If you go through a travel agency, see that the charge is run through the cruise line's account rather than the agent's, protecting you in case the agency should go under with your money in the till. Paying with a credit card also allows you to cancel payment if the cruise is not provided as promised.

Other Cruises

Large cruise ships are not the only way to go to sea. Check out the interesting and offbeat itineraries offered by smaller ships sailing scenic waters at home and abroad.

CLIPPER CRUISE LINE
11969 Westline Industrial Drive, St. Louis, MO 63146;
(314) 655-6700 or (800) 325-0010; www.clippercruise.com (EE)

Clipper's four ships, the *Yorktown Clipper* (138 passengers), the *Nantucket Clipper* (100 passengers), the *Clipper Adventurer* (122 passengers), and the *Clipper Odyssey* (128 passengers) cover a wide range of territory. Destinations include the Caribbean, Costa Rica, Panama, South America, eastern Canada, Alaska's Inside Passage, Mexico and Central America, western Europe, Antarctica, the Baltic, Scandinavia, the British Isles, Greenland, the Northwest Territories, Australia, New Zealand, the Far East, and, closer to home, Florida and the Great Lakes. Historians and naturalists are on board to enhance the experience. Their free catalog, "Small Ship Adventures," details all the itineraries.

INTRAV

7711 Bonhomme Avenue, St. Louis, MO 63105; (800) 456–8100 or (314) 727–0500; www.intrav.com (EE)

INTRAV, which owns the Clipper Cruise Line detailed above, also publishes a catalog called *InTrav Adventures.* The catalog provides information about other upscale small-ship cruises offered on the great rivers of Europe. It also lists a variety of luxury excursions on land.

River Cruises

This is a relaxed way to see the sights along some of the most scenic rivers in the world, up-close and in comfort. Ships are small, so they can pull right into town, allowing you the choice of getting off and strolling at your own pace or following a guided tour. In larger cities, it is a treat to be so close to things, with no need for a bus to get into town. In smaller villages, this is almost like touring by car, spending a couple of hours enjoying the sights, then moving on. And like all cruising, you have the advantage of unpacking once and having the comforts of a floating hotel.

VIKING RIVER CRUISES

21820 Burbank Boulevard, Woodland Hills, CA 91367; (818) 227–1234 or (877) 568–4546; www.rivercruises.com

Viking is the world's largest operator of river cruises, with a fleet of twenty-three ships covering rivers in France, Germany, Holland, Belgium, Austria, Hungary, the Ukraine, and Russia, as well as the Yangtze River in China. Ships average 150 guests, so it is easy to meet people. Viking offers a money-saving bonus; guided shore excursions are included in the price of the trip.

PETER DEILMANN CRUISES

1800 Diagonal Road, Suite 170, Alexandria, VA 22314; (800) 348–8287 or
(703) 549–1741; www.deilmann-cruises.com (EE)

The most luxurious of the river cruises, Deilmann ships sail the great rivers of
Europe—the Danube, Elbe, Rhine, Moselle, Rhone, and Saone—with a fleet
of nine ships small enough to be sociable but large enough (accommodating 58 to
204) to offer a variety of companions and amenities such as attractive lounges,
panoramic windows, and swimming pools. Best of all for solo passengers, all the
ships offer attractive single rates. The company also owns the *Lili Marleen*, a fifty-
passenger luxury sailing yacht, and the *MV Deutschland*, a five-star luxury liner.

C O M M E N T S E.B.: *I have sailed on two Deilmann ships and find the service,
food, and itineraries first rate. I loved being able to walk from the ship into town,
even in big cities such as Vienna and Budapest, without having to sign up for a
tour. Be aware that the line is German owned, so at least half the passengers are
German. This is not a problem since all announcements are in both languages and
English tours are offered at every stop, but it does limit the socializing possibilities.
And know that these trips, like most river cruises, seem to be most popular with
older passengers, averaging age 50 and up.*

EUROPEAN WATERWAYS

35 Wharf Road, Wraysbury, Staines, Middlesex TW19 5J9, England; (800) 394–8630;
www.gobarging.com (E–EE)

A barge cruise is an intimate, placid way to see Europe, with congenial small
groups and plenty of time to sightsee at each stop. The barges move at about
4 miles per hour, so it's easy to get off and bicycle, walk, or jog along towpaths or
go into nearby villages and catch up with the ship at its next stop. Ships hold six to
twelve passengers.

The company arranges trips on rivers and canals in France, Italy, Germany,
Scotland, England, and Ireland.

Freighter Cruises

If you have the time for long voyages, freighter travel is an adventurous way to visit foreign ports at a reasonable cost and in surprising comfort. Many retired people and teachers and others with long vacations sign on. Trips may range from twenty to seventy days.

Most cargo vessels accommodate no more than twelve passengers, so the experience is very personal. Staterooms are spacious and have views, and, unlike cruise liners, many freighters have large, single cabins. This is travel for the self-sufficient, for there are no shipboard activities and evening entertainment usually means conversations, cards, and games. Rates may average as little as $100 a day, including meals shared with the ship's officers. Passengers may also use the lounge and deck. Possible destinations include Australia and New Zealand, the Norwegian coast, South America, the South Pacific, Africa, Europe, and the Orient.

To learn about freighter travel, contact:

**TRAVELTIPS CRUISE AND FREIGHTER
TRAVEL ASSOCIATION**
163–07 Depot Road, P.O. Box 580188, Flushing, NY 11358;
(800) 872–8584 or (718) 939–2400; www.travltips.com

Members receive the *TravLtips* magazine, which includes firsthand accounts of other members' journeys. These stories provide great armchair adventures. There is also a listing of upcoming freighter itineraries as well as discounts on special-value regular cruises. A modest membership fee is credited toward the first voyage. The Web site answers many questions about freighter voyages.

Sailing Cruises

The best bet if you are looking for single company on a ship is to board a sociable, no-frills windjammer sailing cruise, where many passengers are unattached. (See page 105 under Try Adventure Travel for more details.) A more luxurious option is:

WINDSTAR CRUISES

300 Elliott Avenue West, Seattle, WA 98119;
(206) 281–3535 or (800) 258–7245; www.windstarcruises.com (EE)

The beautiful, tall-masted, luxury sailing yachts of this company accommodate 148 to 305 passengers and attract sophisticated, active individuals ages 25 to 65. Destinations include the Caribbean, the Mediterranean, Costa Rica, the Panama Canal, Tahiti, the Greek Isles, and Italy's Amalfi coast. These trips are less expensive than you might expect, but singles do pay a 175 percent supplement and they are a very small percentage of the passengers.

Cruise   Expeditions

Small ships that are able to get off the beaten path to such exotic locales as Antarctica, Africa, Polynesia, Micronesia, Melanesia, and Indonesia offer exciting excursions for adventure-minded travelers. These trips are expensive, but they are also once-in-a-lifetime experiences. Since the numbers of passengers are small and the visits are thrilling, the groups quickly become close, making these seemingly remote excursions very easy to enjoy on your own. Some of my most memorable travel experiences have been on expedition cruises. Operators report that many passengers come by themselves.

The following are among the great expedition cruises I can personally recommend:

Cruising the Nile

A trip on the Nile is an unforgettable experience, offering a chance to see life on the banks of the river and to visit the astonishing ruins and the tombs of the pharaohs with expert guides. The narrow ribbon of gentle river allows a close-up view of village life while at the same time providing a graphic illustration of the Nile's importance—beyond the border of green irrigated by the river, barren desert begins.

Longer cruises begin in Cairo; shorter ones begin in Luxor or Aswan (reached by plane from Cairo). The major sights lie between the cities. Sightseeing stops include the Temple of Luxor and the awesome ruins of the Temple of Karnak as well as the Valley of the Kings, where the tombs of Tutankhamen and other pharaohs were found; you will also see the Valley of the Queens and the Tombs of the Nobles, which contain some of the most important art of ancient Egypt.

Besides the many international expedition cruise companies, a number of local Egyptian operators run cruises, as do the major Cairo hotels. Among the most popular operators for Americans is Sonesta Hotels (www.sonesta.com). They have three cruise ships on the Nile and also operate several hotels in Egypt.

The Coastal Express: Cruising the Fjords of Norway

The ads call this "The World's Most Beautiful Voyage," and it's hard to argue as you cruise along Norway's breathtaking coastline. Wending into steep and narrow fjords, gliding past glaciers, farms, and fishing villages, and crossing the Arctic Circle, the Coastal Express fleet goes where larger cruisers cannot venture. Although cabins are comfortable and newer ships in the fleet are a bit more luxurious, these are not ordinary cruise ships. They are working cargo ships, the vital lifeline for the hardy fishers and farmers in the more remote northern villages along the coast. As they pick up and deliver mail, supplies, and passengers at thirty-five towns and villages along the way, the ships provide a true close-up look at local life. Talks on board tell a lot about the country and its people.

The sail is all the more fascinating because the panoramas change daily on the way to "the top of the world." From the home port of Bergen to Kirkenes at the end of the line, trees give way to Arctic tundra, mountains to flats, and, depending on the season, the light may change from night and day to all night or all day. The music of Edvard Grieg on the loudspeaker announces the most dramatic entry into the narrow, steep-walled Trollfjord, where mountains loom almost close enough to touch.

Tromsø, the gateway to the Arctic, and Trondheim, Norway's third-largest city and one of the oldest, are major stops with many sights to see. Other ports are so tiny it takes no more than five minutes to walk the town, but often there is a pleasant surprise—a whimsical statue, a little park, or simply the chance to watch fishing boats and people going about their daily routines. The final stop in Bergen is best of all. Cradled by steep mountains, filled with cobbled lanes and quaint wooden houses, Bergen delights everyone.

While the Bergen Line has added more luxurious ships with more deck space and some cabins with balconies and Jacuzzis, this is not a typical cruise ship. There are no floor shows and no midnight buffets. Meals are not extravaganzas, but they do feature absolutely delicious fresh seafood. Don't sign on if you want the usual cruise ship experience; do come aboard for the experience of a lifetime. If you can't spend the entire twelve days, fly to Tromsø and take the homeward voyage to Bergen.

For information, contact Bergen Line, Inc., 405 Park Avenue, New York, NY 10022; (212) 319–1390 or (800) 323–7436, www.bergenline.com.

Cruising the Sepik River, Papua New Guinea

Papua New Guinea is like nowhere else on earth, a fantastically varied island, a bird and flower lover's paradise still widely unblemished by humans. The country's finest native art, such as masks, carvings, and bark paintings, can be found in villages along the Sepik River. This route is served by two modern and comfortable small boats, the *Melanesian Discoverer,* a catamaran accommodating forty-eight passengers that departs from the port of Madang, and the *Sepik Spirit,* an eighteen-passenger vessel that leaves from the art-filled Karawari Lodge, the country's oldest and best-known tourist lodging.

The serpentine Sepik River provides the only route of transportation in this region. Its twists and turns provide a new vista around every bend—exotic birds, luxuriant vegetation, families traveling by dugout canoe, and thatched-hut villages where you can go ashore to see traditional ceremonies.

While Papua New Guinea is remote, it is a perfect add-on to a visit to Australia and a truly unforgettable travel experience. It is one of the few remaining places on earth where you can see tribes living as they have since the Stone Age. In many areas, they have had contact with the Western world for less than fifty years. The cruise can be combined with a land package for further exploration in the beautiful highlands.

The best source of current tour and cruise information is the Papua New Guinea Business Directory, www.pngbd.com/travel or www.airniugini.com.pg

Finally, cruising the Galápagos Islands or Antarctica are among the ultimate travel experiences. Read about them in Get Back to Nature, pages 127 and 125, respectively.

Expedition Cruise Operators

Better-known cruise companies that roam the globe from the Arctic to the Amazon using smaller ships are listed on page 128.

Cruise References:

THE UNOFFICIAL GUIDE TO CRUISES: 2004 EDITION
Kay Showker, Bob Sehlinger, Macmillan General Reference, New York.

BERLITZ OCEAN CRUISING VERSUS CRUISE SHIPS, 2004
Douglas Ward, Berlitz Publishing, London, England.

The Singles Scene

W ITH THE NUMBER OF SINGLE TRAVELERS GROWING SO RAPIDLY, IT IS only natural that enterprising folks will find ways to serve them. This chapter is a potpourri of advice and services of interest to singles—tours and resorts where singles mingle, publications and Web sites aimed to help the single traveler, and ideas for finding a compatible roommate to beat the high cost of traveling solo.

Because younger travelers might prefer the company of their contemporaries, there is a section on age-specific programs for the 20 to 35 age group that get a high percentage of single participants. The growing number of trips and services just for women is detailed in the next chapter, followed by a survey of the burgeoning list of possibilities for those over age 50.

Let's look at some of the possibilities for all ages.

Newsletters and Web Sites

The best way to keep track of current special opportunities for solo travel is with a newsletter via mail or online. Subscription rates change, so be sure to inquire about current prices before sending a check!

Connecting: Solo Travel News (689 Park Road, Unit 6, Gibsons, BC V0N 1V7, Canada; 604–886–9099; www.cstn.org) is one of the most valuable resources for single travelers. Published by Diane Redfern, a Canadian, the twenty-page, bimonthly newsletter is packed with up-to-the-minute information on upcoming tours of interest to singles in the United States, Canada, and worldwide. This is the best up-to-the-minute listing of cruises with single cabins and tours without a single supplement. Readers share their firsthand travel experiences and finds, suggest singles-friendly lodgings, and post ads seeking travel companions or offering hospitality to visitors.

The most unique service from *Connecting* is the annual **Single-Friendly Travel Directory,** listing descriptions for every tour operator, resort, or cruise line with special offerings for solo travelers. The directory is in looseleaf form to allow for regular updates, which appear in the newsletter. The directory is free to subscribers, or can be ordered separately for $5. Annual subscriptions to *Connecting* are $45; sample issues, $5. E-members who receive their newsletters online pay $28.

solodining.com (P.O. Box 1025, South Pasadena, CA 91031; 800–299–1079 or 323–257–0026) is a Web site edited by Marya Charles Alexander, devoted to "taking the bite out of eating alone." She offers tips on dining alone comfortably and features solo-friendly restaurants in different cities. Visitors also contribute their finds. The same editor offers links to useful travel sources at a sister Web site, www.solotravel portal.com.

travelchums.com This is a free online service that promises to help find "like-minded companions whose personalities, interests, and plans mesh with yours." Members fill out an extensive profile describing personality, interests, travel likes and dislikes, and future travel plans. For a $15 fee, you can become a subscriber, posting photos and sending private messages to other members. The service has more than 28,000 members.

journeywoman.com See page 189 for this excellent newsletter geared to women but of interest to all.

Travel Companion Exchange (www.travelcompanions.com), a longtime publisher of a bimonthly newsletter and the oldest and largest organization devoted to pairing singles who want a travel partner, has been temporarily suspended due to a family emergency. To be notified when they are resuming operation, send your full name and address to TCE@travelcompanions.com.

Trips for Singles

One way to ensure meeting other single people is to sign up for a tour designed expressly for singles. The number of tour companies offering trips has increased in recent years. Additional options are operators listed in other sections of the book who offer, along with general programs, special trips designated for singles. All of these groups will try to arrange for shares, but there may be a surcharge if you request single occupancy. Here are some of the possibilities:

THE SINGLE GOURMET
Find a nearby chapter by entering "Single Gourmet" into a Web browser.

This nationwide organization dedicated to good eating and sociability started in 1982 and now has chapters in many U.S. locations and three Canadian cities. Restaurant outings are arranged regularly in each city, and a few trips are offered to all members each year. The trips include a full sightseeing agenda but concentrate on dining, visiting the very top restaurants in each location. Lodgings are also deluxe. Recent trips included San Francisco and the Napa Valley, New Orleans, Rome, Paris, China, and a New Year's Eve journey to Spain. Travelers are paired at no charge. Members may attend dinners in other member cities when they travel. The age range of membership is from 20 to 70, with most age 40 or older. Women outnumber men 5 to 2. Since many trips are planned by the New York chapter (www.singlegourmetny.com; 212–980–8788), many of the trip participants are from the Northeast, but there is a representation from all the chapters. Members say the trips are well run and sociable, and the days are flexible enough to allow for free time. Other chapters are found in Chicago; Philadelphia; Minneapolis/St. Paul; Tampa and South Florida; Houston; Phoenix; Norfolk and Richmond, Virginia; Boston; Atlanta; Austin; New Orleans; Dallas; San Diego, Orange County, and Los Angeles, California; and more cities to come. Membership fees vary by chapter, from $59 to $125 yearly.

AMERICAN JEWISH CONGRESS
(see page 155)

The highly respected cultural organization offers several tours for singles ages 29 to 49 to Israel and many other destinations.

CRUISE TOURS
(Page 165)

See listings for several "singles only" groups on regularly scheduled cruises, guaranteeing a roommate and congenial company.

BACKROADS
(page 95)

Offers many walking and biking trips for singles in the United States, Europe, Asia, and the Pacific. The itineraries are identical to regular offerings.

THE WORLD OUTDOORS
(page 96)

Combines biking and hiking with rafting and horseback riding on singles trips to the Colorado Rockies and the Southwest. Singles tours attract younger participants, with 35 the most common age.

WINDJAMMER BAREFOOT CRUISES
(page 105)

Sets aside several cruises each year for singles. They cut off registration when one gender reaches 50 percent, so there's always an even mix.

NIKE AMHERST TENNIS CAMP
(page 13)

Special weeks are designated for singles at this popular tennis camp.

OUTDOOR ADVENTURE RIVER SPECIALISTS (O.A.R.S.), INC.
(page 109)

Singles excursions include rafting trips and multisport adventures.

SEASCAPE SAILING PARTY, LTD.
15127 Northeast Twenty-Fourth Street, Redmond, WA 98052; (877) 273–2722 or (425) 445–1367; www.seascape-sail.com (I–M)

Explorers who want the fun of sailing from island to island in the Greek Isles and along the Turkish coast on a 50-foot sailing yacht may enjoy this group. The boats accommodate eight guests in four cabins. Half a dozen trips are labeled "mostly singles" and draw mostly sociable passengers from late 20s to mid-40s (though older folks are welcome, too).

For Young Singles

CONTIKI HOLIDAYS
801 East Katella Avenue, Anaheim, CA 92805; (888) CONTIKI or (714) 935–0808; www.contiki.com (I)

For more than forty years, Contiki has served adventure-minded passengers ages 18 to 35 with trips to Europe, Australia, New Zealand, North America, and the South Pacific. Most participants are in their 20s; 50 to 60 percent are single, and they come from English-speaking countries all over the world. Contiki offers a roommate matching program to avoid the single supplement. The average male/female ratio is 40/60, but according to one insider, males outnumber females on many U.S. and South Pacific tours, while European trips tend to be

Singles Tour Specialists

O Solo Mio Tours, 160 Main Street, Los Altos, CA 94024; (800) 959–8568; www.osolomio.com. Formed in 1991, this company organizes singles tours and arranges for roommates, eliminating the single supplement. Trips have included safaris, cruises, fall foliage in Canada, and tours in Spain, Portugal, England, Italy, Australia, New Zealand, Belize, Greece, Israel, and the Riviera. You can be on the mailing list for notice of coming trips by phoning or sending an e-mail.

All Singles Travel, c/o Travel Services Worldwide, 2300 Lakeview Parkway, Suite 700, Alpharetta, GA 30004; (770) 645–3241 or (800) 717–3231; www.allsinglestravel.com. This off-shoot of an Atlanta travel service formed in 1996 has grown to offer a variety of trips each year with roommate matching that guarantees no single supplement. Many cruises are on the roster, as well as destinations such as eastern Europe and western Europe, Costa Rica, Peru, and Chile. Average age of participants is 30s to 50s. The Web site has links to other singles trips, including Christian singles, Jewish singles, and trips for senior singles age 60 and up.

Singles Travel International, 310 North State Street, Lockport, IL 60441; (877) 765–6874 or (815) 836–9951; www.singlestravelintl.com. A former flight attendant and travel agent founded this company over seven years ago, offering upscale travel for singles. Six to eight trips per year are scheduled to destinations from New York and New Orleans to Paris and Spain's Costa del Sol, including multisport trips to national parks and a variety of cruises. The Web site has a valuable section of specials, listing current cruise bargains and, sometimes, resorts temporarily waiving single supplements.

Travel Time for Singles, 5970 Deer Springs Lane, Acworth, GA 30101; (800) 469–0091 or (678) 574–4006; www.traveltimeforsingles.com. An offshoot of the Travel Time Agency begun in 1995, this service plans trips for professionals age 30 and up. A roster of cruises includes popular New Year's holiday sailings. Tuscany, Scotland, Brazil, and a Mexican spa were recent tour destinations.

Going Solo Travel Club, 629 11th Avenue S.W., Calgary, Alberta, Canada T2R 0E1; (800) 475–3755 or (403) 298–3532; www.goingsolotravel.com. There *is no fee to become a member of this Canadian club for singles who love to travel. Recent group trips have included Spain, New Orleans, Las Vegas, Australia, Mexico, and a Caribbean cruise.*

Adventures for Singles, Inc., *1907 Daniel Green Court, Smyrna, GA 30080; (877) 813–9421 or (770) 432–8225; www.adventuresforsingles.com. Several moderately priced trips are put together each year by this group formed in 1990. Brazil, France, Italy, Costa Rica, Tahiti, and a South African safari have been recent offerings, along with cruises.*

Singles in Paradise, *3959 L. Honoapiilani Road, #601, Lahaina, HI 96761; (800) 954–5453 or (808) 662–1212; www.singleinparadise.com. Based in Hawaii, Singles in Paradise plans several trips each year to Maui for young, active singles. Hiking, sailing, snorkeling, kayaking, and whale watching are included on the itineraries. Other special outings such as Greece, Carnival in Rio, exploring Peru, and Windjammer cruises are offered.*

Jewish Singles Vacations, *P.O. Box 211, Brookline, MA 02446; (617) 782–3396; www.tourgroups.com/jsv. Trips to Hawaii, Europe, Canada, and around the United States have been on the agenda for Jewish singles ages 35 to 55. Average trips number 30 to 40 people. The group has been in operation since 1990.*

More information on tours for solo travelers is available on Internet sites such as www.ask.com, where a long listing for singles is available by typing "singles travel."

more heavily female. The trips are by motor coach. For tours labeled "Superior," accommodations are in hotels and resorts. Budget travelers stay in Contiki-owned chalets and villas, cabins, and hotels, sometimes four to a room. All "superior" rooms have private baths, while budget travelers share facilities. Said one young woman recently returned from her first trip to Europe: "I can't think of a better way to go."

Resorts Recommended for Singles

CLUB MED

This is still the first place that comes to mind when you ask a travel agent to suggest a solo vacation, though Club Med is far from the "swinging singles" scene of a few decades ago. The original guests have grown up and so has the club. Turkoise and Cancun are the only clubs still designated "for adults only." Families are courted, honeymooners are welcomed, and seniors get special discounts. Increasingly, Club Med is promoting more exotic locations such as Bora Bora. And for this pioneer in all-inclusive resorts, competition from an increasing number of newer resorts means upgraded rooms and value rates, good news for the many loyal fans of Club Med.

Does that mean Club Med is no longer a good choice for solo vacationers? Not at all. The greatest appeal of Club Med remains. The first resorts to cater to singles remain beach vacations where you can be absolutely comfortable by yourself and never have to dine alone. Singles still make up a big percentage of the membership, and many of them welcome the fact that the social pressure at many clubs is less than it used to be.

Those who knew the Club Meds of old will be pleasantly surprised at new and remodeled clubs with larger and better-appointed rooms. Columbus Isle in the Bahamas is the most lavish of the new breed, filled with fabulous folk art and antiques; it even offers TV and telephones in the rooms, a far cry from the spartan original Club Meds. Cancun, Sandpiper, and Punta Gorda clubs have also had multimillion-dollar renovations. Over sixty villages worldwide have been updated.

Many clubs have kept up with the times by offering aerobics classes and fitness centers with the latest in exercise equipment. You can have a massage at many clubs. And you can learn anything from sailing, scuba diving, and windsurfing to tennis and skiing to circus skills such as juggling, acrobatics on a trampoline, or tricks on a trapeze. With the exception of scuba diving, horseback riding, and golf, sports instruction is included in one all-inclusive price, along with gourmet meals and an open bar.

While many guests still prefer to save by having a roommate assigned, single rooms are now available with an added supplement; this can be a modest 10 to 20 percent off-season.

The best deal at Club Med is to take your chances with the Wild Card option. You pick the week for a set, money-saving price; they pick the place. Vacationers reap the benefits of allowing Club Med to even the numbers at its various resorts. Singles are never sent to family-oriented clubs.

Because Club Med is such a well-known choice for single vacationers, it deserves special space and description, pro and con.

Life at Club Med

Life at Club Med villages is meant to be carefree. There's no cash to worry about. You are given a card when you arrive that allows you to charge any expenses and settle up at the end of your stay, so your money can go into the safe until you leave. Rooms usually aren't provided with clocks, so bring a watch and an alarm clock. Lessons are scheduled at specified times, and if you don't get there on time, you'll miss out.

With the many activities offered, days can be jam packed—or you can ignore all the activities and find a quiet spot on the beach. Meals are all-you-can-eat extravaganzas with dozens of choices. Some dishes are better than others, but if you don't like your first selections, you can always go back and find reliable alternatives, such as roast beef, lamb, or turkey served from carving stations. The cuisine has been seriously upgraded in recent years, and food is now available all day.

A hostess seats everyone at big round tables, making it very easy to meet people. You can then make reservations to dine together with your new friends in the smaller specialty dining rooms.

But Club Med is not for everyone. If you hated summer camp and you are not turned on by the idea of group lessons, line dancing, and the "Hands Up" theme song with hand motions, you may not be Club Med material. "Olympics Day" is really a grown-up version of a "color war"—everyone is divided into teams for competitions that include everything from basketball to beer drinking.

In all fairness, though, no one forces you to do anything. You can stay under a palm tree with a book if you like and go for a walk on the beach after dinner, but you can't avoid the music and activity around you or the sound of the loudspeaker announcing daily in English and in French contests such as volleyball and water polo tournaments.

The voice belongs to a GO (*gentil organisateur*), one of the bouncy, good-looking young men and women who do everything they can to make their enthusiasm contagious to their flock of GMs (*gentils members*). The GOs work hard, giving sports instruction, being sociable, leading trivia contests before dinner and group dances afterward (no partner necessary). Then they put on the evening entertainment, which can be surprisingly good for amateurs. Sophisticated? Not really, but you have to admire their energy.

Club Med
Locations for Adults

Clubs open to all ages, but with no special facilities for children:
- *Columbus Isle, Bahamas*
- *Bora Bora, French Polynesia*

Adults over age 18 only:
- *Turkoise, Turks and Caicos*
- *Cancun, Mexico*

Choosing a Club

If you decide to give Club Med a try and look at their big catalog, you'll see plenty of tempting properties. After all, two of the club's main attractions are great locations and interesting architecture. Management makes it easier by pointing out which clubs are primarily geared to families, which to adults, and which are open to all ages but have no special facilities for children (which discourages families with younger kids).

If you have a particular sport or activity in mind, one way to ensure that you'll enjoy the week is to choose Club Med villages with a specialty. Tennis camps are featured at Sandpiper and Punta Cana; horseback riding is offered at Caravelle, Punta Cana, and Cancun; and scuba diving is available for a fee at Turkoise and Columbus Isle. Golf is available at half a dozen locations at an added fee, and some clubs offer free instruction. Sandpiper hosts golf clinics while Turkoise, Cancun, and Sandpiper offer circus programs. You'll find more current offerings in the catalog.

One final bit of personal advice: Don't choose a club with a location that requires several plane changes or long bus rides. The journeys are tiring and expensive and use up valuable vacation time. Check travel time carefully when you make your plans. Club Med one-week packages via charters save time and money; you'll probably save even if you have to pay for an overnight in the departure city in order to make connections.

The ambience at the various clubs depends entirely on the current crop of GOs (they shift assignments every six months) and the makeup of the guests, which changes from one week to the next. Like any vacation, you take your chances on whom you will meet when you choose a Club Med location—but judging from the enormous number of people who return time and again, the chances are good that you will make friends. The club reports that more than 40 percent of their guests are repeaters.

To enroll in any Club Med, you must pay an annual fee. The travel sections of major newspapers frequently carry ads from tour operators who buy space in bulk and promise discounts on rates, so check before you reserve.

For more information and a catalog, contact any travel agent or Club Med direct at (800) CLUB–MED.

COMMENTS E.B.: *I recently spent a week at Club Med Turkoise, wanting to see firsthand the changes since my last visit to a Club Med several years ago. This remains the best beach vacation I know for a single person. The general atmosphere is very friendly; by the time you've had a few meals and taken part in a few activities, you know a number of people. Many of them are interesting and have diverse professions, and since Club Med is international, guests come from all over the United States, Canada, and Europe.*

Turkoise attracts many singles in their 20s and early 30s, but the age range went well into the 60s when I was there, so no one needed to worry about feeling out of place. Some of the younger guests were intent on drinking and partying, but other than creating a few noisy tables in the dining room, they didn't affect the other guests.

Undoubtedly, those who get the most from the Club Med experience are the sociable, fun-loving types who enjoy the line dancing and group songs and who take advantage of the many sports available. But there was ample room to escape on one of the loveliest beaches in the Caribbean, and even a section of quieter beach where classical music was piped in each afternoon.

The most positive change I found was the food. The choices were really impressive. At every lunch and dinner, there were half a dozen meat and poultry entrees, two kinds of pasta, and nearly twenty kinds of vegetables. Each night featured a different theme—French, Italian, Caribbean, and Tex-Mex, to name a few. Seafood night brought caviar, smoked salmon, crab legs, and tons of shrimp—and these were just the appetizers! Every meal offered bountiful fruit and cheese displays, a tempting array of desserts, and breads so delicious, they were a peril to the waistline.

The entertainment was also better than I remembered, thanks to a clever choreographer who knew how to make the most of his amateur cast. Some of the most exciting entertainment came on the night when guests showed off what they had learned at the circus workshop, displaying high-wire balancing and acrobatic feats that were nothing short of amazing. The circus emphasis adds to the spirit of fun at this particular club; wherever you go, you find people practicing juggling and other tricks.

The clubs are now totally all-inclusive, but remember to add in the cost of departure taxes and transfers from the airport to the club.

Most of the people I met had been to several clubs and planned to come back again. Why do they keep returning? Here were some of the comments:

"No surprises. I know the food will be good and the staff will be great."

"I come for the diving. It is much more reasonable than at other resorts, and since I don't do it often, I like the fact that I am so well supervised."

"I like meeting people from all over."

"I like having so many sports options without having to worry about what they cost."

"So easy to meet people, so friendly."

SuperClubs

SuperClubs operates adults-only, all-inclusive resorts in Jamaica, Curacao, the Dominican Republic, Brazil, and the Bahamas. All welcome singles, but two, Hedonism and Breezes, attract the largest numbers.

Beautifully located in Negril, Jamaica, along a 7-mile swath of beach, Hedonism II has attractions similar to those offered by Club Med—rates that include all meals and an open bar, plus tennis, sailing, water-skiing, windsurfing, volleyball, a Nautilus gym, squash, snorkeling, scuba diving, bicycling, horseback riding, aerobics, and arts and crafts classes. In addition, they offer nighttime entertainment that includes top local bands and performers. The long beach at Negril is shared by several hotels, convenient if you want to take a walk into town or sample the local nightlife.

Hedonism's unique lure is the freewheeling Jamaican spirit and contagious reggae beat that permeate the island. "Let's party" is the motto, right from the rum punch you are handed as you arrive. All this attracts a young crowd, averaging between 21 and 35 and about 65 percent single. There is a nude beach and a "prude" beach. One observer noted with surprise that it was the young who tended to be covered; older guests, who ranged into their 60s, seemed to be on the nude beach, unconcerned with appearances. Much of the food is grown locally, and menus feature a lot of native fruits and vegetables.

Hedonism III, on Jamaica's Runaway Bay, is perhaps even less inhibited than its sibling.

Breezes resorts have a more sophisticated ambience and strong emphasis on sports, including golf, tennis, and scuba instruction. They are located in Jamaica on the North Coast and in Montego Bay, in Curacao, and on Nassau in the Bahamas. The newest location is on the coast of Brazil, and more additions are planned. For more information on all these resorts, contact SuperClubs (877–467–8737) or check the Web site at www.superclubs.com.

Le Sport

This lavish St. Lucia resort combines the pleasures of a Caribbean vacation with the benefits of a spa. And they not only welcome solo guests, but have built accommodations specifically for them. Their beautifully furnished garden rooms with queen-size beds cost about the same as half the rate for a twin room. I've been to Le Sport and I can't imagine a better choice for a solo traveler.

Le Sport calls itself "the Body Holiday," and they make good on the claim with one of the most lavish spas in the Caribbean and an enormous choice of activities, all included in the price along with three meals, bar beverages, nightly entertainment, and one spa treatment daily. Active vacationers can choose from swimming, sailing, canoeing, windsurfing, archery, tennis, volleyball, a gym with personal trainers, and a wide range of fitness classes, including aqua-fitness in the pool. The golf school uses the facilities of a nearby eighteen-hole championship course.

The hilltop spa, inspired by Spain's Alhambra, offers delicious ways to relax—excellent massages, facials, beauty treatments, and daily sessions of yoga, t'ai chi, and meditation. The only extra fees are for Ayurvedic treatments, which can include a massage done by two persons, an experience so heavenly you won't be sorry you invested.

Of course you are also free to do nothing, just laze on the beach.

Le Sport is expensive, but you get your money's worth. For information, phone (800) 544–2883 or (758) 457–7800, or check the Web site at www.thebody holiday.com.

For Women Only

NE OF THE MOST NOTICEABLE TRENDS IN TRAVEL IS THE GROWTH OF activities for women only. There have always been spas for women, and as mentioned, almost every major ski area has begun offering special ski weeks for women. But the desire for comfortable, non-competitive, nonpressured travel has spawned a dramatic increase in options for women, and there are more publications and organizations than ever to encourage women to take to the road. There's even a Web site, Christine Columbus, that specializes in travel gear for women.

Trips range from sightseeing to shopping to spirituality. Many of the most popular women-only trips fall into the active, adventure category. These trips are challenging, but they supply a supportive atmosphere and eliminate the need to keep up with macho males. The companionship and sharing on strictly female trips is another major lure; participants report firm friendships that last long after the trip ends, a big plus for participants whether single or not.

Carole Jacobs, in *Shape* magazine, aptly described the appeal of these journeys. "Women-only adventure travel is more than a girl's night out . . . There's no better place to find yourself than on top of a mountain, no better time than when you're climbing a cliff to discover that your better half is not the one you left behind, but the one you found within."

Here are some of the varied resources and trips available for women.

Information and Contacts for Women Travelers

Journeywoman (www.journeywoman.com), a free online quarterly, describes itself as a networking magazine for female travel enthusiasts. Subscribers come from all over North America and from as far afield as Europe, Hong Kong, Israel, Vietnam, and Turkey, making for a wonderful exchange of travel tips and stories. For those with access to the Internet, this magazine is chock-full of valuable information and resources, from hotels welcoming singles to tours for women. Many of the advertisers are American. An article on "Safe and Solo in Turkey" includes suggestions on dining, names a Turkish bath reserved for women only called Tuesdays, and reminds that women must cover their heads on entering a mosque. A story on Tucson tells of a women-only golf instruction program, social hikes for those over 50, and women-led desert walks.

WOMEN WELCOME WOMEN WORLDWIDE
c/o Sharon Giese, P.O. Box 648, Westport, CT 06881; (203) 866–4774; www.womenwelcomewomen.org.uk

This organization was formed in 1984 in England to foster international friendships by enabling women of different nations to visit one another. There are some 2,800 participants from seventy-two countries, ages 16 to over 80. Each new member fills out a form asking to be a hostess, a traveler, or both. Questions on the form include age, occupation; religion, politics, and languages spoken. Details from these applications are included on a worldwide membership list, divided by countries. Visits are arranged individually, initiated by travelers writing to prospective hostesses. The organization recommends continued correspondence to become acquainted a bit before an actual visit and suggests that the first stay be short, in case expectations are not met.

Members also sometimes arrange to get together. Thirteen women from the United States, England, Australia, Scotland, Holland, and Belgium gathered a few years ago in Westport, Connecticut, with each woman housed in a volunteer's home. Such gatherings are publicized in a newsletter published three times a year with news of forthcoming events, reports of members' travels, and requests for touring companions. In 2004, gatherings were held in Brittany, France, London, Scandinavia, Australia, and Manchester, England.

This is purely a voluntary organization, funded by its members' dues and donations. Minimum dues are $47.

Women's Tours

As with any program, before you sign on to one of these tours, ask for reference names and numbers of former participants.

THE WOMEN'S TRAVEL CLUB
36 West 20th Street, Suite 301, New York, NY 10011; (800) 480–4448 or (646) 201–9405 (M–EE)

With more than 1,000 members nationally, ages 30 to 70, this club, founded in 1992, offers a wide variety of small-group trips to interesting places such as Italy, Africa, India, Spain, Mexico, and Costa Rica, as well as U.S. destinations. Spa visits and cruises are also on the agenda. Trips vary from four days to two weeks. They will always try to arrange shares, and a bulletin board on the Web site allows members to seek travel companions. Membership is $35, which includes a monthly newsletter.

WOMEN TRAVELING TOGETHER

1642 Fairhill Drive, Edgewater, MD 21037; (800) 795-7135 or (410) 956-5250; www.women-traveling.com (E–EE)

This group founded in 1996, has a wide variety of offerings on some thirty trips each year: tours, weekend getaways, spas, adventure travel, and personal enrichment retreats. Groups are limited to ten to fifteen in size and offer a nice combination of free and structured time. Shares are guaranteed, but those who request singles pay a supplement.

GUTSY WOMEN TRAVEL

10650 West Charleston Boulevard, Summerlin, NV 89135; (866) 464-8879; www.gutsywomentravel.com (E–EE)

A division of long-established Maupintour (see page 152), this group offers some intriguing choices, including shopping in Hong Kong; an antiquing and culinary trip to Paris; trips to India, Australia, and Italy; and a "New England gems tour" taking in Cape Cod, Nantucket, and Newport. Groups are limited to twenty; the age range is 30s to 60s.

WOMEN'S TRAVEL NETWORK

c/o Travelpoint Enterprises, 8990 Yonge Street, Richmond Hill, Ontario L4C 6Z7, Canada; (888) 419-0118; www.womenstravelnetwork.ca (E–EE)

Culture, sports, shopping, spa visits, and adventure are among the offerings of this Canadian company. Recent trips include cultural tours of Spain and Hungary, a weekend of New York City shopping, horseback riding in the Canadian Rockies, and golf getaways in Myrtle Beach, South Carolina. Shares are guaranteed, but those requesting a single pay extra. A free newsletter keeps members up to date on upcoming excursions.

SIDE TRIPS, INC.
338 South Sharon Amity Road, No. 222, Charlotte, NC 28211; (866) 334–7731
or (704) 334–7731; www.side-trips.com (E–EE)

Artistic, athletic, and cultural getaways for women over age 30 are the specialty of this group. They offer "by the sea" art, creative writing, poetry, or photography trips to semitropical Daufuskie Island in South Carolina; cooking in France or Tuscany; and wine education in Bordeaux or California. Active itineraries run the gamut from inn-to-inn hiking in Virginia to dogsledding in Alaska. Shorter trips include weekends in Williamsburg or New York City.

SHOP AROUND TOURS
305 East 24th Street, Suite 2N, New York, NY 10010; (212) 684–3763;
www.shoparoundtours.com (E)

If shopping is your favorite sport, join this group that hits the stores in places like Paris and Milan. On an Italian tour, you'll also visit the outlets for Gucci, Armani, Prada, and the like.

SACRED JOURNEYS FOR WOMEN
P.O. Box 8007, Roseland Station, Santa Rosa, CA 95406; (888) 779–6696;
www.sacredjourneys.com (E–EE)

Since 1997, Sacred Journeys has planned trips aimed at enrichment, emphasizing women's spirituality and history. Destinations have included Ireland, England, Scotland, the Greek island of Crete, Hawaii, Bali, Mexico, and California.

Women's Adventure Travel

ADVENTUREWOMEN
15033 Kelly Canyon Road, Bozeman, MT 59715;
(406) 587–3883 or (800) 804–8686;
www.adventurewomen.com (M–E)

Worldwide adventures for women over 30 range from one-week U.S. trips to three-week world journeys. Trips are rated easy, moderate, or high energy. Many trips are designed for beginners who want to

Years in business:	Since 1982
Age range:	30–79
Most common age:	Late 40s, early 50s
Percent alone:	All women; owner says the majority are or have been married and have children
Number of participants:	10–20
Male/female ratio:	All female
No single supplements	

enjoy adventure travel within a supportive and noncompetitive environment. Activities include riverrafting, backcountry horse packing, hiking, and multi-activity trips in the western United States plus safaris in Africa, trekking in Nepal, and walking in Tuscany and Ireland. Also on the roster are cultural travels to places such as India and Vietnam.

COMMENTS **Female, 40s:** *I've gone hiking in the U.K., staying in small family hotels and sharing rooms. I've also gone cross-country skiing in Wisconsin and camping on a glacier in Alaska. The women have diverse backgrounds, but share a love for adventure. They come from all over the U.S. Good organization; will go again.*
Female, 70s: *I've taken four trips, including hiking and canal boating in England. The trips are well organized, and I've always made good friends with women of all ages.*

SHERI GRIFFITH EXPEDITIONS, INC.
(see page 108)

This group offers sojourns into nature with spectacular scenery to quiet the soul and white water for excitement. The adventure is described as a supportive, noncompetitive setting to learn outdoor skills taught by well-trained and personable riverwomen.

OUTDOOR ADVENTURE RIVER SPECIALISTS (O.A.R.S.), INC.
(see page 109)

This long-established company has introduced women-only white-water adventures on Idaho's Lower Salmon River and a women-only fishing excursion on the Middle Fork of the Salmon. On the Lower Salmon's Class III white water, women can choose from paddle rafts or inflatable kayaks or simply float down the river in oar rafts or dories. Trips also include hiking, spotting wildlife, and relaxing on river beaches. Meals are prepared by the guides. The Middle Fork of the Salmon, a federally designated Wild and Scenic River, is a blue-ribbon trout fishery.

WOMANSHIP

137 Conduit Street, Annapolis, MD 21401; (800) 342-9295 or (410) 267-6661;
www.womanship.com (E–EE)

Provides sailing instruction and sailing cruises around Florida's Keys; the Chesapeake Bay from Annapolis, Maryland; Long Island Sound; the Great Lakes; and in Maine, the Greek Isles, Ireland, Turkey, and New Zealand. Ages are from 18 to 82.

EXPLORATIONS IN TRAVEL

2458 River Road, Guilford, VT 05301; (802) 257-0152;
www.exploretravel.com (M–EE)

Outdoor and cultural adventures for women over 40 include biking, hiking, rafting, cross-country skiing, canal cruises, and dude ranch vacations in a variety of locations including New England, Montana, Georgia, New Zealand, Mexico, Puerto Rico, and the Galápagos Islands.

WILD WOMEN EXPEDITIONS (WWE)

P.O. Box 145, Station B, Sudbury, Ontario P3E 4N5, Canada; (705) 866-1260;
www.wildwomenexp.com (I)

Canoe and kayaking trips in northern Ontario are the specialties of this group, plus fly fishing, cycling, and dogsledding and cross-country skiing in winter. Retreats are offered at a restored fishing camp on 200 wilderness acres.

CANYON CALLING TOURS

200 Coral Canyon Drive, Sedona, AZ 86336; (928) 282-0916 or
(800) 664-8922; www.canyoncalling.com (M–E)

Multi-adventure vacations for women over 30 are planned for those at medium fitness levels who want to enjoy the outdoors without hardships. Hiking, biking, and rafting are part of comfortable trips to the Southwest, Canadian Rockies, the Alps, Iceland, Costa Rica, Fiji, and New Zealand; even camping is deluxe.

WOMAN TOURS

Elmwood Avenue, Rochester, NY 14618; (800) 247-1444;
www.womantours.com (M–E)

Biking tours for women in New England, the Shenandoah Mountains, Mississippi, Maine, Arizona, Utah, California, the Tetons, North Carolina's

Outer Banks, New York's Finger Lakes, Hawaii, Southwest canyons, Italy, Vietnam, South Africa, France, and Ireland.

ARCTIC LADIES

P.O. Box 308, Girdwood, AK 99587; (877) 783–1954 or (907) 783–1954; www.arcticladies.com (E)

Alaska is the specialty, with hiking, canoeing, and camping in summer and snowshoeing and cross-country skiing in winter, as well as the chance to see the thrilling Iditarod dogsled race. More far-flung adventure journeys are slated in Peru, Ireland, Greece, and South Africa.

WALKING WOMEN HOLIDAYS

22 Duke Street, Leamington Spa, Warwicks CV32 4TF, UK; 44 (0) 1926–313321; www.walkingwomen.com (M–E)

England, Wales, the Alps, South Africa, Spain, Scotland, Italy, and Greece are among the places visited by WalkingWomen, a British-run company offering friendly group holidays for women in some of the most stunning landscapes of Europe and beyond. Trips are graded for difficulty and all ages are welcome. Occasional theme trips focus on photography or wildlife.

TREK TRAVEL

(see page 96)

This growing program of bicycle tours is adding women-specific tours to California wine country, Vermont, Provence, and Tuscany. The trips will have female guides and, on selected itineraries, a female cycling coach. Participants will use Trek Specific road bikes for women.

SENIOR WOMEN'S TRAVEL

136 East 56th Street, New York, NY 10022; (212) 838–4740; www.poshnosh.com (E–EE)

Women over 50 will find plenty of good company with this group "for women with a passion for travel." Trips cover great cities like Paris, London, Venice, Rome, Madrid, and Barcelona, and other destinations such as the Greek Isles, Peru, Malta, Tuscany, and the Amalfi coast. Food lovers can revel in Paris and Italy. Several tours visit New York. Other U.S. destinations are San Francisco and the Berkshire region of Massachusetts. They also sponsor grand-mother-granddaughter adventures.

Women's Travel Gear

Christine Columbus (www.christinecolumbus.com; 800–280–4775) addresses the special needs of women travelers with an online catalog. Along with handy safety items and handsome accessories, this catalog features items you won't find in other places. For instance, a half-slip with zippered pockets keeps jewelry and money secure and her chic leather tote bag has a hidden compartment in the bottom to stash sneakers and double as a hideaway for wallet and passport.

The Golden Age: 50 and Over

W HY A SPECIAL CHAPTER FOR OLDER TRAVELERS? AGE IS NO DETERRENT on the great majority of the group trips mentioned in this book, and adventurous seniors in their 80s are happily roaming the globe on their own right this minute. So what's so special about the older traveler?

To begin with, there are more of them. With those much-publicized baby boomers entering their fifties, the number of so-called seniors is mushrooming and everybody wants their attention. By 2006, the 55-to-74-year-old age group is expected to be nearly 50 percent of the population.

These are people who tend to have more disposable income and more time to spend it, so it isn't surprising that many people want to tap into that market early. No longer do you have to be 65 to reap discounts. Age 50 has become the "golden age" for many travel benefits.

The American Association of Retired Persons has lowered its age requirement to 50, opening a whole range of travel discounts to those who reach the mid-century mark. Learning opportunities geared to older adults are growing rapidly. Elderhostel, the wonderful educational program for seniors, has lowered its age limit from 60 to 55—with companions of any age. Interhostel offers educational experiences abroad for travelers age 50 and older.

On an active trip, sometimes even the fittest traveler of a certain age may welcome a gentler pace and the comforting knowledge that you don't have to keep up with 30-year-olds. A growing number of operators are meeting this need with "soft adventures" geared to healthy, active over-50s.

For many older singles, especially once-married individuals who find themselves considering solo travel for the first time in their later years, the company of contemporaries may seem reassuring. Numerous group tours labeled "over 50" may be of interest to these travelers, and hotel chains such as Hilton and Sheraton have discounts for seniors. Grandparents also will find they are gaining new attention in the travel world. Organizations listed in the pages ahead, such as Elderhostel and Interhostel, have instituted programs for those who want to share their travels with younger generations, as has the Sierra Club. The Loews hotel group now has "Generation G" packages, and resorts such as FDR in Jamaica and the Aruba Sonesta Resort offer special grandparent rates.

So a special chapter for the over-50 generation seems in order just to recap all the privileges that come with age! Let's look at some of the trips that you can't take unless you're over 50!

ELDERHOSTEL
11 Avenue De Lafayette, Boston, MA 02111; (877) 426–8056; www.elderhostel.org; year-round (I)

Since 1975, this remarkable program has provided intellectual stimulation and good company for adults age 55 and over and their companions of any age who want to continue to expand their horizons. It offers reasonably priced, short-term academic programs at educational institutions around the world. The topics? Cicero to computers . . . politics to poetry. More than 2,000 institutions participate, providing programs in every American state and Canadian province and over ninety other countries. Some 250,000 travelers take part each year; many participants come alone. Living/dining accommodations are on college campuses, in conference centers, or in hotels, and participants have the use of the campus or hotel recreational facilities. The charge for many programs in the United States is about $105 per day. Most last five or six nights. Besides classroom courses, programs include active outdoor vacations such as hiking; biking; rafting; cross-country skiing; cruises; trips for golfers, birders, and choral music singers; arts and crafts; volunteer service; and intergenerational programs to be shared with grandchildren or other young friends, all at reasonable rates. Put yourself on the mailing list, and four times each year you'll get a fat, newspaper-size catalog crammed with possibilities. All current programs are also listed on the Web site. A land-sea program in Alaska, a stay at Trinity College in Wales, a spring sojourn in the Great Smoky Mountains, a jazz course in New Orleans, or a stay in New Delhi—it's enough to make younger folks want to hurry up and age!

Elderhostel recently inaugurated a more upscale Road Scholar program for all ages, still with an educational focus but with smaller groups, a less structured program, and lodging in three- and four-star hotels. While open to anyone over 21, the sponsors expect their core group to be age 50 to 60. Read more about the program on page 156.

SENIOR SUMMER SCHOOL, INC. ✓
P.O. Box 4424, Deerfield Beach, FL 33442; (800) 847–2466; www.seniorsummerschool.com (I)

Senior Summer School is an eighteen-year-old program designed for seniors who want to get a feel for life in a college town. It offers reasonably priced two- to

ten-week programs in conjunction with summer courses at institutions such as the
University of Pittsburgh in Greensburg, Pennsylvania; the University of Judaism in
Los Angeles; and Mount Allison University in New Brunswick, Canada. Programs
are also available in Flagstaff, Arizona; Boone, North Carolina; Boston; and San
Diego. Most housing is in apartments or hotels, and the group dines together, usually cafeteria style. Exercise facilities and computer centers are available for participants at most programs, along with access to tennis courts, swimming pools, and
golf courses. Fees include housing, three meals a day, courses, and some area sightseeing. Participants include a good number of singles. They also hold popular programs over the New Year's holiday in warm climes like Tampa, Florida, and Palm
Springs, California.

SENIOR VENTURES

Southern Oregon University, 1250 Siskiyou Boulevard, Ashland, OR 97520;
(800) 257–0577 or (541) 552–6378; www.sou.edu (use index to find current Web page) (I)

Southern Oregon pioneered the Senior Ventures concept for adults age 50 and
over in the Northwest in 1983. Their emphasis is on the well-known Oregon
Shakespeare Festival in Ashland, with classes on the theater taught by OSF company professionals. A second program visits the Stratford and Shaw Festivals in
Canada. Courses run six nights to two weeks. Some programs include other subjects; one popular combination features bridge classes. Reasonable rates include
dorm accommodations, all meals, and theater tickets.

INTERHOSTEL

University of New Hampshire, 6 Garrison Avenue, Durham, NH 03824;
(603) 862–1147 or (800) 773–9753; www.learn.unh.edu/interhostel (E–EE) Year-round

Another education-oriented group operating since 1979, Interhostel study tours
for adults over age 50 (and companions 40 or older) are held in the United
States and many countries abroad. More expensive than Elderhostel, these trips still
are a good value, with rooms usually in comfortable hotels and all meals and airfare
included in the fee. Several programs feature Christmas and New Year's abroad.
The most recent catalog lists more than fifty options, from Argentina to Austria,
Alaska to Australia. Hosts in each city give insight into the history, politics, natural
environment, and culture of the region. Excursions to sites of historic or cultural
significance supplement classroom learning, and the itinerary includes social activities. Familyhostel programs for parents and grandparents are a new addition.

Interhostel tries to find roommates, but if no share can be found, there is a single supplement, often no more than 15 percent more than the double rate.

ELDERTREKS
597 Markham Street, Toronto, Ontario M6G 2L7, Canada; (416) 588–5000 or
(800) 741–7956; www.eldertreks.com (I–E, plus airfare)
Year-round; guaranteed shares

Outdoor adventures for people age 50 or older have been the specialty of this group for more than sixteen years. They travel on foot or by boat, always with an emphasis on both nature and culture of the places visited. The United States—from Maine to Alaska—and Canada—from the Rockies to Newfoundland—are prime destinations. In Europe the recent roster of countries has included England, France, Iceland, Ireland, Italy, Norway, Scotland, Slovenia, and Spain. Going farther afield, the group has visited Africa, Central and South America, Australia, New Zealand, the Arctic and Antarctic, and many countries in Asia, including India, China, Tibet, Mongolia, and the Silk Road countries. There is no single supplement charge for those willing to share a room.

WALKING THE WORLD:
OUTDOOR ADVENTURES FOR PEOPLE 50 AND OVER
P.O. Box 1186, Fort Collins, CO 80522; (970) 498–0500 or (800) 340–9255 (M–E)
Will try to arrange shares

Name a beautiful place and chances are this group will take you hiking there. Designed for active, outdoors-oriented older travelers, this group, founded in 1987, features eclectic worldwide destinations including Asia, Costa Rica, Switzerland, Newfoundland, New Zealand, Ireland, Tuscany, Norway, Portugal, the Italian Alps, the Czech Republic, Banff and Jasper National Parks in Canada, and Hawaii. Closer to home, walking tours range from the coast of Maine to Zion and Bryce National Parks in Utah, and the Arizona desert to California wine country. Hiking is not difficult but does cover some high elevations. Trips are from eight to twenty-one days; distances covered daily range from 3 to 10 miles. Trips are rated, easy to challenging. Depending on the destination, accommodations may be bed-and-breakfasts, hotels, motels, or country inns; a few trips involve camping, with shared responsibilities for setting up camp and cooking.

INTERNATIONAL BICYCLE TOURS
(page 100)

Easy, picturesque terrain and a leisurely pace characterize this company's tours to Holland, Italy, and Austria, which attract many older bicyclers.

Also see Senior Women's Travel on page 195.

Tour Operators Serving Seniors

If you want to see the world with fellow travelers in your own age group, consider these tours aimed at those who have passed their fiftieth birthdays.

GRAND CIRCLE TRAVEL

347 Congress Street, Boston, MA 02210; (800) 959–0405 or (617) 350–7500; www.gct.com (M–E) Will try to match roommates; single supplements vary; many are low and they are waived entirely on some departures and several cruises

Begun in 1958 to serve members of the AARP, Grand Circle opened its trips to all in 1985 and now offers more than 200 trips serving over 120,000 mature travelers each year. The company boasts that 95 percent of their passengers say they will travel with them again. Tours take in North and Central America, Africa, Australia, Europe, and Asia, including river and ocean cruises and safaris. They offer adventurous travel through their overseas adventure travel subsidiary.

VANTAGE DELUXE WORLD TRAVEL

90 Canal Street, Boston, MA 02114; (617) 877–6000 or (888) 652–7104; www.vantagetravel.com (M–E)
Will try to arrange shares; shares are guaranteed on many trips

With more than twenty years of experience planning trips for mature travelers, Vantage offers a wide range of trips, from land tours to cruises. Recent destinations included U.S. national parks, New England, Canada, Italy, Spain, Portugal, eastern Europe, Croatia, South America, and China.

GOLDEN AGE TRAVELERS CLUB

Pier 27, The Embarcadero, San Francisco, CA 94111; (415) 286–0151 or (800) 258–8880; www.gatclub.com

Founded in 1969, the club, which has over 30,000 members, organizes many cruises for seniors, as well as land tours to Spain, Portugal, England, Ireland, Italy, Costa Rica, Greece, and other destinations. It is under the auspices of You and Leisure, a travel agency that promises seniors discounts and savings.

For more senior savings, see:

- *Unbelievably Good Deals and Great Adventures That You Absolutely Can't Get Unless You're Over 50,* Joan Rattner Heilman, McGraw-Hill, 2005–6.
- *Free Stuff and Good Deals for Folks Over 50,* Linda Bowman, Santa Monica Press, 2003.

Taking Advantage
of Senior Discounts

- *Join the American Association of Retired Persons as soon as you turn 50. AARP dues are small, and membership entitles you to many benefits, including discounts at almost every major hotel, motel, and car rental chain in America, as well as some airlines.*
- *Even if you don't belong to an organization, always ask hotels if they offer senior discounts. They won't bring it up unless you do; they have no way to know your age.*
- *Ask for the discount when you make your reservation; many places won't honor it later. At hotels, remind the clerk of your discount when you check in.*
- *Carry your driver's license or other proof of age when you check in, just in case you are asked.*
- *Compare rates. Sometimes special promotions at hotels are a better deal than the senior discount.*
- *Check with your auto insurance company; many companies offer a discount on car insurance after you pass your fiftieth birthday. Ditto for banks and retailers like Sears.*
- *Ask tour operators and resorts whether they offer a senior discount. Among the many who do is Club Med (page 183).*
- *Look for senior discounts at museums around the world.*
- *Are you a skier? Recognizing that older skiers are good business, almost every area now offers discounts, with the qualifying ages ranging anywhere from 50 to 60.*

More Perks at 62

Getting a bit older has its own advantages:
- *Amtrak takes 15 percent off its lowest fares for passengers 62 and over.*
- *For $10, you can buy a Golden Age Passport that admits you to all the national parks, forests, refuges, and monuments free for life. Seniors get half off on fees for camping, parking, and tours, as well. Passports are sold at all parks. For details write to the National Park Service, P.O. Box 37127, Washington, DC 20013.*
- *While most airlines have discontinued their senior discounts, some have not and it always pays to ask.*

Section TWO

SOLO TRAVEL

Know-How

Some General Advice

f I'd traveled with a group or even another person, I wonder what memories I'd have missed. Would the man with the box of pigeons at his feet on the Polish train have offered to show me his town? The man at the tiny restaurant in Switzerland probably wouldn't have invited me to polka, and I am quite certain the hotel owner in Saba wouldn't have joined me for dinner, his treat.

—Letters to the Editor, *Travel Holiday*

GROUP VACATIONS MAY PROVIDE GREAT EXPERIENCES AND WONDERFUL companionship, but many independent souls still prefer to set their own pace and agenda. If you've always wanted to see the Statue of Liberty or the Eiffel Tower or the Duomo in Florence, there's absolutely no reason why you cannot blaze your own path, design your dream trip, and happily do and see exactly what you please. One of the special privileges of solo travel is being able to tailor a trip to your own special likes and dislikes. Sleep as late or get up as early as you please. If you love antiques or bookshops or offbeat museums away from the main tourist track, you can indulge to your heart's content. If you want to savor a sunset, no one will say "Let's go." If you hate cathedrals, you need see nary a one!

It will take more planning to go your own way, yes—but often that very planning is a part of the fun of travel. Advance research is the best way to start learning about your destination. The more you know beforehand, the more you will get out of your trip.

Will you meet people on your travels? Probably more than if you were with a partner. You'll try a little harder to make friends than if you had a built-in companion, and you will be more approachable than if you were deep in conversation with your friend or spouse.

What are the best destinations for a first trip on your own? Whenever anyone asks me that question, my answer is, "Head for a city." Every great city has its own intriguing rhythms and personality, and often you can actually sense these best when you are alone, when you have no distractions and plenty of time to stroll, eyes wide open and antennae turned on high. Staying in one place also gives you a chance to get your bearings and begin to feel confident about getting around.

The best time to plan a city trip alone is during warm weather, when sociable outdoor cafes are in high gear. But, if you can avoid it, don't travel alone during the peak vacation season in July and August. Hotels and restaurants are least happy to see single guests during these months because this is when they are busiest and best able to fill tables and rooms with two or more instead of one. All the sights you want to see are also most crowded in high season. Late May, June, September, and early October are the ideal times to enjoy good weather without encountering hordes of tourists.

Pick your city carefully. Don't go alone to places like Los Angeles where you must drive unfamiliar streets or freeways to get around. Choose towns with a vital, walkable center and plenty of intriguing neighborhoods that can be explored on foot, plus an efficient and inexpensive public transportation system to get you from one place to another so that you won't need a car. Cities fitting this description usually meet another important criterion that makes for easier travel on your own—they have large single populations and many informal neighborhood restaurants to serve them.

Among the cities in the United States that meet these qualifications well are Boston, New York, Philadelphia, Chicago, Seattle, and San Francisco. Charming historic smaller cities like Charleston, Savannah, and New Orleans are also easy to cover on foot. The best bets in Canada are Montreal, Toronto, and Vancouver. Almost any major city in Europe is a likely candidate, though places where English is spoken are probably the best choices for a first foreign venture. This doesn't mean you must limit yourself to London, wonderful city though it is. Think also of Dublin or Edinburgh, where English comes with a delightful brogue; Amsterdam, where the multilingual Dutch will welcome you in your own tongue; or Copenhagen or Stockholm, where English is the second language. I'll zero in on some of my favorite cities in the next chapter, but first let me share some techniques that work for me when I get ready to visit any new town.

Sizing Up a City

If you allow yourself to arrive alone in a new city without specific plans, you can feel lost and confused. To feel in control, your days should be mapped in advance. Start at home by contacting the local tourist office for information and maps of city streets and transit systems. Next, get the best guidebooks you can find and, if possible, a copy of the city's local magazine. If you don't have access to a newsstand that sells out-of-town publications, get the address and phone number of the magazine from the tourist office and order a copy by phone. If your community does not have a good travel bookstore, order by mail from those in the resource list on page 289. The Internet is another valuable resource for information and books.

When you have assembled your materials, read the brochures and books to learn about the character of the city and its special attractions for tourists. Use the magazine to find out what the people who live there are doing and where they are going right now.

Now make a list of the places you most want to see and circle them on the street map. Although it is hard to get an accurate sense of scale from a map of a strange city, you can easily see which attractions are close together and plot your days by grouping places in the same geographic area. Check the transit maps against the street map to see which places can be easily reached by bus or tram.

Next, make a tentative day-by-day schedule of what you hope to do and see, ranking the sights each day from most to least important. That way, if something proves fascinating, you can find extra time by dropping the least important items on the agenda. If a top choice turns out to be a disappointment, you have plenty of options to fill your time.

In a brand-new city, I always start the first day with a local sightseeing tour. This gives you a quick sense of the locations of important sites and streets. These tours often include inconvenient areas that you may not get back to easily on your own. Sometimes when I actually get a look at a place that sounded wonderful in the guidebooks, I realize it is not so great in reality, and I strike a second visit off my list.

I also like to leave time on my schedule for guided walking tours in interesting or historic areas of the city. Walking tours have fewer people than bus tours and are far more personal and interesting; they are an excellent way to meet people. In foreign cities, walking tours with English-speaking guides are the best way to seek out fellow travelers as well as a welcome respite from struggling to speak the language. With a really knowledgeable local guide, you'll get colorful inside information that isn't found in any book. The best current walking tours aren't always listed in guidebooks, but they are usually included in city magazines. You can also ask about these at your hotel or the local tourist office after you arrive.

Schedule plenty of time just to wander when you explore a new city—this is one of the great pleasures of solo travel. As long as you stay in safe neighborhoods, don't worry about getting lost. (Ask at your hotel about parts of the city that should be avoided.) Some of the best discoveries may lie on little side streets that don't show on the map. Even in a foreign city, if you write down the name and address of your hotel and mark it clearly on the street map, you will be able to get directions or find a cab when you want to return. One of the pleasant discoveries when you travel alone is that people everywhere seem particularly willing to go out of their way to help a solo visitor.

When you go exploring, you may find you get more out of your journey by pretending that you are a travel writer who will want to bring the place alive for your readers. Take your time, look closely, window-shop, talk to people, ask questions, take mental notes, and make written ones. Make lists of the unusual shops and galleries you pass, take photos, and keep a nightly journal of your impressions. A journal is fun—it keeps you company, and it will vividly bring back the pleasures of your trip every time you open the pages back home. If you return to the city in the future, your journal will become your personal guidebook leading you back to the best places.

How much time you allot to shopping beyond souvenirs for friends and family depends on your own disposition. If you are like me and seldom find time for relaxed shopping at home, an afternoon to yourself for browsing stores in a new city is a treat. When I buy clothing or unique local handicrafts on a trip, they come with a bonus of happy memories. Some of my favorite souvenirs have been paintings or folk art purchased on my travels. Looking for them invariably means talking to people and learning a lot about the local scene.

Choosing a Place to Stay

The circles you've marked on a city street map will help you choose a convenient area for your lodging. There are a few ways to consider accommodations when you are alone; the ultimate choices are dictated by budget and personal preference—and whether you are in the United States or abroad.

U.S. Accommodations

If you can afford the splurge, it's a special pleasure to stay at a top hotel when you are traveling alone. Being surrounded by luxury is even more of a treat when you are by yourself, and the better hotels offer an important practical advantage as well: the concierge.

Now found widely in hotels in the United States as well as Europe, the job of the concierge is purely and simply to make your stay more pleasant. Besides taking care of all your transportation and ticket arrangements, a good concierge should know the city inside out—the best places to shop, the best ways to sightsee, and the places where single diners will feel comfortable. Well-connected concierges provide a lot of business to the city's restaurants, and when they phone in a reservation and

City Smarts:
An Assortment of Tips
on U.S. Cities

- San Francisco has an exceptional number of small, well-priced hotels. Especially recommended for solo travelers are the Kimpton and Joie de Vivre chains. These lodgings are attractive, conveniently located, and moderately priced. Kimpton's complimentary wine reception each afternoon provides a chance to mingle with other guests. Many also offer coffee or a continental breakfast in the morning. The hotels I've personally inspected include Monaco, Monticello Inn, Triton, Villa Florence, and the Tuscan Inn. Recommended Joie de Vivre properties include the Maxwell and two budget properties, the Bijou and the Commodore.

- In Chicago, the choicest hotel location is on or near North Michigan Avenue's "Magnificent Mile," where fine dining and most of America's top retailers are found within a 20-block stroll, and buses can be boarded to all the city museums. Surprisingly situated in this posh neighborhood is a high-rise Red Roof Inn, one of the city's best buys.

- Charleston, one of America's most beautiful strolling cities, is an ideal destination for solo travelers since most of the lodging, dining, and sightseeing is in the easily walkable Historic District. If you can afford the tab, Charleston Place, a luxury hotel in the center of things, is ideal. Their restaurants offer a Single Diner program to encourage solo guests to come to dinner, including special wine and appetizer tastings and special visits by the manager and chef on duty. They even present a silver tray with a selection of magazines, papers, postcards, and books to keep you occupied between courses. Among dozens of appealing smaller inns, my top recommendation (when the budget allows) is 2 Meeting Street.

- Wherever you go, look for multiday passes on city transit systems; they invariably save money.

say a good word, you can be sure that you won't be shunted to a cramped corner or ignored by your waiter. A good way to determine the quality of the concierge service in advance is to find out whether the head concierge wears the golden keys of Le Clef d'Or, the prestigious international concierge association.

At the other end of the scale, the small, charming budget hotels available in Europe just don't exist in most cities in the United States. With a few exceptions, our budget lodgings are at best impersonal and at worst, shabby and dreary. Luckily, now that the bed-and-breakfast craze has moved into big American cities, there is a cheerier choice when funds are limited. A bed-and-breakfast apartment or home in a pleasant neighborhood provides an insider's advice on the city from your host, plus someone to talk to at breakfast and when you get home at night. As a bonus, you get a better sense of the real life of the city away from the business district. Dining is almost always more reasonable in the neighborhoods than in the business center of town—if you have fellow lodgers, you may even wind up with company for dinner.

Bed-and-breakfast reservations can be made through services that handle a large number of locations in each city. You'll find a sampling of these services in the box on page 212, and there are plenty of books with further suggestions. The lodgings themselves vary from lavish to modest, with either private or shared baths. Be very specific about your needs and desires when you make your reservation. Most of all, be sure the location is convenient to public transportation. If you think there may be times when you will return to your lodging late at night, find out whether cabs are readily available from midtown and the approximate fare to your destination.

Another plus for bed-and-breakfast accommodations is that, unlike hotels, they often give a generous break to single travelers. It isn't that hotels don't like singles, but the overwhelming majority of their rooms are designed for two people, and they seem to feel it is not good business to lose the extra revenue. That means one guest pays a single supplement, making the rate almost the same as for two.

When you do get a single room in a hotel, it may be the smallest and least attractive in the place. Don't be afraid to speak up and ask for a better one.

The single supplement remains the biggest gripe of solo travelers, so perhaps if enough people write to hotel managers or major hotel chains to complain, some savvy hotels will begin to change this discriminatory policy.

While they may not have done much about improving their single rates, a number of U.S. hotels have begun offering a few services that make life pleasanter for their guests who are traveling alone. These amenities are aimed at attracting business travelers, but they are equally welcome to vacationers. One innovation commonly available in large hotels is a special "executive floor" where continental breakfasts and complimentary hors d'oeuvres are served in a special lounge. You pay extra for a room on this floor, but the lounge is a very easy setting for finding company, and the complimentary breakfast and snacks are pleasant money-savers. Executive floors also tend to provide extra security, with floor concierges on duty and special elevator keys.

European Accommodations

Bed-and-breakfast homes have long been available in Europe, but, unlike in the United States, there's also a good chance of finding small and reasonable hotels that have local character and at least a modicum of charm. I favor a hotel rather than a bed-and-breakfast home in a city where I don't speak the language, because I feel more secure in a central location when I don't know my way around. Most tourist offices as well as guidebooks offer listings of both small hotels and bed-and-breakfast lodgings.

By choosing smaller accommodations, you can hold down the cost of traveling on your own, but you may have to make arrangements yourself by mail, fax, e-mail, or phone. Travel agents are businesspeople, after all, and these time-consuming reservations usually pay no commission. It's a simple matter to make your own arrangements, and the fax and e-mail make it easy to make contact. If you must communicate by mail, allow plenty of time for letters to make their way across the ocean and back.

If you are willing to make a move after you arrive, you can try another technique. Make a hotel reservation for the first night or two, and then take a morning to check out a list of small, less-expensive hotels in person, reserving a room in your favorite for the rest of your stay. If you find that you have booked a hotel that is disappointing, do the same—pay for the first night and look for a more pleasant alternative. Having the option to look around for lodgings is another reason to avoid traveling during busy peak seasons, when desirable hotels are likely to be filled.

When you are hotel-shopping, don't hesitate to ask to see rooms—or to ask if a less expensive room is available. Contrary to what many people think, room prices are often negotiable if the hotel is not filled.

U.S. City
Bed-and-Breakfast Registries

• **New York**

City Lights B&B Ltd., P.O. Box 20355, Cherokee Station, New York, NY
10021; (212) 737-7049; www.citylightsnewyork.com.
At Home in New York, P.O. Box 407, New York, NY 10185;
(212) 956-3125 or (800) 692-4262; www.athomeny.com.

• **Boston**

Host Homes of Boston, P.O. Box 117, Waban Branch, Boston, MA 02168;
(617) 244-1308 or (800) 600-1308; www.hosthomesofboston.com.
Greater Boston Hospitality, P.O. Box 125, Newton, MA 02456;
(617) 393-1548; www.bostonbedandbreakfast.com.

• **Chicago**

At Home Inn Chicago, (800) 375-7084 or (312) 640-1050;
www.athomeinnchicago.com.
Chicago Bed and Breakfast Association, www.chicago-bed-breakfast.com;
site has direct links to over a dozen bed-and-breakfast homes.

• **Washington, D.C.**

Bed & Breakfast League/Sweet Dreams and Toast, P.O. Box 9490,
Washington, D.C. 20016; (202) 363-7767.

• **Philadelphia**

A Bed and Breakfast Connection/Bed and Breakfast of Philadelphia,
P.O. Box 21, Devon, PA 19333; (610) 687-3565 or (800) 448-3619;
www.bnbphiladelphia.com.

• **San Francisco**

Bed & Breakfast San Francisco, P.O. Box 420009, San Francisco, CA 94142;
(415) 899-0060 or (800) 452-8249; www.bbsf.com.

For a list of reservation services in other cities, contact The National Network
(TNN), P.O. Box 44, Devon, PA 19333; (800) 727-7592; www.go-lodging.com.

Making Your Own Travel Arrangements

Saving on Airfare

If you are making your own travel arrangements, one way to save on transportation costs is to investigate some of the consolidators who offer bargain airfares. You'll see ads from these companies in almost any big-city newspaper, listing fares to major cities that are far below the going official rate. How do they do it? They buy blocks of seats that the airlines do not expect to be able to sell themselves, mostly on international routes. A good example: Air India flies to Bombay from New York with a stop in London. There are often empty seats on the New York–London leg that will be occupied in London. Consolidators can offer the trip to London at a big discount.

Some of these companies may specialize in specific regions such as Hawaii or the Orient. Rates and dates vary from one firm to another, so comparison shopping is essential.

There can be drawbacks to dealing with a consolidator. It is more difficult to get a refund, and you may not always get frequent-flyer mile credit. You may not be transferred to another carrier in the event of a cancellation or delay of a flight, and you may have to juggle your dates to coincide with the flights that are available.

Consolidators are not recommended for inexperienced or nervous travelers who might panic if complications arise. For those who feel confident about coping in case of emergencies, however, the consolidators offer flights on regular scheduled airlines at a very substantial savings.

Dealing with a reputable consolidator is important. A few that come well recommended are:

TFI Tours
34 West 32nd Street, New York, NY 10001; (800) 745–8000 or (212) 736–1140; www.tfitours.com.

CHEAP TICKETS, INC.
(800) 377–1000; www.cheaptickets.com.

LOWESTFARE.COM
(800) 569–3783; www.lowestfare.com.

Remember also that many tour operators offer independent tours that do not require traveling with others. They simply give you the benefit of a group rate for airfare and hotels and sometimes a free sightseeing tour. The hotels tend to be commercial, but you may want to compare these group rates with those you are quoted on your own.

Priceline.com

Priceline.com is the site where you offer a price for flights, hotels, or rental cars and wait to see if anyone accepts. Here's how it works for hotels: You specify the city, neighborhood, number of stars in the rating, and what you want to pay. If someone meets your price and you agree, only then do you find out the name of the hotel. With flights, you specify the day, the airports you want to use, an airline if you wish, and the amount you want to pay. After you agree to the price, you get the details. In both cases, a comparison list from lowest to highest price will give you an idea of the best prices available to guide you in making your bid. You can definitely save money this way, though it is a bit of a gamble. You have no control over the time of flights or whether there are stops en route. There are no refunds on these agreements, and no frequent flyer miles on the air portions.

Internet Bargains

Some of today's best travel bargains are found on the Internet, and every savvy traveler should learn how to use it. If you have no computer at home, use the public library. It takes a little comparison shopping, but you can save a lot. Every airline offers discounts and sometimes extra frequent flyer miles to those who will reserve on the Internet, saving expenses for the carrier. You can also sign on for a weekly e-mail from each airline listing upcoming weekend fare bargains. Three Web sites (**www.travelocity.com, www.expedia.com, www.orbitz.com**) are the most useful tools for comparing airfares from several airlines, as well as for finding good rates on hotels, rental cars, and travel packages. All three should be checked and compared against the airline's Web site, as they do not always give the same rates. If you travel to one place frequently or plan a future vacation to a specific place, sign on with Travelocity and they will send you an e-mail alert every time the fare changes to your destination so that you don't miss special sales. This service is free.

Savvy Travel Tips
for Solo Travelers

- Always ask for the corporate rate at a hotel, even if you don't work for a big company. It usually saves you 20 percent. Few hotels ask for I.D. when you arrive, and if they do, a business card is usually all you need to show.
- Don't call the 800 number to reserve at big hotel chains; they don't always know about local specials.
- Don't accept the first rate offered at a hotel; always ask if something cheaper is available. If they aren't full, most hotels are amenable to a little bargaining. Be sure they incorporate lower weekend rates into your bill.
- In the United States, big savings are available from hotel discount services, sometimes as much as 50 percent off the published rate. Three major services are **Express Reservations** (800–407–3351; www.express-res.com) for New York and Los Angeles; *Hotels.com* for major U.S. cities, Paris, and London; and **Quikbook** (800–789–9887; www.quikbook.com) for Atlanta, Boston, Chicago, Los Angeles, New York, San Francisco, and Washington, D.C. **Hotel Reservations Network** (800–715–7666; www.hoteldiscount .com) handles hotels in Europe, as well as many U.S. cities.
- No rooms available at the hotel? Call back after 6:00 P.M.; that's when rooms saved for no-shows become available.
- Can't get through to the airlines during a fare sale? Try calling at 7:00 A.M. or after 11:00 P.M., when you're less likely to get a busy signal.
- During bad weather months, avoid delays by flying early in the day and choosing nonstop flights. When you must change planes, look for winter hubs like Dallas, Atlanta, or Las Vegas rather than northern cities such as Chicago, Denver, or Detroit. Don't book the last flight of the day; if it is canceled, you are out of luck.
- To avoid getting stuck in the middle seat on a plane, always ask for seat assignments when you reserve your ticket. Check in at least twenty minutes before departure in order to hold your seat. Early arrival is doubly important to claim your seat, since advance boarding passes have been eliminated, causing longer lines for check-in.
- Always pay for tickets and tours with a credit card; it is your insurance in case the airline or the tour company goes out of business.

Traveling by Train in Europe

European trains are a pleasant surprise for first-time American travelers. They are fast and comfortable; they run frequently and are almost always on time. Trains like the TGV, running on high-tech tracks, travel 130 to 170 miles per hour—so smoothly that you can hardly believe how fast you are moving. They allow you to relax and see the sights and to arrive at a central location where both taxis and public transportation are usually available. There are no guarantees, but trains sometimes can be a way to meet people, too.

The Eurailpass is one of Europe's best buys. For a specified period, fifteen days to three months, it allows unlimited first-class travel on speedy trains that go almost everywhere in seventeen countries. Since distances are small and trains run often, you can cover a lot of ground in a short time. The pass must be purchased in this country before you leave; it is not available in Europe.

If you want to base yourself in cities and do day or overnight trips, the Eurail Flexipass is ideal, allowing a certain number of travel days within a two-month period. For those under the age of 26, the Eurail Youthpass offers economy second-class travel. But there is nothing second class about those second-class seats—they are perfectly comfortable and recommended for anyone who wants to save a bit of money on travel.

You can adapt a train trip to almost any kind of European itinerary. I had a wonderful journey recently, seeing Swiss mountain villages on day trips from Lausanne, then whizzing to Paris in three and a half hours on the TGV, that amazing high-speed superliner. After several days in Paris, a one-and-a-half-hour train ride took me to Blois, which became my home base for an excursion into the Loire Valley chateau country. I didn't need a car in Blois—there were daily bus excursions from the railroad station to the great chateaus of Chambord, Chenonceaux, and Amboise. Blois itself was a charming, small medieval town with its own famous chateau within walking distance of my hotel.

Stays in the countryside also provide a way to stretch your budget, since hotels and restaurants are far less expensive than those in big cities. In Blois I stayed at a stylish, modern, three-star hotel where three-course gourmet dinners were half the price of comparable meals in Paris.

Each European country has its own national railroad featuring special money-saving passes; you can learn about these from the local tourist office. If you plan to visit only one country, these may be a better choice than a Eurailpass.

A great thrill is taking the Eurostar, the train that runs through the tunnel beneath the English Channel to whisk you from the center of London to midtown Paris or Brussels. It is just as quick as flying (if you include time getting to and from

Tips on European Train Travel

- Most trains can be boarded without reservations, but the TGV and certain other special trains require advance seating. These are clearly marked with an R (meaning reservations required) on Eurail timetables, so be sure to check.
- Remember that if all your travel is within one country, the national rail is often cheaper than Eurail.
- Porters may not turn up when you need them, but many stations have an ample supply of luggage carts. It takes exact change to get one, however, so find out in advance what coins are required and have them ready.
- Some European cities have more than one train station. Paris, for example, has six. Be sure to find out from which station your train is leaving.
- Avoid travel on Friday and Sunday afternoons when weekending Europeans jam the trains.
- Remember that the Eurailpass can be purchased only in the United States.

For more information on Eurail train travel packages and reservations, see a travel agent or contact Rail Europe, 44 South Broadway, White Plains, NY 10601; (877) 257–2887 or (888) 382–7245; www.raileurope.com. BritRail and other single-country rail passes can be purchased through Rail Europe.

airports) and much more fun, since you can watch the countryside as you whiz by; the actual time in the underground tunnel is very short. Rail Europe has excellent packages that include the "Chunnel" trip as does BritRail, the British rail service, which also issues passes for unlimited train travel in Ireland, Scotland, and Wales. When all of your travel will be in one country, the local rail pass is often the most economical choice.

Because trains in Europe run more frequently than they do in the United States, it is possible to tour short distances with almost as much flexibility as you would by car, and train stations are often centrally located for sightseeing in the old parts of the cities.

My first European travel on my own, in fact, was a one-week, low-budget train trip through Holland, a compact country that is ideal if you want to see a lot in a short time. I used a suitcase small enough to fit into station lockers, and traveled much the way I might have by car. Fifteen minutes out of Amsterdam, I got off the train, checked my bag, and went out to see the charming city of Haarlem, walking the old square and visiting the Franz Hals Museum.

(Finding your way around is a cinch in Holland, since the VVV, the local information office near each train station, provides walking maps and has an English-speaking staff.)

After lunch in the square, I reboarded the train for the old university town of Leiden, another short ride away, where I did more browsing. Later, I boarded a train for The Hague, where I settled in for a couple of days. From there, day trips by train took me to Delft, Gouda, and Rotterdam, and a trolley ride brought me to the seaside resort of Scheveningen. The entire journey was inexpensive and easy, and I never felt nervous for a minute.

Famous scenic tours can be taken by train. The Bernina Express, the Glacier Express, and the Golden Pass Route in Switzerland, the Bergen Express in Norway, and Loisrail in France follow routes through magnificent scenery that you can sit back and enjoy from your picture window. Most long-distance trains either have a dining car or will serve meals at your seat. You can also reserve a sleeper—your own little bedroom—and use the train as your hotel, making the most of your travel time.

You'll find that train travel is not intimidating in most foreign countries. Signs in stations are easy to read; pictures point out lockers and checkrooms. Reservations offices are marked with a big *R* and information offices with a big *I*. In larger cities there is always someone in either of those offices who speaks English. The trains, their track numbers, and departure times are clearly listed on big boards. Even in countries where you can't understand the loudspeaker announcements, you need only spot the track number, line up at the right place, and you'll know when to board when you see the crowd starting to move.

With most major trains, it's hard to make a mistake, since the side of each car bears an identification panel showing the name of the city where the train originated, the final destination, and the major stops in between. Trains sometimes switch cars en route, so always check the destination on your car. First- and second-class cars are identified with large numbers, and a smaller number clearly identifies the cars with reserved seats.

Traveling by Train in North America

Amtrak trains are an underrated resource for people traveling alone in the United States. Getting to and from centrally located train stations is much easier than the hassle today of traveling to airports. Seats are wide and comfortable, and you can walk to the lounge car for refreshments or conversation if you get restless.

Trains can also substitute for driving alone when you want to tour. Well-priced All Aboard America fares are good for a thirty-day period in one of three regions (the eastern, central, or western United States) with three stopovers permitted. Amtrak offers its own tour packages using local hotels, as well. Trips crossing regions can be arranged for an extra fee.

Roomettes and single slumbercoaches designed for one adult allow you to save money and time by using the train as a hotel and covering many miles while you sleep. Fares include all meals while you are on board; tea, coffee, or fruit juice and a newspaper are complimentary in the morning.

Along the eastern corridor, Boston, New York, Philadelphia, Wilmington, Baltimore, Washington, Fredericksburg, and Richmond are a straight run from conveniently located midtown stations. The trains run often, making for easy city tours. The new high-speed Acela trains cut the time between Boston, New York, and Washington, D.C.

You can also let Amtrak do the driving while you enjoy the scenery on some fine fall foliage routes. The *Adirondack* runs from Manhattan through New York's Adirondack Mountains to Montreal. The *Vermonter* goes through the Green Mountains. Both the *Vermonter* and the *Ethan Allen Express* can take you to Vermont ski areas, avoiding the worry of winter driving to the slopes.

In the western United States, bilevel superliners allow you to sit back and enjoy the scenery through big picture windows, and Sightseer Lounges with windows extending all the way into the roof are great places to meet people. The *Empire Builder* from Chicago to Seattle takes you right through Glacier National Park.

Canada's Rocky Mountaineer offers one of the most spectacular train routes—the journey from Vancouver to Calgary through Jasper, Banff, and the Canadian Rockies. You can also tour comfortably on VIA, the national railway, from Montreal to Quebec City to Toronto at a speedy 95 miles per hour. Canrail passes allow twelve days of travel within a thirty-day period, allowing for plenty of sightseeing time. Like Eurail passes, these must be purchased before leaving home.

For information on Amtrak service, call (800) USA–RAIL (www.amtrak.com); for Rocky Mountaineer, (800) 665–7245 (www.rkymtnrail.com); for VIA Rail Canada, (800) 561–3949 (www.viarail.ca).

Some excellent guides to train travel include:

- *U.S.A. by Rail* by John Pitt, The Globe Pequot Press, Guilford, CT
- *Traveling the Eurail Express (Traveling Europe's Trains)* by Jay Brunhouse, Pelican Publishing Company, Gretna, LA

Top Scenic U.S. and Canada Train Routes

If you don't want to tour the whole seaboard or crisscross the country, consider some of these choice segments:
- *New York to Albany along the Hudson River*
- *New Haven to Boston along Long Island Sound*
- *Philadelphia to Harrisburg through Pennsylvania Dutch country*
- *Chicago to Seattle crossing over the Mississippi River, the Continental Divide, and the Columbia River Gorge*
- *Chicago to San Francisco via the Rocky Mountains*
- *Chicago to Portland/Seattle via Glacier National Park*
- *Vancouver to Calgary through the Canadian Rockies*

- *Eight Great American Rail Journeys: A Travel Guide* by Karen Ivory, The Globe Pequot Press, Guilford, CT
- *Great American Rail Journeys* by John Grant, The Globe Pequot Press, Guilford, CT
- *Europe by Eurail: Touring Europe by Train* by La Verne Ferguson-Kosinski, The Globe Pequot Press, Guilford, CT
- *Britain by BritRail* by La Verne Ferguson-Kosinski, The Globe Pequot Press, Guilford, CT

Meeting Local People Abroad

Spending time in a new country is always far more meaningful if you are able to meet and really talk to the people. When you are traveling alone, the chance to visit with local residents is doubly welcome. A few organizations help make this possible.

U.S. SERVAS COMMITTEE, INC.

11 John Street, New York, NY 10038; (212) 267–0252; www.usservas.org

This nonprofit, interracial, and interfaith group, now into its sixth decade, is affiliated with the United Nations as a nongovernmental organization. Its purpose is to promote peace through person-to-person understanding and friendship, which they do by opening doors for travelers to "homes and hearts" in more than 15,000 homes in over 140 countries.

Servas maintains a roster of approved hosts abroad (and throughout the United States) who welcome foreign visitors to stay in their homes, usually for two nights; no money is exchanged. To apply for membership, each applicant fills out a detailed form, which subsequently serves as a letter of introduction to hosts. This form must be submitted with two letters of recommendation. A personal interview by a volunteer is required before a new applicant is accepted for the program. If approved, members pay an annual fee of $85 plus a refundable deposit of $25 for host directories in specific countries. Travelers then write or phone these hosts to ask for hospitality, giving each reasonable notice.

Members are asked to learn as much as possible in advance about the customs and cultures of the places they plan to visit. They are also requested not to stay only in major cities since hosts in suburbs and smaller communities often have more time to welcome visitors. The purpose of visiting is to share yourself, your country, and your interests, and travelers are urged to be respectful of their hosts' values and customs. When the program works well, lifelong friendships can be formed, and many hosts eventually visit former guests.

FRIENDSHIP FORCE INTERNATIONAL
34 Peachtree Street, NW, Suite 900, Atlanta, GA 30303; (404) 522–9490;
www.friendshipforce.org

This nonprofit cultural exchange organization begun in 1977 is dedicated to promoting friendships across the barriers that separate people, through personal visits. Nearly 3,300 people in sixty countries have participated in their homestay programs of one or two weeks. The backbone of the group is a global network of some 275 clubs of volunteers who organize exchanges in their areas, with the support of the professional staff in Atlanta. Clubs aim for at least fifty members. There are some 117 active clubs in the United States, from Alabama to Wyoming. They are part of over 350 clubs in fifty-one countries and regions, including Mexico, Canada, western and eastern Europe, South America, Africa, Asia, the Middle East, Australia, and New Zealand. Members pay dues established by their clubs plus $10 dues to the national organization, for which they receive a bimonthly magazine. The group also sponsors Festivals of Friendship, combining informative seminars with five- to seven-day homestays. Planned sites for the 2005 festivals are Chicago and a location in Asia. The best way to get involved is to check the Web site and find the nearest club.

Meet the People

Several tourist offices keep lists of local people who are happy to meet with visitors and spend a few hours showing them the city. Usually there is a match with someone who has an occupation or interests similar to the visitor; in foreign countries, these friendly volunteers are bilingual. Local tourist offices can put you in touch with these organizations, which include:

- *Big Apple Greeters (New York City) (212) 669–8159; www.bigapplegreeter.org*
- *Chicago Greeters, Chicago Office of Tourism (312) 391–2000;*
  www.chicagogreeter.com
- *Meet the People Program (Jamaica) (800) 233–4582; www.visitjamaica.com*
- *People to People Program (Bahamas) (242) 323–1853; www.bahamas.com*
- *Japan Goodwill Guides (212) 757–5640;*
  www.jnto.go.jp/eng/gj/travelsupport/list_volunteerguides
- *Melbourne Greeter Service (Australia) 61 (03)–9650–6168;*
  www.melbourne.vic.gov.au/greeterservice (listed under tourism services)

FRIENDS OVERSEAS

68-04 Dartmouth Street, Forest Hills, NY 11375; (718) 544–5660 (between 9:00 and 11:00 A.M. or 5:00 and 7:00 P.M. Eastern time)

American tourists can write to this organization if they would like to meet Scandinavians, couples or singles, during their visits to Denmark, Sweden, Norway, and Finland. American participants receive the names and addresses of Scandinavian members who are eager to meet compatible Americans and begin a correspondence before the visitor leaves the States. This can lead to invitations to an evening out or a day of sightseeing, and perhaps an invitation to visit a home. Sometimes accommodations in homes may be offered. Send a self-addressed, stamped, business-size envelope for full information.

FRIENDS OVERSEAS—AUSTRALIA

68-01 Dartmouth Street, Forest hills, NY 11375; (718) 261–0534

This meet-the-people program introduces Americans to residents of Australia who are willing to give advice by mail and personal guidance in their country.

AMERICAN INTERNATIONAL HOMESTAYS, INC.
P.O. Box 1754, Nederland, CO 80466; (303) 258–3234 or (800) 876–2048;
www.aihtravel.com/homestays

Since 1988 this organization has organized homestays with English-speaking families in somewhat unusual destinations abroad. About 200 American travelers ages 40 to 70 take advantage of this opportunity for in-depth and inexpensive travel each year. You can choose bed-and-breakfast arrangements or have a home-cooked dinner with your host family each night. The countries of Central Europe and the Baltics, as well as Russia and China, are included.

WOMEN WELCOME WOMEN WORLDWIDE
(see page 190)

Offers homestays for women in many countries around the world.

Dining Alone

The part of traveling solo that people seem to dread most is dining alone. Even the most worldly travelers may hate it. Some people refuse to travel by themselves just to avoid it.

In part, this is understandable since it is undeniably a lot pleasanter to share a meal. But often the reluctance is strictly a matter of point of view. When *Travel & Leisure* magazine talked to businesspeople who frequently travel alone, many of them said that after a hectic day it is actually a relief to be able to relax and not have to make conversation with strangers. Many also considered a room service dinner a wonderfully indulgent luxury.

The same can be true after a busy day of sightseeing. It really isn't so bad relaxing over a drink by yourself and thinking back over the day—unless you think it is. Some diners are so self-conscious they bury themselves in a book, thereby missing out on the pleasure of people-watching in the restaurant—or maybe even starting up a conversation with someone at the next table.

One of the reasons that solo diners may feel ill at ease is that busy restaurants don't always seem pleased to see them. It's that same old problem—most tables are designed for two. The smaller tables inevitably seem to be stuck back near the kitchen. And, understandably, it may be true that waiters would be happier getting tips from two instead of one. If you make the effort to be friendly, however, explaining that you are a solo traveler, and enlisting advice about the menu and

Travel on a Shoestring

Short of travel funds? Not to worry. If you don't demand luxury, you can still travel happily on a tight budget. **Hostelling International-American Youth Hostels (HI-AYH)** is not only for the young. Many a canny traveler takes advantage of their rock-bottom rates for dorm rooms (divided by sex) and shared cooking facilities. Lodging goes for $8 to $25 per night; in some locations, when available, you can even splurge on a private room (chosen usually by couples) and still save a bundle over other lodging choices. Ante up $28 a year to join AYH (free for under 18, $18 for seniors), and you can make reservations with a credit card at one hundred U.S. locations and take advantage of nearly 4,000 hostels in sixty countries around the globe. (Hostels are open to nonmembers, as well, for slightly higher fees per night.)

In the United States, HI-AYH uses many interesting converted historic sites, such as an ironmaster's home built in 1827 in Pennsylvania, a Victorian mansion in Sacramento, an old lifesaving station on Nantucket, and an art deco hotel on Miami Beach. Some locations even have recreational facilities. The organization has won the National Preservation Honor Award from the National Trust for Historic Preservation for its contributions to preservation in saving these historic properties.

If you will be sharing a dorm with strangers, it only makes sense to leave valuables at home and to keep your money and camera with you at all times. Most large hostels have lockers, so bring along a padlock. With a bit of care, hostels can be a sociable and money-saving opportunity. For information, phone (202) 783-6161 or check www.hi-ayh.org.

Another way to travel on the cheap in summer is to go back to school. Many colleges and universities worldwide open their residence halls to tourists. These dormitory lodgings, while not posh, are more private than hostels, and private bathrooms are sometimes available. Some schools have central locations and the savings can be huge.

Some recent examples:

- **Trinity College Dublin** (353–1–608–1117; www.tcd.ie/conferences/visitor). About 800 rooms are available. A single room with a private bath and shower is around $50; includes breakfast.

- **London School of Economics** (44–207–955–7676; www.lse.ac.uk/vacations). Five properties in London range from high-rise apartments to row houses; residences have kitchen facilities, another saving. Singles start around $40; $65 with private bath.

- **McGill University,** Montreal (514–398–5200; www.residences.mcgill.ca/summer). Convenient single rooms with shared baths are available from May 15 to August 15 for around $28.

- **University of California at Berkeley** (510–642–4444; www.housing.berkeley.edu/conference/summervis.) In the heart of Berkeley and an easy commute to San Francisco, single dorm rooms with shared baths run about $53.

even about what to see and do in the city, you may find a staunch ally in your waiter.

Sometimes I shift my schedule so I can eat an early dinner before restaurants are filled and when I know they are happier to see a solo diner. Often I'll have this early meal in the neighborhood where I spent the afternoon, which gives me a chance to try places in areas I might not venture into on my own later in the evening.

When I want to eat at a really posh place by myself, I usually go for lunch. This is not only cheaper than evening dining but usually leaves me wanting very little for dinner that night. I've found that if you stop by in advance and explain to the captain that you are in town alone and ask which day they might best be able to accommodate you for lunch or dinner, you'll likely get a more cordial reception—and a reservation. Don't try this visit during the height of the lunchtime rush.

I have a female friend with another technique. She phones to reserve tables for one under the name of "Dr. Glenn." Somehow the title seems to do the trick; she isn't turned down, and she is welcomed when she arrives.

Though you don't want to miss out on some of the really great restaurants in a new city, as a rule, when you travel alone, it is a lot more comfortable going to smaller, more casual dining places. The less formal dining rooms in large hotels are always a good bet for single travelers, since management is quite used to serving them; you'll notice that these rooms tend to have a lot of small tables. You don't have to be staying in a particular hotel to take advantage of its dining facilities, so you can have a number of comfortable evenings simply by surveying the local hotel scene.

If I am looking for variety and I have no concierge to guide me, I always scout the blocks around my hotel during the day for promising little places within walking distance. This may or may not be successful, depending on the neighborhood and the city.

A surer technique is to seek out the trendy city neighborhoods that attract a lot of browsers. Usually as you stroll along you can count on finding small cafes in these areas. Watch for outdoor terraces with empty tables or little cafes with lots of small tables by the windows or along the walls. These are often used to serve single diners; you will probably spy some who have arrived before you.

Other best bets in every city are restaurants with bars serving complete meals as well as beverages. These may be among the city's most popular restaurants, as you'll see from some of the places listed beginning on page 227. Sushi bars are always fine for dining alone, as are restaurant bar areas and wine bars in many cities that also serve light meals. I've found that Chinese restaurants tend to be relaxed places where single diners need not feel self-conscious.

If you want extra guidance, you can consult a new book series, *Table for One: The Solo Diner's Restaurant Guide,* published by Contemporary Books, a division of McGraw Hill. Guides available so far are for New York, Chicago, and Los Angeles. Log on to www.diningsolo.com for more information.

The www.solodining.com Web site mentioned on page 178 is another resource, as are the Zagat restaurant surveys, which are made up of opinions from local residents and always include suggestions for dining alone as well as listings of places where local singles gather. The Zagat guides are available for most major U.S. cities. For ordering information contact Zagat Survey, 4 Columbus Circle, New York, NY 10019; (800) 333–3421 or (212) 977–6000; www.zagat.com.

One other option: Take an evening sightseeing tour that includes dinner and you'll definitely have company. That's the way I saw San Francisco's Chinatown for the first time.

Wherever you go, you'll be better received in a restaurant if you are reasonably well dressed. I met one traveler who told me she always dresses up when she goes out to dine by herself. She also carries a notebook and asks lots of questions about the restaurant and the menu. She hopes she will be mistaken for a food critic, and so far, she says she has been treated well wherever she has tried her little game.

Another way to find dining companions in a city in the United States is to look into the meeting dates of the local chapters of any professional organization or alumni club you may belong to, or the scheduled dinners of the local Single Gourmet group. Contact the national Single Gourmet organization listed on page 178 for local addresses. And don't hesitate to look up friends of friends.

The best way to find nightlife is to read local publications. If you are 35 or under, look for alternative papers such as the *Boston Phoenix* or the magazine *Time Out* in New York. If you are hesitant about venturing alone, check into nighttime tours.

Singles bars still exist, but they are far less attractive to travelers in this age of AIDS. A brief romance in a strange city once might have seemed romantic, but today it is a bit like playing Russian roulette. A good rule for females always is to pay your own way at bars or in restaurants. If you are meeting someone you don't know well, always do so at a public place, never at your hotel.

For those who prefer specific dining destinations to browsing, here are some solo suggestions from restaurant critics who were kind enough to share their expertise on three major U.S. cities:

Boston

Mat Schaffer, a former restaurant critic for *Boston Magazine,* offers these suggestions:

DAILY CATCH
(323 Hanover Street in the North End; 617–523–8567) specializes in seafood, especially squid—fried, stuffed, sautéed, even minced into marvelous meatballs served in tomato sauce over linguini. Located in the city's Italian neighborhood, the tiny dining room is conducive to meeting diners at adjoining tables.

JAE'S
(520 Columbus Avenue, 617–421–9405, 212 Stuart Street, and 1281 Cambridge Street, Cambridge, 617–467–8380) has three locations with an excellent, reasonably priced Pacific Rim menu of Thai, Korean, and Japanese dishes. If you dine at the sushi bar downstairs on Columbus Avenue, you're guaranteed to strike up a conversation with the person next to you.

CHARLIE'S SANDWICH SHOP
(429 Columbus Avenue; 617–536–7669) is a neighborhood breakfast and lunch spot where everyone shares tables. Be ready for long lines on Saturdays, and be sure to order the turkey hash.

STEPHANIE'S ON NEWBURY
(190 Newbury Street; 617–236–0990) dishes out terrific American comfort food, sandwiches, and salads to a fashionable clientele in a *très chic* setting. Alfresco dining on the sidewalk out front features some of the city's best people-watching.

HAMERSLEY'S BISTRO
(553 Tremont Street; 617–423–2700) is nationally recognized as one of Boston's finest restaurants. The roast chicken is spectacular. Chef Gordon Hamersley is the lanky guy in the open kitchen with the red hair and ever-present baseball cap. The intimate seating makes it virtually impossible not to spark up a conversation.

LALA ROKH
(97 Mount Vernon Street; 617–720–5511) is a Persian restaurant in the basement of a Beacon Hill townhouse. Allow the well-informed wait staff to guide you through the pleasures of an exotically delicious cuisine with influences from the Near East to the Far East.

RIALTO
(in the Charles Hotel, 1 Bennett Street, Cambridge; 617–661–5050) serves the foods of southern Spain, France, and Italy. Make a reservation—Jody Adams is rightfully considered one of Boston's most accomplished chefs. The lounge is a good place to meet the local intelligentsia.

MR. & MRS. BARTLEY'S BURGER COTTAGE
(1246 Massachusetts Avenue, Cambridge; 617–354–6559) is a Harvard Square landmark that has been serving huge hamburgers to Harvard students forever. Every other customer dines solo—many with his or her head in a book.

COMMENTS E.B.: *When I am in Boston alone, I always head for Legal Seafoods. They are only found now in commercial locations like Copley Place or the Prudential Center, but the chowder is still the best. If you can't get there in town, you'll also find them at Logan Airport.*

A trendy favorite with a dining bar, Mistral (221 Columbus Avenue; 617–867–9300), is a great-looking South End spot known for fine food.

Another possibility is Durgin Park, a longtime landmark in the North Building of Quincy Market (617–227–2038), where diners are seated at long communal tables and served big portions of roast beef and other hearty American fare by waitresses renowned for their grumpiness. It's definitely touristy, but do it once, anyway.

Chicago

Penny Pollack, dining editor of *Chicago Magazine,* recommends:

BERGHOFF
(17 West Adams; 312–427–3170) is a genuine Chicago institution, serving traditional German cuisine and house-made brews since 1898!

BIG BOWL CAFE
(6 East Cedar; 312–640–8888) is a casual, fun Asian cafe created in the noodle-house tradition. Simple, fresh noodle-based dishes are the mainstay here. An interactive stir-fry bar adds to the fun.

ED DEBEVIC'S DINER

(640 North Wells at Ontario; 312–664–1707) provides 1950s nostalgia, burgers served to the blare of rock and roll, and a gum-cracking, smooth-talking wait staff.

FRONTERA GRILL

(445 North Clark; 312–661–1434) serves the most sophisticated Mexican food in town. Single diners may sit at the bar, and often avoid a daunting line for tables.

BLUE CRAB LOUNGE

(21 East Hubbard; 312–527–2722) is under the same roof as Shaw's Crab House. It offers raw-bar items plus a few more ambitious entrees served mostly at high stools along the bar. If you prefer table seating, Shaw's is a good choice, too.

CAFE SPIAGGIA

(980 North Michigan; 312–280–2750) treats you to all the flavors of Northern Italy in a casual-chic setting overlooking Michigan Avenue—and for less money than in its elegant next-door sibling, Spiaggia.

SEASONS CAFE

(at the Four Seasons Hotel, 120 East Delaware; 312–649–2349) provides a cozy nook off the main dining room where you can enjoy expertly prepared soups, grilled fish, pastas, and salads.

BISTRO 110

(110 East Pearson; 312–266–3110) is a lively spot just off Michigan Avenue serving typical bistro standards accompanied by crusty baguettes.

MITY NICE GRILL

(at Water Tower Place, 835 North Michigan Avenue; 312–335–4745) has the decor and feel of the forties and the comfort food of today. The perfect stop after shopping on Michigan Avenue.

MRS. PARK'S TAVERN

(at the Doubletree Guest Suites at 198 East Delaware; 312–280–8882) is a sophisticated spot in a sophisticated neighborhood. The kitchen benefits from the talent and style upstairs at the pricier Park Avenue Cafe.

BRASSERIE JO
(59 West Hubbard; 312–595–0800) is a sizzling, bustling River North hot spot for robust Alsatian food and custom-brewed beer.

CHEESECAKE FACTORY
(in the John Hancock Center at 875 North Michigan Avenue; 312–337–1101) sports eclectic, over-the-top decor and provides great people-watching, an enormous California-style menu, and delectable cheesecakes. But be perpared for a wait.

312 CHICAGO
(136 North La Salle Street; 312–696–2420), attached to the Allegro Hotel in the ever-evolving Chicago Loop, makes singles feel welcome. Whether you are seated at the counter fronting the kitchen or comfortably ensconced in a tapestried arm-chair, light-handed American interpretations of French and Italian techniques make for a pleasing bill of fare.

C O M M E N T S E.B.: *Chicago pizza is not to be missed. Local critics say it isn't as good as it used to be, but as an out-of-towner, I'm still impressed with Giordano's (at 747 West Rush Street [312–251–0747] or at 1840 North Clark Street [312–944–6100], the place that made "stuffed pizza" famous.*

A few additional singles suggestions from the Metromix Web site (http://metro mix.chicagotribune.com) include the attractive Ritz-Carlton Café (160 East Pearson Street; 312–266–1000), Vinci (1732 North Halsted; 312–266–1199), an Italian restaurant, and Ben Pao (52 West Illinois Street; 333–222–1888), serving a Chinese and pan-Asian menu.

San Francisco

Patricia Unterman, a respected restaurant reviewer, suggests these singles-friendly places:

IL FORNAIO
(1265 Battery Street; 415–986–0100), a bustling Italian trattoria with a comfortable counter, is part of a popular chain.

LITTLE JOE'S

(523 Broadway; 415–443–4343) is a busy, old-fashioned Italian restaurant known for its pasta and veal; it's inexpensive and has a counter.

HAYES STREET GRILL

(320 Hayes Street; 415–863–5545) specializes in fish and has a number of smaller tables for singles. Zagat ranks it among the city's best for seafood.

VICOLO

(201 Ivy Street; 415–863–2382) is an upscale pizzeria with counter seats and many small tables.

VIVANDE PORTA VIA

(2125 Fillmore Street; 415–346–4430) is a wonderful Italian deli and cafe with a counter and small tables. Note that it is open only until 7:00 P.M.

HAWTHORNE LANE

(22 Hawthorne Street; 415–777–9779) is in the blooming SOMA area. It's pricey but well recommended.

Ms. Unterman adds that many San Francisco restaurants now feature a bar or counter where you can stop in for a fine meal alone, including Kuleto's (221 Powell Street; 415–397–7720). Designer Pat Kuleto, whose imaginative settings are found in many of the city's favorite dining places, has made eating bars one of his trademarks. They can be found at Boulevard in SOMA (1 Mission Street; 415–543–6084), Farallon near Union Square (450 Post Street; 415–956–6969), and Jardiniere near the Opera House (300 Grove Street; 415–861–5555). Another favorite with a dining bar facing the kitchen is Rose Pistola in North Beach (532 Columbus Avenue; 415–399–0499).

You won't be bored dining alone at Foreign Cinema (2534 Mission Street; 415–648–7600), where shorts, foreign films, and independent films are served up along with good French bistro fare; the heated courtyard setting includes many communal tables.

Four Favorite Cities

EVERYBODY HAS HIS OR HER OWN FAVORITE CITIES. I'VE CHOSEN Amsterdam, Montreal, Paris, and New York, not only for their beauty or excitement but because I have found them to be especially easy cities to be in by myself. My descriptions are not meant to be used as a substitute for a comprehensive guidebook—they are simply personal impressions to share what I've found most enjoyable when traveling on my own.

Amsterdam

There's a fairy-tale quality to the tilty, gabled townhouses on the tree-lined canal streets of Amsterdam. Though apartments, boutiques, and cafes may hide behind the historic facades, the beautiful, old city has not changed since the seventeenth century. No matter how many times you walk along the canals, they are always enchanting, even in busy midday when traffic and whizzing bicycles dispel the old-world illusion. The loveliest times for walking are on a silent Sunday morning or on a summer evening when the old facades are floodlit.

The contrasting aspects of this city equally well known for its Rembrandts and its red-light district are endlessly fascinating. And the contrasts continue to grow as the Docklands area of the city becomes a showcase of avant-garde architecture, and the city's cutting-edge fashion boutiques add to the new appellation, "cool Amsterdam." See the wonderful old city first, but save time for the new.

Amsterdam is small, so you can cover most of it on foot, savoring such details as the charming, no-two-alike gables atop the houses, the growing number of kicky boutiques, the many art galleries, the tempting bakeries, and the masses of flowers in the colorful, floating flower market. Outdoor markets for everything from postage stamps to parakeets to "junk-tiques" are another intriguing part of the cityscape that you need no company to enjoy.

Amsterdam's polyglot population is another part of its appeal. The freewheeling atmosphere makes everyone, young and old, feel at home. The street music characterizes the happy spirit of the city. On one recent stroll in Amsterdam I counted six kinds of music from various music makers: a classical violinist outside the concert hall, a folksinger-guitarist near the Van Gogh museum, a rock group in front of the train station, a carillon ringing from a church steeple, an organ concert wafting from an open church door, and the tinkly tunes of a barrel organ in Dam Square. All are typically Amsterdam.

Several things make Amsterdam particularly easy for solo travelers. First, everyone speaks English. Second, if you stay within the confines of the old city, you can easily walk to see the Rembrandts in the Rijksmuseum and the priceless collections in the Vincent van Gogh Museum, as well as to concerts and restaurants. If you tire, cheerfully clanging trolley cars are waiting on every major street. To save money, buy the trolley tickets that are good for a whole day or get a strip of tickets good for a number of rides. Tickets are also available for individual rides if you think you won't make good use of the more economical multiple-ride tickets. For a wonderful way to see the city, sign up for a bicycle tour and join the Dutch on their bikes. Check with the tourist office for current offerings.

Because the center of the city is small, almost any hotel is conveniently located, but two with particularly sociable bars are the American Hotel, an art deco landmark at 97 Leidsekade (31–20–624–5322), and the Pulitzer, an amalgam of seventeenth-century townhouses at 315 Prinsengracht (31–20–627–6753). The newest luxury hot spot is the chic, modern Blakes at 384 Keizersgracht (31–20–520–2010). The Ambassade at 341 Herengracht (31–20–324–5321), made up of six patrician canal houses, is one of the most charming canal-house hotels, along with the Canal House at 148 Keizersgracht (31–20–622–5182). Less expensive hotels along the canals include the Hotel Agora at 462 Singel, the Amsterdam Weichmann Hotel at 328–332 Prinsengracht (31–20–626–8962), and Seven Bridges at 31 Reguliersgracht (31–20–623–1329).

What's best of all about Amsterdam when you are by yourself is that it is a city where people like to "hang out"—in sidewalk cafes in summer and in coffee shops and local taverns, known as "brown bars," in winter. There's always a place where you can comfortably have a cup of coffee, a drink, or a meal without feeling out of place because you are alone. And if you need to, it is easy to watch your budget. At dozens of restaurants, you'll see the knife-and-fork symbol indicating a tourist menu, which means a price-fixed three-course meal. You'll no doubt make your own dining discoveries as you wander, but the following are some recommended spots.

The busy square called Leidseplein is the center of Amsterdam's nightlife, and together with the side streets perpendicular to its edges it offers a wide range of cafes from casual to chic. The following cafes deserve special recommendation:

CAFE-RESTAURANT AMERICAIN

(in the American Hotel at 97 Leidsekade) is a high-ceilinged art deco rendezvous for everything from reading a newspaper over a cup of coffee to indulging in a full dinner menu. Theatergoers, actors, musicians, and tourists all can be found here or on the big terrace cafe outside. One of the city's most popular gathering spots, it's perfect when you are alone.

OESTERBAR

(10 Leidseplein) offers a top seafood restaurant upstairs with an informal, tiled dining room on the street level with tables and a counter.

You might also try these nearby restaurants:

HAESJE CLAES

(275 Spuistraat) is small, narrow, wood-paneled, atmospheric, and inexpensive.

DE KNIJP

(134 van Baerlestraat) offers a range of choices from quiches to six-course feasts in a pleasant spot with a garden.

CAFE LUXEMBOURG

(Spui 22–24) has a relaxing ambience and large portions of good food at good prices.

CAFE PULITZER

(in the Pulitzer Hotel at the corner of Keizersgracht and Reestraat) has rattan furnishings, contemporary art, and a menu that runs the gamut from snacks to substantial meals.

KEUKEN VAN 1870

(4 Spuistraat) has the plainest Dutch cooking at the lowest prices. Patrons share tables, so it is a good place to meet Amsterdammers.

CASA DI DAVID

(426 Single) is a family-run Italian restaurant overlooking the canal. It offers reasonably priced homemade pastas and pizza.

PANCAKE BAKERY
(191 Prinsengracht) is a restored canalside warehouse with more than fifty kinds of Dutch pancakes—great for lunch or a light dinner and very light on the pocket-book.

GRAND CAFE L'OPERA
(27–29 Rembrandtsplein) is a split-level art deco restaurant-cafe and bar with a big, popular terrace.

KANTJIL EN DE TIJGER
(291 Spuistraat) is the place to sample a multidish Indonesian rijsttafel.

SPANJER & VAN TWIST
(60 Leliegracht) is a friendly spot with good Dutch food and a canalside terrace.

HOLLANDS GLORIE
(220–222 Kerkstraat), longtime local favorite, serves up popular-priced food in a wonderful Old Dutch setting of copper and tiles.

For further information on Amsterdam, contact the Netherlands Board of Tourism (NBT) at 355 Lexington Avenue, New York, NY 10017, or 225 North Michigan Avenue, Chicago, IL 60601, or call (888) 464–6552 (www.goholland.com). Recommended guides include *Eyewitness Guide to Amsterdam,* Dorling Kindersley, London and New York, and *Cadogan Amsterdam,* Cadogan Books, London.

Montreal

Here's a touch of French *joie de vivre* right over the border—and you don't even have to know the language. Montreal is an easily manageable city of 1.8 million people with the life, charm, and sophistication of a metropolis many times its size. Promenaders on the streets and laughter in the sidewalk cafes last well into the night!

Recently there has been another incentive to discover Montreal—an exchange rate that makes the American dollar go far in Canada.

The setting is unusual and scenic: an island in the middle of the St. Lawrence River, with a little mountain, Mont Royal, providing acres of greenery right in the middle of town. The street and shop signs, much of the food, and the ambience are strictly French and foreign, yet almost everyone in Montreal is bilingual, so you'll not have to open your phrase book unless you want to.

The marvel of Montreal is its Metro, a subway system that is not only clean, safe, and speedy but a tourist attraction in itself. Buy a day pass for a discount, and ask for a free pocket-size map card of the city and the Metro system. Miles of the Metro's wide, well-lit, attractive corridors connect the city's main shopping complexes and offer hundreds of shops in the corridors themselves. The system provides something to do no matter what the weather. The entertainers who make your strolling and waiting time tuneful are top-rate musicians who have auditioned to compete for their spots.

The efficient train system makes it easy to visit attractions outside the city center. It's not hard to get to the Olympic Stadium or the Parc Jean-Drapeau, a green island oasis in the midst of the majestic St. Lawrence River that was the site of Expo '67, the 1967 World's Fair. During summer, the park offers both Quebec's largest amusement park (La Ronde) and one of the world's most beautiful fireworks competitions. The French pavilion from Expo '67 is now the elegant Casino de Montreal and the American pavilion is now the Biosphere, where the St. Lawrence–Great Lakes ecosystems come alive. Not to be missed is the city's marvelous Garden Botanical, one of the world's largest and most spectacular.

Quaint Old Montreal on the banks of the St. Lawrence is the city's tourist mecca. Browsing is pleasant, though many of the shops are decidedly commercial. For a fascinating history tour of the area, take one of the walks given daily from late June through September with one of Guidatour's English-speaking guides. For information, call (800) 363-4021.

The city's history is displayed in the Pointe-a-Calliere Museum of Archaeology and History of Montreal, located on the site of Place Royale, where the city was founded. The upstairs cafe has a wonderful view of the port.

Self-guided walking tours printed in the free official Tourist Guide take you through some of the city's other neighborhoods—the elegant Sherbrooke Street area that boasts the city's top hotels and boutiques and the handsome McGill University campus; Saint-Denis, the lively "Latin Quarter" of student life filled with boutiques and cafes; Avenue Laurier, a burgeoning area of upscale shops and restaurants; and Boulevard Saint-Laurent with its mix of nationalities, trendy bistros, discos, and cigar bars. Everywhere you go, you'll find sidewalk cafes where you can have a rest and a view of the passing scene.

On Sherbrooke, the Montreal Museum of Fine Arts is housed in two buildings. The spectacular newer pavilion was designed by noted Israeli architect Moshe Safdie with a fourth-floor atrium that offers a grand view of the city. The collections range from Rembrandt to Rodin.

Shopping is one of this city's greatest pleasures, and one you need no company to enjoy. The fashions are French and the prices are Canadian, a great combination for travelers with American dollars. Boutiques and department stores on Sainte-Catherine Street vie with the most elegant of those to be found at city shopping centers anywhere. Ogilvy's, for one, is an old-world treasure filled with five floors of lovely boutiques.

Two centers are modernistic dazzlers and good places for informal meals as well. Les Cours Mont-Royal, a former hotel on Peel Street, has been converted to a fourteen-level elegant mall of interior courtyards, skylights, fountains, and glittering chandeliers. The mall is shared by more than eighty fine shops, condominiums, and offices. Among the dining places in the food court, Guyet Dodo Morali is a recommended choice.

Place Montreal Trust, between McGill College Avenue and Mansfield, boasts a number of cafes and boutiques on its five multicolored levels, including such names as Zara, Esprit, Mexx, and Crabtree and Evelyn, as well as dozens of shops featuring exclusive designer creations.

If you have dreamed of buying a fur coat for yourself or to give as a gift, Montreal is definitely the place. The selection and the prices are superior, and the American dollar goes far. The fur district is centered around Mayor Street.

Where to stay? Three top-of-the-line hotels are on Sherbrooke West, the Ritz-Carlton at 1228 (800–426–3135), the new Sofitel at 1155 (514–285–9000), and the Omni at 1050 (800–228–3000). They are top-notch and conveniently located near the cafes on convivial Crescent Street. Loews Hotel Vogue at 1425 Rue de la Montagne (800–465–6654) is another top luxury choice, and the 101-room Le Germain is a chic choice for those who prefer small boutique hotels (2050 rue Mansfield; 514–849–2050). The more moderately priced Holiday Inn Montreal Midtown (800–387–3042) is about 6 blocks away at 420 Sherbrooke West. Château Versailles (1659 Sherbrooke West; 800–361–7199), a small hotel comprising four Victorian houses, is also a good value. Auberge du Vieux Port, 97 rue de la Commune Est (514–876–0081), is a charming, small old city inn in an 1880s building. Auberge les Passants du Sans Soucy, 171 Rue St-Paul Ouest (514–842–2634) is another small charmer.

The safe and efficient Metro makes this an ideal city for bed-and-breakfast lodgings. For reservations, contact Montreal Bed and Breakfast, 2033, St-Hubert, Montreal, Quebec, H2L 3Z6 Canada; (514) 738–9410 or (800) 738–4338; www.bbmontreal.com.

When it comes to restaurants, you can hardly go wrong in Montreal. The gastronomic capital of Canada, it is a city all but dedicated to wining and dining. This is a sophisticated city, and no one raises an eyebrow when you enter a restaurant alone. Take your pick of the places in the following areas.

Crescent Street between Sherbrooke and Sainte-Catherine is a favorite area of Montreal's over-30 smart set. A host of good, informal choices await, many with outside terraces. **Les Halles** at 1450 Crescent is one of the city's old-fashioned gourmet landmarks; it's probably a better bet at lunchtime if you are alone. Excellent newer choices in this general area include Europea, 1227 Rue de la Montagne, and Renoir in the Sofitel Hotel.

The lower part of Saint-Denis Street near the University of Quebec draws younger patrons to its wall-to-wall lineup of cafes of all nationalities. The farther up the hill you go, the more sophisticated the restaurants and the older the crowd. During the late-June Jazz Festival, the lower street sings with impromptu concerts. Suggestions in this neighborhood are:

L'EXPRESS
(3927 Saint-Denis) classic French bistro.

COCAGNE
(3842 Saint-Denis) highly rated French cuisine.

Prince Arthur Street and Duluth Street, not far from the Saint-Denis area, are filled with Greek and other ethnic restaurants with big outdoor patios. They're all inexpensive and strictly BYOB—bring your own bottle of wine. Prince Arthur is also a pedestrian mall where guests enjoy street entertainment along with the modest dinner tabs. Just pick a place with an empty seat out front.

You'll find more tourists than locals in Old Montreal, but you'll also find street musicians and a host of outside cafes.

LES REMPARTS
(93 rue de la Commune Est) French contemporary, one of the old city's best.

LA GARGOTE
(351 place d'Youville) pleasant bistro amid stone and brick walls.

LE BOURLINGUEUR
(363 St-François-Xavier) good four-course meals at good prices.

Le Cafe de Paris in the Ritz-Carlton Hotel has delicious food and a beautiful outdoor garden in summer. The gracious Ritz staff will make you comfortable, but if you are shy about dinner, come for lunch, a fabulous breakfast, or high tea.

Restaurant critic Alan Richman recently wrote an extensive article about dining in Montreal, and while he wasn't concentrating on solo dining, some of his recommendations sound well worth considering. They include La Binerie Mont-Royal, 367 Avenue du Mont-Royal East for comfort food; Bu, 5245 Boulevard Saint-Laurent, a combination wine bar and good French food; Restaurant Delfino, 1231 Avenue Lajoie for seafood; Au Pied de Cochon, 536 Avenue Duluth East, for bistro fare; and Schwartz's, 3895 Boulevard Saint-Laurent, for good deli food.

Still more recommendations from friends who live in the city (often the best advice of all):

- The Bistro on the Avenue, 1362 Greene Avenue, Westmount
- Cassis, 1279 Avenue du Mont-Royal East
- Le Paris, 1812 Saint Catherine Street West
- Jardin du Nord, 78 de la Gauchetiere Street West (Chinese)
- Koji Kaizen, 4120 Saint Catherine Street West (Japanese)

For further Montreal information, send for the free Tourist Guide and other excellent materials put out by the Tourisme Montreal. You can find them at www.tourism-montreal.org or get information at (877) 266–5687.

Paris

Can the most romantic city in the world really be a good place to be alone? I know none better. Paris is dazzling, incredibly beautiful, and interesting at every turn. There are never enough days to begin to cover all the neighborhoods to be explored, all the fascinating shops for browsing, and all the incredible museums to be visited. No matter how many times you go, there is always something new to see. The splendid additions to the Louvre, the soaring d'Orsay Museum filled with Impressionist works, and the charming Picasso Museum are visual treats. The old Place de Vosges neighborhood grows more beautiful each year. And since there is always some controversial modern building going up, it's fun to have a look and form an opinion about places like the Pompidou Center, the newly remodeled Les Halles, the pyramid entrance at the Louvre, and the Bastille Opera.

Of course, a visit to Paris may be more enjoyable if you speak a modicum of French. Some lessons before you leave home are helpful, and a phrase book is a necessity. On my last visit I noticed that a remarkable number of Parisians now are willing to speak some English, and I found residents extremely kind and helpful. The three-star restaurants may not be overly warm to American-speaking guests, but in the less-rarified stratas of the city, in my opinion, Paris no longer deserves its longtime reputation for coldness.

Unfortunately, you can't always count on the cab drivers to speak English. When I travel around Paris, I always carry the indispensable street guide, the little red *Paris Practique,* which locates every single address in each of the city's *arrondissements,* or districts. It also includes a detailed map of each arrondissement as well as maps of the Metro subway system and the bus routes. All you need to do is add an *X* to mark your spot, and you'll always be able to find your way. You can find it in larger U.S. bookstores, or you can buy one when you arrive in Paris at almost any newsstand.

The Metro is simple to figure out. Stations are marked with a large *M,* and many have elegant turn-of-the-century art nouveau entrances. You can buy *un carnet* ("uhn kar-*nay*"), a book of ten tickets good for train or bus at a discount. If you will be in town for five to seven days, a better bet is the Carte Orange, which gives you a week or a month of unlimited travel; come prepared—you'll need two passport-size photos of yourself. Whichever you use, remember to take your ticket when the machine returns it. You sometimes need it to exit.

If you plan to visit outside the city center, consider the Paris Visite pass, which allows unlimited travel for one to five days by Metro, bus, or railroad, including transportation to the airports and Versailles.

To find the right train, find your destination on a Metro map and trace the line by following the color coding and the number of the line. At the end of the line you will see the number of the last stop—it will guide you to the right train. The name of the last stop is also indicated on the platform. Inside the train is a chart of all the stops, so you can follow your route. You'll find a neighborhood map at almost every Metro exit.

You might prefer to take your time and ride the bus, since every route in this city makes for a scenic tour. A bus map is available at the big tourist office on the Champs-Elysées. Each bus is clearly marked with a route number and its final destination. Traveling across town by bus may require more than one ticket; ask the driver. Just a few of the outstanding sightseeing routes are:

- Line 24, which crosses the Seine four times and passes most of the city's famous sites
- Line 29 from the Opera to the Bastille
- Line 38 from Les Halles across Ile de la Cité and up boulevard Saint-Michel to the Luxembourg Gardens
- Line 63, a Left Bank route through the Saint-Germain-des-Pres area

- Line 84 from the Madeleine up rue Royale, around the Place de la Concorde through the heart of the Left Bank to the Luxembourg Gardens and around the Place de Pantheon
- Line 96 from Montparnasse through Saint-Germain-des-Pres to Saint Paul

Check a current map before you board to be sure that routes have not changed, and remember that bus service is limited on Sundays and evenings.

Not even the most magnificent ride will satisfy for long in a city made to order for walking. One of the best ways to get to know Paris on a first visit is with Paris Walking Tours, run by a personable young English couple. Ninety-minute tours, which vary from week to week, may take in Notre-Dame, Sainte-Chapelle, the Luxembourg Gardens, Hemingway's Paris, the old village of Montmartre, medieval Paris, the Invalides, Paris of the Impressionists, the Ile St.-Louis and the Seine, the Marais, and the Opera House. The company also does bus trips to Malmaison and Versailles. Reservations for walks are not necessary; groups meet at a designated Metro stop. For information, phone (33–1) 48–09–21–40 or check out www.pariswalkingtours.com.

It's also nice for those of us who haven't mastered French that the Louvre offers regular tours in English. Check at the information desk for the time schedule.

Besides tours, the many English-language bookshops afford an excellent way to find other English-speaking people in Paris. **Brentano's** (37 avenue de l'Opera) is the largest of these and a good place to pick up information through postings and newsletters with activities of interest to Americans.

My favorites of the English-language bookstores are **W.H. Smith's** combination restaurant, tearoom, and bookshop at 248 rue de Rivoli (also a fine place for a meal or a snack), and **Shakespeare and Company,** 37 rue de la Boucherie, an atmospheric gem of a used bookstore on the Left Bank. When I last visited the latter, you could borrow (they'll ask you to leave a deposit) a copy of *Pariswalks,* one of the best guides to self-guided walking tours, and have free tea upstairs on Sunday afternoons at 4:00 P.M. If you are staying in the city long enough, you might want to sign up for language lessons at the Alliance-Française, 101 boulevard Raspail, another place to meet your countrymen.

Of course you haven't come all the way to Paris only to meet other Americans, but when you have no companion in a city where few people speak your language well, it is a relief to take a break occasionally and talk freely to someone from home.

While you're in Paris, read all you can about the city to discover some of the special small pleasures that you might overlook, such as the concerts held at Sainte-Chapelle, illuminated by daylight through the church's glorious stained-glass windows. Check the "Bests" section in the guidebook *Paris Access* for other treasures favored by a number of noted Paris visitors. The "Star Sights" noted in the *Eyewitness Guide to Paris* offer a good roundup of special sights not to be missed.

Any guidebook can tell you about the grand hotels of Paris, but there are many small, reasonable hotels with some amount of charm (albeit small rooms) where you can be comfortable by yourself and not spend a fortune. Among those that have been recommended to me are: the Hotel de la Bretonnerie, 22 rue Ste-Croix de la Bretonnerie (01–48–87–7763), in the lovely Marais district; Hotel Des Deux Iles, 59 rue St. Louis-en-L'Ile (01–43–26–1335), on the Ile St. Louis; Hotel Burgundy, 8 rue Duphot (01–42–60–34–12), two converted 1830s townhouses on the posh Right Bank; Hotel L'Abbaye St. Germain, 10 rue Cassette (01–45–44–38–11; www.hotel-abbaye.com), a one-time convent turned into a boutique hotel on the Left Bank near the Luxembourg Gardens; and two other delightful St. Germain choices on the Left Bank, Hotel Verneuil, 8 rue de Verneuil (01–42–60–82–14) and Hotel de Danube, 58 rue Jacob (01–42–60–34–07).

Unless you are determined to try the famous culinary palaces of Paris, dining alone in this city is a snap. There are cafes and bistros in every neighborhood, many with big outdoor terraces, and dozens of tiny eateries where solo diners are commonplace. Attractive tearooms are perfect places for lunch, as are wine bars. And though the street has become a bit tacky, the Champs-Elysées offers a lineup of reasonably priced cafes offering the traditional steakfrites (beef steak and French fries); lone diners are not at all unusual in this neighborhood.

An expensive but wonderful way to enjoy French cuisine with company—and to take home the ability to cook it yourself—is to sign up for the Gourmet Sessions at the famous cooking school, Le Cordon Bleu (8 rue Leon Delhomme). Courses are available from a half day to a month. A one-day class of particular interest for visitors is a visit with chefs (and an English interpreter) to a city market, followed by a light buffet and a cooking demonstration in the afternoon. Demonstration lessons are also open to the public. For a schedule and information in the United States, phone (800) 457–CHEF. Le Cordon Bleu also supplies students with a list of hotels where they receive special rates.

Another possibility is the well-known Ritz-Escoffier School of French Gastronomy at the posh Hotel Ritz, 15 Place Vendôme, where classes as short as one week are offered for amateur chefs as well as courses for serious students. If you don't want a course, demonstrations are given with samplings of the dishes prepared. Phone 01–43–16–30–50 or (800) 966–5758 for a schedule or see www.ritz.com.

Check the *Michelin Guide to Paris* if you want the latest count on star chefs in Paris; if you can afford the bill, you can probably eat better in this city than anywhere in the world. This small selection concentrates on atmospheric neighborhoods where you can roam and almost take your pick of comfortable spots to dine. Here are a few specific recommendations, broken down by neighborhoods:

The Marais

BOFINGER
(5 rue de la Bastille) is a lively and pretty landmark brasserie dating back to 1864.

CHEZ JO GOLDENBERG
(7 rue de Rosiers) is on the main artery of the old Jewish ghetto, a local landmark.

Ile de la Cité

BRASSERIE DE L'ILE ST. LOUIS
(55 Quai de Bourbon) a popular newly chic old-timer dating to the 1880s.

Saint-Germain

AU PACTOLE
(44 Boulevard St. Germain) a fine chef; fixed-price menus can be good value.

LE PETIT ZINC
(11 rue Saint Benoit), an art deco beauty, is known for good food and always busy.

LA FERMETTE MARBEUF
(5 Rue Marbeuf) is worth a trip for the fabulous art nouveau decor.

The famous brasseries where Sartre, Hemingway, and other literary lions once assembled are now said by many to be overpriced and filled with nothing but tourists, but they are landmarks I wanted to see on my first visit to Paris and perhaps you will, too. You will find three on boulevard St. Germain: Café de Flore at 172, Aux Deux Magots at 170, and Brasserie Lipp at 151. La Coupole is at 102 boulevard du Montparnasse.

Other Recommendations

You might also try:

MUSÉE D'ORSAY RESTAURANT
(62 rue de Lille) is in the marvelous d'Orsay Museum and is open for lunch and dinner.

CAFE DE LA PAIX
(12 boulevard des Capucines, Place de Opera) is a restored national landmark. Come for meals or tea between 3:00 P.M. and 6:00 P.M. The terrace is a prime spot for people-watching.

FAUCHON
(26 Place de la Madeleine, 8th arrondissement). This is the best cafeteria in Paris. You'll eat standing up, but it's still a "don't miss" for lunch.

CAFÉ DROUANT
(18 Rue Gaillon) is the sibling of a famous restaurant and offers good value, given the quality of the food. The shellfish motif on the ceiling is famous.

RUE DE LA HUCHETTE, a Left Bank street near the Shakespeare and Company bookshop, is lined with inexpensive, small Greek restaurants—good to know about if your budget is running low.

Yahoo! lists the following ten most popular restaurants in Paris. Some are touristy, one or two are among the most expensive, but every one is worth a visit.

LA TOUR D'ARGENT (1517 Quai de la Tournelle), a perennial favorite dating to the 1850s, expensive but noted for fine cuisine and panoramic views of Notre Dame.

MAN RAY (32/34 Rue Marbeuf), trendy Asian, Thai, and Japanese, owned by actors Johnny Depp, Sean Penn, and John Malkovich.

LE VIEUX BISTRO (14 Rue du Cloitre-Notre-Dame), a popular bistro on the Ile de la Cité.

AU PIED DU COCHON (6 Rue de Coquillier), a restored brasserie near the old market of Les Halles.

CAFÉ BEAUBOURG (Beaubourg Plaza), moderately priced cafe with a big terrace for people-watching and views of Beaubourg Centre.

TAILLEVENT (15 Rue Lamennais), the "hautest" of haute cuisine.

LA COUPOLE (102 boulevard du Montparnesse), classic brasserie.

GEORGES (top of the Pompidou Centre), worth visiting for the views.

CHEZ PAUL (22 Rue de la Butte-aux-Cailles), bistro classics in a corner of Old Paris.

LE GRAND COLBERT (Rue Vivienne), beautiful Opera district brasserie in the restored Galerie Colbert.

If you are really low on cash and homesick, there are dozens of McDonalds and Burger Kings, plus scores of sound-alikes all over Paris. What is the culinary world coming to?

Guides to Paris

EYEWITNESS GUIDE TO PARIS, Dorling Kindersley, London and New York. Wonderful photographs and guided walking itineraries.

ACCESS PARIS, Access Press, HarperCollins, New York. Detailed neighborhood walking tours that include sights, shops, and dining places where you need them.

MICHELIN GUIDES, PARIS. The old standbys, with green for sightseeing, and red, with those much-desired star ratings, for dining. The guides stay popular because they tell you what you need to know quickly, and the narrow size is easy to carry in your pocket or purse.

For free information, contact the French Government Tourist Office, 444 Madison Avenue, New York, NY 10022; (212) 838–7855; www.france tourism.com.

New York

This is my city. Almost all of us who live here have a love-hate relationship with the place. We grumble about the traffic, the subways, the rents, the prices, and the crowds. What keeps us here, however, are the same elements that make New York a fabulous place to visit: It is one of the most diverse and exciting cities in the world, overflowing with cultural riches, theater magic, marvelous food, and wares from around the globe. The old saying is true: If you can't find it in New York, it probably doesn't exist.

Even the sad events of September 11, 2001, could not dim the spirit of New York for long. The pace and pulse of the city are tangible, maybe daunting at the start but eventually drawing you in to pick up your step and share the excitement. If you can't have a wonderful time here, you just aren't trying.

The New York subway is intimidating to strangers and sometimes even to natives. To feel secure getting around the city, familiarize yourself with the bus system. Buses are slow but sure, and they provide a great inexpensive way to see the sights as well as the natives. You won't mind the traffic nearly so much if you aren't watching a taxi meter tick. You'll need exact change before you board, and no bills are accepted, so bring lots of change with you. Better yet, go down into any subway station and buy a Metrocard, which is also accepted on all buses. Each ride is automatically deducted when you board and slide the card through a slot. A "Funpass" card gives unlimited rides all day. (It is available from participating merchants all over the city; watch for the Metrocard symbol.)

Contrary to what many out-of-towners expect, getting your New York bearings is easy because most of Manhattan is laid out on a straight grid, with avenues running north to south and streets running east to west. The central business district is only about 16 blocks wide, and you'll spend most of your time within eight to ten of them. Bus transfers are free if you need to change from a "crosstown" (east-west) bus to one heading uptown or downtown (or vice versa). This is automatic with a Metrocard, but without one you have to ask for a transfer when you board the first bus, not when you are getting off. Metrocards also allow free transfers between buses and subways; without the card, you pay twice.

Bus routes are clearly marked on maps at most bus stops. A bus map is also printed on the back of the subway maps available free at token booths at the main city stations, or you can write to the New York Convention and Visitors Bureau (see page 251).

No one should miss a heart-stopping, skyscraper-high view of the city at night. Nothing else shows you so vividly why New York is unique. The Empire State Building observatory is open until midnight (last tickets sold at 11:25 P.M.). You

Only-in-New York Pleasures

Some favorite New Yorkers' pleasures that can be shared by visitors include:

- *Biking the car-free roadways on the weekend or jogging around the reservoir any day in Central Park (both activities recommended for daylight hours only).*
- *Sitting on the steps of the Metropolitan Museum of Art on Sunday afternoon and watching the street performers and the passing parade.*
- *Visiting the farmer's Green Market in Union Square on Wednesday, Friday, or Saturday.*
- *Weekend brunching and shopping in SoHo along Broadway, West Broadway, and the cross streets between.*
- *Wandering Eighth Street, West Fourth Street, Bleecker, and other Greenwich Village streets along with young and young-at-heart New Yorkers.*
- *Walking the promenade along the East River from the World Financial Center through Battery Park City, with the Statue of Liberty in view all the way.*
- *Evenings at the city museums. The Metropolitan Museum of Art is open until 9:00 P.M. on Friday and Saturday; the Museum of Modern Art until 8:00 P.M. on Friday (pay what you wish); the Whitney Museum until 9:00 P.M. on Friday (pay what you wish after 6:00 P.M.); the Guggenheim to 8:00 P.M. on Friday (voluntary donation after 6:00 P.M.); and the American Museum of Natural History Rose Center to 8:45 P.M. on Friday.*

might want to have a drink in the lounge of the Rainbow Room on the sixty-fifth floor of the RCA building or atop the Beekman Tower Hotel at First Avenue and 49th Street. A magical time to see the city from above is at dusk, when you can watch millions of city lights go on. For a dramatic view of the city from the water, there's nothing better than the free ride on the Staten Island Ferry from the Battery at the tip of Manhattan Island.

New Yorkers are champion walkers and they like exploring their city as much as visitors do, so when it comes to seeing specific neighborhoods on foot, you'll find a great choice of walking tours around almost every part of the city each weekend from late spring through fall. Some of these groups also offer bus excursions that make it easy to visit suburban attractions. Here are some of the leading organizations that offer guided walks and tours:

MUNICIPAL ART SOCIETY, 457 Madison Avenue at 50th Street, New York, NY 10022; (212) 935–3960.

92ND STREET Y, 1395 Lexington Avenue, New York, NY 10128; (212) 996–1105.

BIG ONION TOURS, (212) 439–1090.

Two of the city's landmarks offer free tours—the magnificent public library at Fifth Avenue and 42nd Street each Saturday at 11:00 A.M and 2:00 P.M., and the beautifully restored Grand Central Station, 42nd Street and Lexington Avenue, each Wednesday at 12:30 P.M.

Central Park is one of the city's glories, a beautiful site and the best place to see a microcosm of city life from baby strollers to rock concerts. In summer it is the scene of free concerts by the Metropolitan Opera and the New York Philharmonic, free Shakespeare in the Park, and a whole series of popular and rock music known as Summerstage. The park is perfectly safe in daylight and is filled with hundreds of people for performances. If you are nervous, however, join one of the guided Urban Park Ranger tours; schedules are available at The Dairy building in the park near 64th Street.

On a first trip to New York, Chinatown can be confusing and might well be better seen on a guided walking tour. But here are some suggested neighborhoods to roam safely on your own to get a sense of the city and its diversity (buy a book of self-guided walking tours to find out who lived where as you wander):

- The posh Upper East Side residential streets, roughly between 70th and 90th Streets from Fifth to Park Avenues
- The charming West Side neighborhoods from Central Park West to West End Avenue between 68th and 86th Streets
- The chic Madison Avenue shops from the 60s to the 90s
- The overpriced but enticing boutiques on Columbus Avenue from 68th to 81st Streets
- The winding streets and historic townhouses of Greenwich Village, the old heart of literary New York
- The dozens of galleries in Chelsea loft buildings west of Tenth Avenue, roughly between 19th and 26th Streets

- Evening strolls where New York's trendy young pack the streets to dine and drink in the old Meat Packing District north of Greenwich Village, west of Ninth Avenue between Little 12th and 14th Streets.

Shopping is a favorite New York pastime. Besides the special merchandise carried by the hundreds of small shops, out-of-towners often find the variety of wares in the big department stores such as Macy's, Saks Fifth Avenue, and Bloomingdale's a revelation. Most of the branches in major cities can't compare with the home stores. And the advent of superstores like Bed, Bath and Beyond means stocks so enormous you can hardly get through the whole store.

Designer boutiques are to be found on Fifth Avenue between 55th and 57th Streets, on 57th Street between Fifth and Madison Avenues, and on Madison above 59th Street. The new, hip designers are selling their wildly expensive wares on 14th Street between Ninth and Tenth Avenues in the Meat Packing District.

For bargains, if you know your labels, you can venture down to the Lower East Side. Bargains do still exist, but you will also find that trendy boutiques have invaded the old neighborhood. Note that stores are closed on Saturday in this once-Jewish neighborhood, and Sunday is the busiest shopping day. Free guided tours by the Lower East Side Visitor Center leave every Sunday at 11:00 A.M., April through December, from Katz's Delicatessen, 205 East Houston Street. Phone (888) 825–8374 for information. Without a tour, it is a good idea to go armed with one of the special shopping guides to the area sold in most bookstores.

Another pleasure not to be missed by book lovers is the city's trove of wonderful specialized bookstores. Among the many stops providing hours of happy browsing are the beautiful Rizzoli store at 31 West 57th Street; specialty shops such as The Biography Bookshop at 400 Bleecker Street; The Drama Book Shop for theater books at 250 West 40th Street; Kitchen Arts & Letters at 1435 Lexington Avenue between 93rd and 94th Streets; The Military Bookman at 29 East 93rd Street; Hacker Art Books, 45 West 57th Street; and Murder Ink., a treasure trove of mystery novels at 2486 Broadway at 92nd Street. Check the Yellow Pages for addresses of the big Barnes and Noble and Borders superstores now found all over town, most with a coffee bar for browsers and favorite meeting spots for single New Yorkers. Used-book treasures are available at the Strand at 828 Broadway at 12th Street, the Argosy at 116 East 59th Street, and the Gotham Book Mart at 41 West 47th Street. The Yellow Pages will guide you to dozens of other specialists for everything from comic books to collectors' volumes.

No trip to New York is complete without a visit to the theaters and concert halls. To avoid spending a king's ransom, take advantage of the TKTS booth (Times Square Ticket Center) at 47th Street and Broadway. Half-priced tickets for Broadway and off-Broadway shows are sold on the day of the performance starting at 3:00 P.M., and at 10:00 A.M. for matinees on Wednesday, Saturday, or Sunday. If you happen to be sightseeing downtown, there is a branch of TKTS, usually with much shorter lines, at South Street Seaport.

Contrary to another popular belief, everything in New York does not cost pots of money. Television shows are one favorite free pastime, but you must get your request in early—at least one month in advance and often as much as six months ahead for the hot shows. Some networks will mail out ticket requests received by phone; others ask you to send in a postcard. At times, standby tickets may be available the morning of the show. Singles have a good shot. You can also pick up same-day tickets on occasion at the New York Visitors Bureau at 810 Seventh Avenue at 53rd Street or the Times Square Visitor Center, Broadway between 46th and 47th Streets. A complete list of contacts for tapings in New York can be found on their Web site, www.nycvisit.com, under "Things to Do." For up-to-date information on your favorite show, it's best to phone. Network numbers are: ABC, (212) 456–3054; CBS, (212) 975–2476; NBC, (212) 664–3057. Everyone is welcome to watch the *Today* show through the window daily 7:00 to 9:00 A.M at Rockefeller Plaza and 49th Street.

It won't cost you a cent to take in a master class or attend high-quality, free concerts by faculty and students at the noted Juilliard School; phone in advance for schedules and ticket information at (212) 799–5000. Thursday morning rehearsals of the New York Philharmonic at Avery Fisher Hall are open to the public for a modest fee.

There are numerous free concerts as well in building atriums (such as the glorious Winter Garden at the World Financial Center), museums, and outdoor plazas around the city. Check *New York* or *Time Out* magazines or the Convention and Visitors Bureau at (212) 484–1222; for a free guidebook, phone (800) NYC–VISIT (www.nycvisit.com).

Any guidebook will list the city's leading hotels. If you can't afford the top listings, but you prefer a small hotel to bed-and-breakfast homes, here are a few inexpensive and moderate recommendations. All are area code 212.

PICKWICK ARMS
(230 East 51st Street; 355-0300) offers no frills at all but a good, safe, East Side location.

HOTEL METRO
(45 East 35th Street; 947-2500) is breezy and cheerful and offers complimentary breakfast.

EDISON
(228 West 47th Street; 840-5000) is a refurbished hotel in the heart of the theater district; it saves searching for cabs after the show.

WYNDHAM

(42 West 58th Street; 753–3500) provides big, pretty rooms, dated plumbing, and the best values in town. It has new owners, so things may change; best to check.

New York has a growing number of chain hotels at moderate prices. Apple Core Hotels is a reservation service for several of these, including Best Western, Comfort Inn, Super 8, and Ramada (800–567–7720; www.applecorehotels.com). Most include breakfast, a nice savings.

Affinia Hotels (866–246–2203; www.affinia.com) offer spacious studios and suites and kitchens in several locations, for the price of many moderate hotel rooms. They are good values.

Consider leaving the midtown business center and seeing New York like a native by taking advantage of the city's bed-and-breakfast registries (see page 212). They'll show you what real life is like in the Big Apple, where in warm weather people sunbathe in the parks on Sunday and sit around in sidewalk cafes. Having checked out a number of these lodgings for a recent article, I was surprised at the lovely apartments available as B&Bs. It says a lot about the price of housing in New York that so many people are welcoming paying guests.

Where to dine alone in New York? There are plenty of options. If you want ambience, you'll find cafes even in some of the tiniest hotels. Check the Zagat guide for a long list of restaurants with dining at the bar. You'll no doubt make your own discoveries as you walk around, but some suggested havens for dining alone, by neighborhood, include:

Midtown

THE OYSTER BAR

(lower level in Grand Central Station, 42nd Street and Lexington Avenue) provides counter service and a number of small tables; it's tops for seafood.

THE HUDSON CAFETERIA

(356 West 58th Street) is a dramatic space in the trendy Hudson Hotel, with long tables where it is easy to strike up a conversation.

ASIA DE CUBA

(237 Madison Avenue between 37th and 38th Streets) is a trendy favorite for its fusion menu and a singles favorite for the big communal table.

CARNEGIE DELICATESSEN

(854 Seventh Avenue between 54th and 55th Streets) is a New York landmark with wisecracking waiters, long, cramped tables, and legendary corned beef and pastrami sandwiches.

CHEZ NAPOLEON

(365 West 50th Street) is a homey, family-run French bistro, convenient for theatergoers.

OSTERIA DEL CIRCO

(120 West 55th Street) has playful circus decor, tasty (if a bit pricey) Italian food, and a most convivial dining bar. Men love the female bartenders.

LA VINERIA

(19 West 55th Street) is a small, friendly Italian cafe with excellent food and reasonable prices.

EDISON CAFE

(at the Hotel Edison at 228 West 47th Street) offers potato pancakes, blintzes, matzo ball soup, and the chance that show-biz biggies will stop in between shows.

LA BONNE SOUPE

(48 West 55th Street) is good for a light dinner.

BRASSERIE

(100 East 53rd Street) has a long bar where you can enjoy the inventive menu and the chic decor.

DERVISH TURKISH RESTAURANT

(146 West 47th Street) serves good food and has a bargain pre-theater prix fixe menu.

Upper West Side

Browse Columbus Avenue and its side streets between 65th and 81st Streets for limitless possibilities—just pick a cafe that doesn't have a line spilling out the door! If you aren't going to Lincoln Center, come after 8:00 P.M. when the crowds are smaller. A few recommendations:

CAFE FIORELLO

(1900 Broadway between 63rd and 64th Streets); have a seat at the antipasto bar and feast before an evening at Lincoln Center, just across the street.

PASHA

(70 West 71st Street) is calm and attractive and serves excellent Turkish food. Convenient to Lincoln Center.

SCALETTA

(50 West 77th Street) is a spacious, old-fashioned Italian restaurant with quiet ambience.

Upper East Side

Browse Second Avenue between 74th and 86th Streets, and 86th Street east or
west of Second Avenue, and you'll have experienced a mini world tour of cuisines.
Try one of these:

SEL & POIVRE
(853 Lexington Avenue between 64th and 65th Streets), a pleasant French restaurant,
offers good value prix fixe dinners.

EJ'S LUNCHEONETTE
(1271 Third Avenue at 73rd Street), a neighborhood favorite, serves all three meals at
agreeably moderate prices.

WU LIANG YE
(215 East 86th Street between Second and Third Avenues) is one of the best of the
neighborhood's many Chinese choices.

LE PAIN QUOTIDIEN
(1131 Madison Avenue between 83rd and 84th Streets) serves breakfast, lunch, and
early dinner (to 7:00 P.M.) at a congenial 26-foot-long communal table.

BELLA CUCINA
(1293 Lexington Avenue at 87th Street) is a pleasant, reasonably priced Italian
eatery.

VIAND
(300 East 86th Street and also at 1011 Madison Avenue and at 673 Madison Avenue) is
an upscale coffee shop with wide-ranging diner-style menus and surprisingly good
food. The upper Madison Avenue address is ideal if you are visiting the
Metropolitan or Whitney museums.

Greenwich Village/SoHo

Pick any block and you'll likely find tiny, welcoming restaurants. Here are some
possibilities:

NEXT DOOR NOBU
(105 Hudson Street) serves the same great food as its pricey namesake. No reservations, so come early.

JOHN'S PIZZERIA
(278 Bleecker Street) is generally agreed to be New York's best, as attested by the
long lines. Come at an off-hour.

WHITE HORSE TAVERN
(Hudson and 11th Streets) is a neighborhood classic over a century old.

ZOE
(90 Prince Street) has a popular counter where diners can watch the chef in action.

CHEZ BRIGETTE
(77 Greenwich Avenue) is a hole-in-the-wall spot with counters—and incredible French food. Great for onion soup at lunch.

BABBO
(110 Waverly Place), a busy trattoria, usually has seats at the handsome bar and excellent wines by the glass to go with the pasta.

NORTH SQUARE
(103 Waverly Place) has snug ambience, good food, and good prices.

Don't leave the Village without sampling its coffee houses. Two suggestions are:

CAFFE RAFAELLA
(134 Seventh Avenue) has salads as well as coffee and dessert.

CAFFE REGGIO
(119 MacDougal Street) offers incredible desserts.

The East Village

Here's where young New York eats on a budget. A few favorites follow:

"Little India," covering all of 6th Street between First and Second Avenues, and spilling over onto First Avenue, is lined with tiny Indian restaurants, most BYOB. There are at least a dozen to try. **Mitali East** at 334 East 6th Street gets good reviews—or just pick the decor that pleases you; some people joke that they all use the same kitchen, anyway. Better Indian food, still quite inexpensive, is found on **"Curry Hill,"** Lexington Avenue between 27th and 29th Streets. One recommendation: **Curry Leaf** at 99 Lexington.

CHRISTINE'S
(208 First Avenue between 12th and 13th Streets) has zero decor but is noted for inexpensive and hearty Polish home cooking.

TERESA'S
(103 First Avenue at 6th Street) is another downtown Polish choice.

A Tip about Tips

Most New Yorkers find it easiest to just double the tax (8¼ percent) on their restaurant bills and leave a 16.5 percent tip. The difference from the usual 15 percent is negligible, and it saves lots of mental arithmetic.

Union Square Area

UNION SQUARE CAFE
(21 East 16th Street) This is a stylish cafe—one of the city's favorites—with an innovative menu and a long bar where singles dine comfortably.

GOTHAM BAR & GRILL
(12 East 12th Street, 620–4020), another of the city's top restaurants, welcomes with special trays that attach to the bar to make single diners comfortable. Their prix fixe lunch ($20.05 or $20.06, depending on the year) is a great deal.

Guides to New York

Recommended guides to the city are:

Eyewitness Guide to New York by Dorling Kindersley (London and New York)

Nooks and Crannies: A Walking Tour Guide to New York City by David Yeadon (Charles Scribner's Sons, New York)

AIA Guide to New York City by Elliot Willensky and Norval White (Harcourt Brace, New York). A knowledgeable architectural guide for walking tours.

Frommer's Irreverent Guide to Manhattan
(Macmillan, New York). An honest appraisal of what's good and bad around the city.

Access New York City
(HarperCollins, New York). Handy street-by-street format.

New York Neighborhoods
(Globe Pequot, Guilford, Connecticut). My own guide for visitors who want to explore the city's ethnic neighborhoods beyond Manhattan.

Bring the Kids

BUSY SINGLE PARENTS WHO TAKE DOUBLE RESPONSIBILITY FOR THEIR kids most of the year really deserve a vacation. They most often want to share that vacation with the children. They look forward to rare relaxed and unscheduled time to have fun together, family time to really talk and share. Having kids for company actually solves certain travel problems, such as solitary meals.

Yet, while shared family vacations can be wonderfully rewarding, single parents also need a break. In fact, each generation benefits from time off for relaxing and socializing with people in their own age group. For parents, that doesn't necessarily mean looking for romance—just a bit of adult companionship and conversation. So, the most successful single-parent outings with the kids offer both the opportunity for togetherness and time to be apart.

For that reason, some traditional family vacations aren't really great for single parents. One parent trying to keep up with two or three kids at Walt Disney World might be exhausted instead of exhilarated. Car trips can be miserable with no one to share the driving or the disciplining of the children. And resorts with children's programs can be populated mostly by couples who are relishing time together while *their* kids are busy, and they are therefore not much company for a parent alone. Luckily, there are options that offer both togetherness and a chance for separate activities.

Some Practical Pointers

Start by planning something *you* really want to do, regardless of the kids. Ranches are wonderful places for family vacations, but if you hate the idea of getting on a horse, life on a ranch isn't going to be any more appealing just because the children are along.

As with any family outing, arrangements generally work out better if the youngsters are involved in the planning and are excited about the trip. If there are choices to be made, even preschoolers can look at color brochures and have some say in what looks great to them. Let the children help write for brochures and information, using their own names so that the mail comes back addressed to them. If you decide on a city vacation, have them participate in making lists of what you hope to do each day. Readers can make a trip to the library to get books about the area you will be visiting.

A productive pretrip activity is to have children put together a scrapbook with space for preplanning and a day-to-day diary with room to paste in souvenirs as you travel. It helps build anticipation beforehand and keeps them busy along the way.

Older kids can also help put together those tried-and-true travel games, such as making a list of states that can be checked off when their license plates are spied. Another family favorite is printing the alphabet down the side of a sheet of notebook paper for each child, with space to fill in objects spotted for each letter. Don't forget to bring favorite books, toys, and other games to keep everyone happily occupied.

When you pack, choose comfortable, fast-drying clothing in dark colors so you needn't nag about keeping clothes clean on vacation. Be sure to include rainwear in case of bad weather.

Two issues that make for crabby tempers on family vacations are fatigue and hunger. Do your best to avoid both. Be prepared with snacks during travel times and in hotel rooms. Unfamiliar beds and schedules and the excitement of new places can wreak havoc with bedtimes, so plan time out for rest each day. It will do you good, too.

Keep traveling time to a minimum. Pack a small bag for each child with pajamas, toothbrush, toothpaste, and a favorite blanket and toy, so they can settle into a new place fast. If you need cribs and high chairs, call ahead to double-check that they are available and in place.

Resources for Single Parents

The growing number of single parents has spawned more interest in their specific needs. One especially useful source is a Web site and newsletter, the *Single Parent Travel Network,* www.singleparenttravel.net. The site includes advice, tips, and travel suggestions, as well as bargains, a free newsletter, and the chance to ask questions or post concerns on bulletin boards. The author, Brenda Elwell, has also published a book, *The Single Parent Travel Handbook,* which includes a list of recommended travel agents. It can be ordered from the Web site for $17.95. Her most recent venture, www.singleparenttours.com, offers trips including ranches and beach and adventure vacations.

Quality Time Travel, (Box 1141, Commack, NY 11725; 888–758–9386 or 631–543–4009; www.qualitytimetravel.com) is another travel agency specializing in single-parent vacations. They offer a dozen trips a year during school vacation periods. Recent options have included a dude ranch, Florida beaches, and a Caribbean cruise.

The Family Travel Forum, a Web site at www.familytravelforum.com, occasionally addresses issues of interest to single parents, such as the advisability of a notarized letter from the absent parent if you are traveling out of the country.

Family Adventure Magazine, (P.O. Box 469, Woodstock, NY 12498; 845–679–9321; www.familyadventuretravel.com) is not geared to single parents, but is a useful resource. The Web site lists and describes dozens of companies offering family adventure travel around the world, and has articles about family trips to exotic places. The companies are indexed by destination and activities, with links to operators.

Single parents looking for adventurous family vacations will find lots of ideas in two books by Candyce Stapen, *National Geographic Guide to Family Adventure Vacations* and *National Geographic Guide to Caribbean Family Vacations.*

Singular Parent Choices

Some of the vacation choices recommended for single adults are equally comfortable for single-parent families. Active adventure vacations are wonderful for youngsters who are old enough to enjoy them. Almost all are appropriate for teens, and some can accommodate much younger children. Ask the operator about the ages recommended. Some groups that explicitly welcome children are listed below, along with learning options that have separate programs for youngsters.

Ranch vacations are made to order for single parents, and all the guidance on page 27 is appropriate for families. Cruising from a family point of view is covered later in this chapter. See page 106 for information on Windjammer cruises. Teenagers love the adventure of these big sailing ships, but restless younger children are not well suited to these trips. For them, stick to the ocean liners. If you want to go to a resort, check for tennis, sailing, or golf schools that are resort-based and have children's programs. Those arrangements will give you a focus, and you can make friends while the children enjoy their own brand of fun.

Here are a variety of vacation suggestions for single parents:

CLUB MED
(See page 183) (M–E)

Club Med doesn't just tolerate children—Club Med welcomes them, and they welcome single parents, too. At Club Med villages that have been designated for families, kids' programs entertain and teach children ages 1 to 11 with nonstop activities, meals, and amusements, supervised and coordinated by a special staff, all at no additional cost. Programs run from 8:00 A.M. to 9:00 P.M. daily, and there are optional kid-pleasing early lunches and dinners to give parents the chance to enjoy conversation with other adults at meals.

Villages for families are found in many locations. Programs are divided by age for youngsters. Kids can stop by for one favorite activity, for an hour, or for the entire day. Baby Clubs take children from 4 months to 2 years; Petit Clubs, from 2 to 4 years, and Mini Clubs, from 4 to 12 years. During school breaks, a Junior Club welcomes teens.

All four programs are available at Sandpiper in Florida and Ixtapa in Mexico. Punta Cana in the Dominican Republic has facilities for all but babies, and Mini and Junior Clubs are available at Caravelle in Guadeloupe and Crested Butte in Colorado, the latter a best bet in winter for families who want to ski.

Baby Clubs are equipped with cribs, playpens, and toys. Strollers, potties, and baby monitors can be borrowed at no extra charge. They even sell diapers in the boutiques. How family-minded can you get?

Activities vary from village to village. Among the fun possibilities are lessons in skiing, waterskiing, sailing, golf, and tennis, plus arts and crafts, archery, boat rides, picnics, trapeze, and swimming.

Ask about special family rates; discounts are often available.

SIERRA CLUB FAMILY OUTINGS
(See page 90) (I)

Introducing families to the joys of camping and the outdoors is one of the missions of the Sierra Club. Many outings each summer are designated especially for families, and single parents as well as uncles, aunts, and grandparents are welcome. The difficulty of the trips varies. Most trips are lodge-based; others are at campsites. All offer opportunities for nature study, day hikes, fishing, swimming, and solitude. The group meets for breakfast and supper; lunch for outings is packed at breakfast. Most activities are informal and unstructured, and the group usually makes its own fun in the evening. Mother-daughter and grandparent-grandkids are among the offerings.

Among recent offerings were lodge-based toddler adventures appropriate for very young children. Other adventures included trips to Hawaii and Alaska with rafting, kayaking, and wilderness adventures.

FAMILY GOES TO CAMP
SHERI GRIFFITH EXPEDITIONS
(See page 108) (M)

The most exciting river runs are recommended for ages 10 and up, but special two- to five-day family trips, fun but not difficult, are open to children from age 5. Camping is on sandy beaches. Hiking excursions are part of the trips. Meals take pint-size tastes into account by including hamburgers as well as steak. After dark come campfires, roasted marshmallows, and plenty of talk and song.

Guides also take the children on separate outings. Parents can join in or take this time for themselves—for quiet relaxation beside the river, a leisurely walk, or a demanding hike. According to the operators, many of the adults are single parents.

FAMILY RAFTING
O.A.R.S. RAFTING ADVENTURES
(See page 109) (I)

For families who want to be introduced to the fun and excitement of river rafting, special discounts are offered on half a dozen selected family dates for trips on the many rivers this company navigates. The regular trips offered by this group also welcome children of specified minimum ages, starting at 4 years for some of the shorter, easier trips and starting at 16 years for the more rugged rivers.

FAMILY RAFTING
DVORAK'S RAFTING EXPEDITIONS
(See page 110) (I–M)

On specified family weeks, this outfitter invites one child under the age of 13 to come along free with an adult. These trips on the Green and Dolores Rivers are planned with kids in mind. Reserve early—they fill up fast.

Other short trips suitable as an introduction to river-running offer discounts for families of three and up.

FAMILY SUMMIT PROGRAM
NATIONAL WILDLIFE FEDERATION
(See page 117) (I)

Most of the programs for adults offer separate supervised activities for children and child care for those younger than preschool age. A nature discovery program for preschoolers includes micro-hikes, touch-and-feel expeditions, and fun-with-nature crafts. "Junior Naturalists," for ages 5 to 12, divide into age groups for nature hikes, stream studies, wildlife investigations, bird walks, folktale hours, outdoor games, fishing, camping, and arts and crafts. A separate Teen Adventure program is adventure oriented, with field trips, camping, hiking, and the chance to learn more about the environment.

CORNELL'S ADULT UNIVERSITY
(See page 45) (I–M)

Although the title says adult, kids are far from forgotten here. Youngsters from all over the United States enroll in the Youth Program, having fun while their parents are learning on their own level. Families always have breakfast and dinner together, but child supervision is available from 8:30 A.M. to 11:15 P.M. for those who want it.

Programming is provided for five age groups. Infants and tots under 3 have no formal schedule, but qualified babysitters are available. Li'l Bears (ages 3 to 5) learn and play in a Cornell preschool facility. Art, music, crafts, expeditions across campus, and time to rest are all part of their fun. (Children enrolled must be potty trained.) Tykes (5- and 6-year-olds who have been to school) have their own similar sessions.

Explorers (ages 7 and 8) have a learning program as well as hikes, games, sports, crafts, and cookouts. Junior Cornellians (ages 11 to 13) and Big Reds (ages 9 and 10) meet in the morning for a choice of classes and have recreational activities, outings to state parks, visits to campus facilities, and presentations and demonstrations by members of the faculty during supervised afternoon and evening programs. They can choose from a variety of classes including music, geology, astronomy, theater, and architecture, as well as sailing, horseback riding, and outdoor adventures.

Teens (ages 13 to 16) have an even wider selection, and they have their own reserved dormitory floor and dining place.

CHAUTAUQUA INSTITUTION
(See page 49) (I–M)

While parents enjoy the multitude of classes and cultural events during the summer at Chautauqua, youngsters can enroll in the diverse children's programs offered. Programs are for one week to a full season.

Children's School, held from 9:00 A.M. to noon daily, is an early childhood center for preschoolers from age 3. It includes language enrichment, pre-reading, early math concepts, and exposure to the arts as well as creative free play. The Boys' and Girls' Club for ages 7 to 15 is organized as a day camp where children get a full schedule of summer recreation such as swimming, sailing, canoeing, arts and crafts, drama, music, archery, basketball, soccer, volleyball, and baseball. The group is divided into sections according to age.

For teenagers, the Youth Activities Center is open daily from noon to 11:00 P.M. It has its own beach (with diving board), a snack bar, amusement machines, Ping-Pong equipment, table games, and color television. Dances, cookouts, guest speakers, and movies are offered at night.

YOSEMITE OUTDOOR ADVENTURES
(See page 122) (I, tuition only)

Activities for families include one-day programs for ages 7 to 13 and family camping "jamborees" featuring walks and hikes and learning about nature.

ANDERSON RANCH ARTS CENTER
(See page 79)

This top arts and crafts center is one of the few with workshops for children as well as adults, at least one offering for each week of the summer program. Ages as young as 6 to 8 can enjoy using clay, painting, or making prints. Printmaking, fused glass, fiber techniques, sculpting, and book-making were recent courses for 9- to 12-year-olds, and ages 13 to 17 can choose ceramics, photography, painting, sculpture, or woodworking. Lodgings in two-bedroom condominiums close to the Center are ideal for families, and the surrounding mountains make for great family hikes.

BACKROADS BICYCLING VACATIONS
(See page 95) (I–M)

Several of this group's tours, both camping and with inn lodging, are designated as family outings. Recent destinations have included Washington State's Puget Sound, the Canadian Rockies, Maine, Vermont, Nova Scotia, and excursions in Europe and Latin America.

COUNTRY WALKERS
(See page 103)

Several family adventures are offered with moderate walking and beautiful destinations from Canada to Costa Rica.

BUTTERFIELD & ROBINSON
(See page 99)

Family biking and hiking trips are offered around the globe, recommended for specific age groups, 8+, 12+, and 15+. A trip for all ages, including tots, is based at a lodge in Provence.

RASCALS IN PARADISE
One Daniel Burnham Court, San Francisco, CA 94109;
(415) 921–7000 or (800) U–RASCAL; www.rascalsinparadise.com (EE)

Hawaii and Honduras, Alaska and Africa, Florida and Fiji are among the far-flung family offerings of this California-based group, whose trips include the Caribbean, Mexico, Central and South America, Europe, the Middle East, Africa, Asia, and the South Pacific. Age minimums vary with the difficulty of the trip and are as low as 3 years for many destinations. To make the experience easier for families, on most trips the group establishes one home base and goes exploring on day trips. Kids have a separate menu, and mealtimes bring familiar foods even in remote climes.

The operators also specialize in booking family-oriented resort vacations at sites such as FDR and Pebbles that specialize in family vacations.

THOMSON FAMILY ADVENTURES
347 Broadway, Cambridge, MA 02139; (800) 262–6255;
www.familyadventures.com (EE)

This is another option for adventuresome (and well-heeled) parents from a company that has been doing adventure travel for over twenty years. They promise small groups of fifteen to twenty for family-oriented trips to Africa, Turkey, the Galápagos and Andes, Costa Rica, Canada, Alaska, and Australia, as well as U.S. journeys to national parks or rafting trips.

FAMILY SAFARIS
(see page 132)

United Touring International, Park East Tours, Micato, and Abercrombie & Kent all include a family safari in their African itineraries.

FDR (FRANKLYN D. RESORTS)
c/o P.O. Box 7499, Freeport, NY 11520;
(888) FDRKIDS or (800) 654–1FDR; www.fdrholidays.com (EE)

A one-of-a-kind Jamaica resort, FDR offers all-suite accommodations and a Vacation Nanny for each family to take the pressure off Mom or Dad. Children's activities such as arts and crafts lessons, shell-collecting, and dress-up parties give adults time to enjoy water sports or shopping trips. Both generations can enjoy trips to Dunns River Falls and the Computer Cyber Cafe, where guests are given computer lessons and may receive e-mail or surf the Internet. A newer property, FDR Pebbles, in Trelawny, Jamaica, offers soft adventure holidays with hiking, cycling, camping, fishing, and other activities for pre-teens and teens, and sometimes offers special deals for families on a budget.

Family Cruise Vacations

Children love cruise ships. They love climbing the steps or riding the elevators from one deck to another; they like the pools and the gyms and all the activities and entertainment on board; they adore scampering down the gangplank to see a brand-new port. The constant parade of food is a treat, especially since it usually includes familiar favorites like hamburgers and ice cream as well as sophisticated fare. Teens enjoy it too—provided they find company aboard. Some ships provide special video/disco centers where they can meet others their age.

Cruising certainly is not an inexpensive family vacation, but it can be a memorable one, and many of the problems of cruising alone are solved when you have your family along.

Almost any itinerary seems exciting, but The Disney Cruise Line (Box 22804, Lake Buena Vista, FL 32830; 800–951–3532; www.disneycruise.disney.go.com)

specializes in families and offers the largest dedicated space for kids at sea, with age-specific programming starting at age 3 from morning to night. Older teens have their own teen club and game arcade. Of course, Disney characters are around to please the kids, and the lavish entertainment is planned for families. Seven-night Caribbean cruises and three- and four-day cruises from Cape Canaveral to the Bahamas are offered, and they can be combined with visits to the Disney theme parks.

Most cruise lines today recognize that families are good business and provide special activities, from babysitters to crafts programs to pizza parties. Many have children's playrooms. Norwegian, Royal Caribbean, Celebrity, and Princess are among the lines with special age-appropriate activities for cruisers ages 3 to 17. On its Alaska cruises, Holland America has offered just-for-kids excursions to fly in a bush plane or kayak around icebergs.

Many cruise lines allow children under 3 to share their parents' staterooms, and most have special children's rates or reduced fares for the third and fourth passengers in a cabin. Reduced rates and children's programs vary with the seasons, and some lines offer them only during school breaks. Choose carefully so that you can look forward to smooth sailing on a family vacation. Cruise specialists listed on page 169 can help.

Ski Weeks

Skiing is a wonderful family sport. Even the youngest children take to the slopes with glee, and thanks to nurseries and lessons for children, parents can find free time to take off at their own ability level. The bigger ski resorts typically have centers that accommodate children from infants to ages 6 or 8. You can leave the children for an hour or two or for the day.

As the kids get older, skiing allows for plenty of independence. After one or two family runs, everyone usually goes off to his or her own challenges, reuniting for lunch and at day's end. If the weather is uncooperative, parents can stay by the fire or read a book in the lodge while gung-ho youngsters brave the elements. In our family, skiing was the one family vacation that remained popular even after my children were in college and traveling on their own.

If you can afford it, the ideal situation for families is a lodge within walking distance of the slopes or one that has shuttle service to the mountain. This means eager beavers can be first on the slopes while parents get needed rest, and everyone can quit and go home when they are ready.

Another good bet is the Club Med at Crested Butte, Colorado.

Every ski area offers money-saving ski week packages with or without lessons, and many have additional savings for children who stay in parents' rooms. Families also may choose less expensive, less crowded, smaller ski areas while children are still young and need less challenge. The best plan is to pick several areas that interest you and write for current programs.

Single Grandparents

Single grandparents and their grandchildren can make great traveling companions. Each generation widens the other's perspective, and a trip affords them a wonderful chance to get to know each other better and bond for life.

GRANDTRAVEL, A DIVISION OF ACADEMIC TRAVEL ABROAD, INC.
1920 N Street NW, Suite 200, Washington, DC 20036; (202) 785–8901 or
(800) 247–7651; www.grandtrvl.com

Grandtravel was the first to make it easier to arrange this type of trip, usually scheduled during school breaks. These escorted tours take care of all travel arrangements, and they provide time for each generation to be alone with their peers as well as ample time together. The kids might go roller skating while the grandparents go out for a gourmet dinner. The grandparents typically are in their 60s or early 70s, the grandchildren ages 7 to 14. Among the U.S. destinations are the western national parks; Washington, D.C.; New York; the desert Southwest; Pacific Northwest; and Alaska. Foreign itineraries have included England, Scotland, Australia, Russia, China, Italy, London and Paris, and safaris in Kenya.

More Options

The Sierra Club (see page 260) also has a special week in its family programs set aside for grandparents. Elderhostel (page 198) and Interhostel (page 199) have added intergenerational outings. And several cruise lines are offering discounts for passengers older than 55 during certain periods.

City Safaris

Parents who prefer an outing solely for their own family would do well to think about visiting a city. Kids really wax enthusiastic about picking a city and planning what to see and do. All you have to do to keep everybody happy is to allot a fair share of time for activities that appeal to youngsters as well as grown-ups.

For the happiest outings, plan an itinerary alternating your choices with those of the children. Intersperse museum visits with trips to the zoo, the beach, or an aquarium, for example. If you insist on shopping with children along, reward them with a performance at a children's theater or a children's movie. Look for boat rides, major league baseball games, and other sure-to-please treats everyone can share. While you are researching reasonable family-priced dining, look out also for the best local ice-cream emporiums. Above all, provide plenty of breaks such as excursions to city parks where kids can run and play or use up excess energy on a rented bike. Parks offer a bonus for parents, for while the smaller members of the family are letting off steam, adults can gain a special perspective watching everyday local life they might otherwise have missed.

The growth of all-suite hotels with two rooms for the price of one is a real boon for families. These are equivalent in price to standard hotels and offer space, privacy, refrigerators, and separate TVs; some even have cooking facilities. While you may not want to spend your vacation cooking, having snacks, drinks, and breakfast ingredients on hand is a real money-saver. Some of the all-suite chains also include a free breakfast.

Most bed-and-breakfast facilities, however, are not good choices for families with young children. Healthy, noisy little ones often feel much too restricted in someone else's home. And somehow, even a budget motel seems more exciting, more of a special outing.

Almost any major city presents opportunities for family adventures, but those with easy and inexpensive public transportation systems offer a special advantage.

Chicago

Chicago is one of my top picks for family fun. It is filled with kid-pleasing attractions, is easy to navigate, and is easy on the budget. You can stay in a high-rise Motel 6 in the heart of the city! Most of the city's museums have a free admission day, and the Lincoln Park Zoo is free whenever you visit. Too much sightseeing? Take a break at Oak Street beach, right in town.

Navy Pier and its 150-foot Ferris wheel is almost reason enough for a visit. The revitalized 1916 pier, a city landmark, is a spectacular playground on the lake with more than fifty acres of parks, an old-fashioned carousel, ice skating in winter, and a big, bright children's museum.

Cruises leaving from Navy Pier and along the Chicago River, which runs through the city to the lake, are a wonderful way to appreciate the great architecture in this town where the skyscraper was born. The Chicago Architecture Foundation runs the most informative river trips.

Another popular perspective on the skyline is from the 103rd-floor sky deck of the Sears Tower, one of the tallest skyscrapers in the world.

The Art Institute, home to many of the world's most famous works of art, has a wonderful interactive introduction to art for kids in the Kraft General Foods Education Center, where paintings are hung at kids'-eye level. Family Days are planned to highlight various parts of the collection.

Allow plenty of time for the Museum of Science and Industry, Chicago's most visited attraction, a vast building covering more than fifteen acres with more than 2,000 exhibits, including the chance to descend into a realistic reproduction of a coal mine, tour an actual U-505 submarine, and be strapped in for a simulated space-shuttle flight.

Grant Park on the lakefront includes three major museums. The Field Museum of Natural History features a four-story brachiosaurus, the world's largest mounted dinosaur, and the Adler Planetarium has a special Sky Show for kids. Everyone enjoys visiting the beluga whales, sharks, sea otters, and penguins at the Oceanarium in the Shedd Aquarium.

Farther north on the lake is Lincoln Park and its thirty-five-acre zoo, home to more than 2,000 mammals. There is a separate children's zoo where many baby animals can be seen and small animals like rabbits can be petted, plus the Farm in the Zoo, a working farm with the chance to see milking every day. All of this is free.

Another family pleasure in Chicago is bicycling along miles of maintained trails. *Bicycle Magazine* selected Chicago as the "Best Cycling City in the United States" in the category of big cities with over one million population.

At dinnertime, sample Chicago's famous deep-dish pizza, or visit the one and only Rock 'n Roll McDonald's.

For information, contact the Chicago Convention and Tourism Bureau, 2301 South Lake Shore Drive, Chicago, IL 60616; (877) CHICAGO; www.choosechicago.com

Boston

Another of my favorite cities to visit with children is Boston, home of the New England Aquarium, with its exciting dolphin shows, a fabulous Children's Museum, and the country's only Computer Museum, a surefire hit with most youngsters. In Boston, kids can have a lively history lesson walking the red line of the Freedom Trail, tossing their own chest of tea overboard on the Boston Tea Party ship, and boarding "Old Ironsides," the USS *Constitution*. A visit to Paul Revere's home and the Old North Church in the North End can be followed by dinner at one of the area's many Italian restaurants, with unbeatable cannoli for dessert.

The National Park Service offers Freedom Trail guided tours from its information center at 15 State Street, or you can sign up for a citywide family tour, Boston by Little Feet (617–367–2345), designed for ages 6 to 12 (accompanied by adults).

A not-to-be-missed adventure is a Boston Duck Tour in an amphibious craft that tours city streets, then does a splash-down into the Charles River for a cruise.

The famous swan boats are out in the Public Garden in warm weather, offering rides near the spot made famous by Robert McCloskey's classic children's picture book *Make Way for Ducklings*. Read the book before you go.

Kids also love visiting the food booths at Quincy Market, where lavish choices for every taste include pizza and brownies as well as a whole world of ethnic fare, all to be enjoyed at outdoor tables to the tune of free entertainment by street musicians. This is also a great city for sports lovers; especially popular are the baseball games at Fenway Park, one of the country's last classic arenas. Game tickets are hard to come by, but tours of the field are fun for all.

Don't overlook the Esplanade beside the Charles River, a great place for watching roller skaters, joggers, rowing crews, and sailboats in action. A walk up Beacon Hill is a wonderful way to see what cities were like in America a long time ago. Trolley tours and double-decker buses allow on and off privileges around the city all day, a good investment at least one day of your visit.

For more information, contact the Greater Boston Convention and Visitors Bureau, Two Copley Place, Suite 105, Boston, MA 02116; (888) SEEBOSTON; www.bostonusa.com.

Philadelphia

Children love Philadelphia—and vice versa. Besides the perennial attraction of the Liberty Bell and Independence Hall, this city makes youngsters welcome with many attractions. The "Please Touch" Museum was the first museum in the nation designed especially for children under age 7. Another surefire favorite is the imaginative Treehouse at the Philadelphia Zoo, where kids can find out how it feels to climb through a 35-foot-high honeycomb or hatch out of a giant egg in the Everglades swamp. The nation's oldest zoo also offers a separate Children's Zoo, where kids can board Noah's Ark to pet the furry passengers, see how cows are milked, ride a pony, or watch a sea lion show.

Philadelphia's Independence National Park is better than ever, with a handsome Visitor Center and a new home for the Liberty Bell completed in the last few years. The Constitution Center gives new understanding of the nation's roots. Another recent addition to the museum scene, the National Liberty Museum, celebrates heroes who have overcome the odds to fight for freedom all over the world, from Jackie Robinson to Jonas Salk, Itzhak Perlman to Nelson Mandela.

History, Philadelphia-style, becomes a hands-on experience at Franklin Court, a fabulous little museum devoted to Benjamin Franklin. A telephone hotline there allows you to call anyone from George Washington to John F. Kennedy to hear what they had to say about the remarkable Mr. F. At Dial-a-Witticism, you can call up a Franklin quip on almost any subject.

Not far away on the river, Philadelphia's waterfront is blooming, with a maritime museum, historic ships for boarding, and a boat that shuttles back and forth to the New Jersey Aquarium just across the Delaware River.

The big Franklin Institute ranks as one of the nation's great science museums. It is full of participatory exhibits: Climb aboard a steam locomotive or take a walk through the chambers of a giant walk-through heart. The Mendell Center is a whirring, blinking world of participatory exhibits that show what we can expect in the future. Here you can stand inside a human cell a million times larger than life or manipulate a robot on the surface of the moon. The museum continues to innovate with exhibits such as the Sports Challenge, where you can try your hand at various sports and learn about the physics involved. The KidScience area takes children ages 5 to 8 on a journey to explore light, water, earth, and air.

For a change of pace, what could be spookier than a visit to the ruins of the notorious Eastern State Penitentiary, including the cell occupied by Al Capone? Philadelphia also offers the nation's largest city park, filled with diversions.

There is good eating both at the family restaurants near South Philly's colorful Italian Market and at Reading Terminal Market, where generations of Philadelphians have shopped for fresh produce and meat—and where knowing locals come for lunch at stands offering everything from freshly carved turkey sandwiches to Greek gyros or hot enchiladas. And don't miss a sampling of Philly's gourmet junk food, the cheese steak, at Jim's at Fourth and South Streets.

Learn more from the Greater Philadelphia Marketing Corporation, 123 South Broad Street, Avenue of the Arts, Suite 2180, Philadelphia, PA 19109; (215) 599–0776; www.gophila.com.

Washington, D.C.

This city is guaranteed fun for both generations, though it is best to wait until children are old enough to be interested in the workings of government. The Tour Mobile allows you to get on and off all day, seeing the many monuments and sights without wearing out shoe leather. If you can, visit when Congress is in session. Stop into your representative's office, and you may get to meet your Congressperson and/or learn from his or her staff just what goes on in an office in the Capitol.

The FBI tour is a special treat for most young visitors, and the Mall allows for stretching young legs. Every kid loves climbing on the prehistoric animals outside the Museum of Natural History and gazing at the spacecraft in the National Air and Space Museum. The National Museum of American History is another popular spot where you can see George Washington's uniform and Abraham Lincoln's top hat or watch the earth rotate an inch or two under the Great Pendulum. Every kind of Americana is found here, from the original set of *Sesame Street* to the inaugural gowns of our First Ladies.

Many hotels are within walking distance of the main sights, but don't hesitate to save by staying outside the city, as long as your accommodations are near a stop on the Metro; it's the cleanest, quietest subway you'll ever ride.

Get the latest news from the Washington, D.C. Convention and Tourism Corportation, 901 7th Street NW, 4th Floor, Washington, DC 20001–3719; (800) 422–8644; www.washington.org.

San Francisco

It almost seems that this city was designed with children in mind. Few amusement park rides can equal the fun of the trolley cars clambering up and down the hills of San Francisco, and harbor seals frisking around Fisherman's Wharf are the best free entertainment around. And how can you match the thrill of walking or biking across the Golden Gate Bridge?

San Francisco also has one of the nation's first and best museums for children, the huge Exploratorium, where you can explore science with dozens of imaginative participatory exhibits, from learning to "paint" on a computer screen to entering the Tactile Dome, a pitch black crawl through a variety of touch experiences.

The area south of Market Street, known as SOMA, has many attractions for families. It is the new location of the California Academy of Sciences, with natural science exhibits and the Steinhart Aquarium housing all manner of intriguing sea creatures. The Cartoon Art Museum displays rotating exhibits spanning the history of comic book art, plus animated movies, magazines, and newspapers. At Sony's Metreon you can try out the latest video games, enter a life-size world of *Where the Wild Things Are* (Maurice Sendak's children's classic), and see a giant-screen IMAX movie.

At the San Francisco Cable Car Museum you can see the actual cable-winding machinery at work as it reels 11 miles of steel at a steady pace of nine and a half miles per hour. Antique cable cars are also on display, including the first one dating from 1873.

Older kids think it is really cool to take the boat trip for a tour of infamous Alcatraz Island; reserve well in advance, for this is one of the city's most popular excursions. Best of all, the places that kids love best in the city have almost equal appeal for moms and dads.

At the west end of Fisherman's Wharf have a look at the figureheads, ship models, and photos in the ship-shaped Maritime Museum in the San Francisco

Maritime National Historic Park and the lineup of historic ships at Hyde Street Pier. Experience some of the excitement of sailing 100 years ago by prowling the passageways of the three-masted 1886 square-rigger *Balclutha,* the last of the historic Cape Horn fleet. You can also tour the engine room of the impressive 1890 steam-powered ferryboat *Eureka.*

On the more commercial side of Fisherman's Wharf, take time out for a chowder and sourdough snack while you watch some of the city's free entertainment— the fishing fleet and the seals. Then take a stroll to see some of the street performers in action around the wharf and its shopping centers, especially at the Cannery. Balloon sculptors seem to win the biggest audience of fascinated kids. If you're feeling flush, your children may lure you into the amusements at Pier 39. The attractions include a Cinemax theater and the Aquarium of the Bay, an aquarium that takes visitors on a walkway through an ocean environment. You can also tour the 312-foot submarine U.S.S. *Pampanito* at Pier 45, or board a boat at Piers 39 or 41 for a harbor cruise, a picnic on Angel Island, or a visit to Sausalito or Tiburon.

Learn more about the city from the San Francisco Convention and Visitors Bureau, 201 3rd Street, Suite 900, San Francisco, CA 91103; (415) 391–2000; www.sfvisitor.org.

The special excitement of any of these great cities will make for meaningful, shared memories for everyone in the family—which is what family vacations are all about.

Traveling Safe and Smart

W HETHER YOU ARE JOINING A GROUP OR TRAVELING ON YOUR OWN, with or without children in tow, when you set out without another adult along, it is doubly important to be a smart traveler. Traveling alone carries some built-in stresses: no one to help watch the bags or read a map, no one to share the aggravations. But there are many practical steps you can take to keep yourself feeling confident and in control.

Practical Packing

R edcaps never seem to be around when you need them most, so remember when you pack your suitcase that every item inside is something you may have to carry. Use the smallest suitcase you can get along with and pack a folding tote bag to hold any extras you might acquire on your trip. If you need a lot of clothing, two smaller bags or a small case on wheels and a garment bag that goes over your arm or shoulder are easier to manage than a giant suitcase.

A soft-sided bag with a frame is the best combination I've found for both light weight and protection. Cordura is an excellent, sturdy choice as a luggage material. Strong wheels make a bag easy to transport. The most stable bags are those with a retractable handle across the wide side of the top and two big wheels that carry the weight when you tilt the bag. Suitcases on four wheels pulled by a strap are easy to tip over. If your luggage lacks wheels, a wheeled carrying cart can be a lifesaver.

Other helps are padded shoulder straps or bags that can convert into a backpack, freeing your hands for finding tickets or change. Don't keep valuables in a backpack, where you cannot see them when the pack is on your back.

Be merciless when it comes to paring your travel wardrobe. Unless you are going to a resort where dressing up is the rule, all a woman really needs for a week of normal travel is three dark skirts or slacks, three daytime tops and three tops for evening, a sweater, a jacket, and a raincoat, preferably one that easily folds up. Pack a folding umbrella, as well—the smaller the better.

A similar basic wardrobe suits men, who may add a tie or two for evening for some destinations. One pair of walking shoes and one pair of dress shoes complete the picture for both sexes, unless you need to add a warmer coat for colder climates. If you need a coat, wear it or carry it, don't try to pack it.

Expect unexpected weather. Be prepared for a cold, rainy spell in July or a January thaw. For extra warmth, bring silk long underwear, the kind that skiers wear; it is lightweight and can be rolled up into almost nothing when you pack. Avoid bulky items as much as possible. If you are going to a cold climate, think like skiers and wear layers—underwear, cotton turtleneck, flat-knit sweater, wind-resistant jacket.

So many hotels have indoor pools these days that you may want to take along a bathing suit no matter what the season. Packing a couple of plastic bags to hold wet or soiled clothing is another good idea.

The best travel advice is that old adage: Bring half as many clothes and twice as much money as you think you'll need.

The most important item in your travel wardrobe is a pair of comfortable walking shoes with nonskid soles—a pair that has been broken in at home *before* your trip. Two important small items are a sewing kit for quick repairs and a travel alarm to be sure you don't oversleep.

Bring plenty of film with you. It's almost always cheaper at home, and you don't want to run out where there are no refills available. Don't trust airport x-ray machines with your precious vacation pictures. Buy a film-shield bag or hand your film (and camera if it is loaded) to the guard for manual inspection.

Before you set off on your trip, be sure your luggage is clearly tagged, and remember to put your name, home address, and next destination address inside your suitcase as well. Tags sometimes get detached, and if your bag is lost, inside identification will help locate you.

It's also not a bad idea to jot down the brand, size, color, and any other aids for identifying your luggage in case it is delayed or lost by an airline. They will ask you to write a description, and sometimes memories play tricks under stress. A close-up snapshot is a reminder that is easy to take along.

Another important tip: Make copies of your tickets, confirmations of hotel reservations, passport, and other important documents, and keep them separate from the originals. The copies will be a big help should you need replacements. Electronic ticketing takes away the worry of lost tickets, but I like to keep a copy of the airline's letter of confirmation, just for my own peace of mind.

Above all, never pack valuables, jewelry, travel documents, or medicines in luggage that you intend to check. Always put them in your hand luggage. Always pack one change of clothes in your carry-on luggage, just in case. If you arrive in a warm climate in winter clothes and your bag is delayed, you'll bless that one lightweight outfit!

Packing Tips

• *Make a packing list. It will keep you from forgetting important items and will come in handy if your luggage goes astray and you need to account for the contents.*

• *Organize your wardrobe around one basic dark color (brown, black, or navy) to cut down on accessories.*

• *Transfer shampoo and lotions into mini-bottles of lightweight plastic. Don't fill them to the top; pressure may cause the contents to expand. Put spillables into a plastic bag, just in case.*

• *Pack heaviest items first; put shoes along the sides or the bottom of the bag.*

• *Pack tightly; don't waste precious space. Fill in spaces with underwear, socks, and hose. Roll pajamas, sweaters, and other casual wear to fit into small spaces.*

• *Pack suits, dresses, shirts, and blouses in plastic dry-cleaner bags to cut down wrinkling, or put layers of tissue paper between garments.*

• *Drape slacks, dresses, and any longer garments across the suitcase with the ends hanging over the sides. Put shirts and blouses in the center and fold the long ends over. The center clothing acts as a cushion to prevent wrinkles.*

• *Pack some old clothes and discard them after you wear them, lightening your load as you go or leaving room for new purchases.*

• *Don't force your suitcase to close; it may mean broken hinges or zippers when you can least cope with them. If the suitcase won't close, remove a few items.*

• *A bright piece of ribbon or yarn will help you spot your bag among the look-alikes on the luggage carousel.*

• *Remove old claim tags so baggage handlers won't be confused about your destination.*

Incidentally, if your bag is delayed more than a few hours, airlines often will advance you cash to buy a few necessities, so always ask; they may not volunteer!

Easy Departures and Arrivals

Be sure to allow extra time for the airport. Check-in and baggage inspection lines are longer and slower now that airlines are taking extra security precautions. Boarding passes can now be printed out at home from airline Internet sites, beginning twenty-four hours before departure, or you can do it automatically using your credit card at airport machines in many cities. Both are time-savers. Extra time means you won't feel panicked about missing your plane. Better to leave calm and collected than in a frantic rush.

Remember to take photo identification with you; you won't be allowed to board without it. And be sure to get seat assignments in advance. Those without assigned seats stand a greater risk of being "bumped" when planes are over-booked.

If you are traveling into an unfamiliar city from the airport alone, you'll find yourself a lot more confident if you know what to expect. Find out from your travel agent, tour operator, or hotel, airport, or airline personnel how long it takes to get into the city and the options for getting there. Is there a convenient bus or limo to your hotel? Does the hotel have courtesy van service? Are cabs plentiful? What is the difference in cost between public transportation and usual cab fare? The *Airport Transit Guide,* available through the Magellan Catalog listed on page 281, can give you much of this information on many cities.

If you take a cab, you will save hassles by knowing in advance the normal rate to town. *Before* you get into the cab, ask the driver what the fare will be. If it is out of line with the expected rate, wait for another cab.

As mentioned earlier, I've learned that, abroad and even sometimes in the United States, it is a good idea to write down the name and address of your destination clearly before you get into a cab and to mark the spot on a street map. You can't assume that foreign drivers know English or that all cab drivers know their cities well.

The more you know and are prepared in advance, the more you will have that all-important feeling of control in an unfamiliar place.

Money Matters

Nobody likes to think of bad things happening on vacation, but the surest way to prevent them is to be prepared. The biggest problem is pickpockets. Overladen solo travelers juggling bags and bundles can be a tempting target. Money holders to hide your cash and guard against pickpockets give great peace of mind when you travel.

Protection comes in many forms. Some money holders are slotted to fit on a belt and tuck into your skirt or slacks; others have straps that hang either around your neck or across your shoulder like a holster or fit around the calf of your leg under trousers. For women, there are half-slips with zip-pockets in the bottom of the hem. Money belts have zip compartments hidden on the inside. There's even a waterproof plastic money holder on a neck cord that solves the problem of where to put your cash if you go swimming alone.

Many travelers use hikers' day packs or a "fanny pack" that fits around the waist. These are convenient, but they identify you as a tourist so may not be the wisest choice. If you do use a fanny pack, look for a strong, wide belt; thieves have been known to come up behind and cut the straps. One safety trick is to loop the strap through your trouser belt loops so that the pack won't fall if someone cuts the strap. Always keep the pack in front, in your sight.

I often carry a lightweight but sturdy cloth tote bag with straps long enough to go over my shoulder but short enough that I can tuck the bag under my arm when I walk. It allows me to bring along a pad and pencil and an extra sweater or umbrella; I keep my wallet and camera in the very bottom of the bag, out of sight.

Try to avoid looking like a tourist. Study the big street map before you go out, and once you are on the street, use only an inconspicuous-size guidebook. Dress down and avoid jewelry. Even a chain that is fake gold may attract thieves.

I picked up a great little tip from the *Travel Companions* newsletter for countries like Brazil where thefts are a big problem for tourists. A reader noted that a Brazilian friend had taught her to carry her camera and valuables in a supermarket plastic bag, which made her look like a native rather than a tourist.

No matter which of these safety measures you find most convenient, the point is to keep your cash, tickets, passports, and valuables safe—and preferably out of sight.

Traveler's checks are still a standby to avoid losing cash, but the prevalence of ATM bank cash machines in the United States and Europe that accept Cirrus, Plus, and other common banking networks means you don't have to carry as much money with you as in the past. Not only can you get money easily twenty-four hours a day, but you get a preferred exchange rate abroad; the bank gets a wholesale rate that is not available to individuals. Most bank machines offer instructions in English. The fee charged for the transaction is also likely to be less than the hefty exchange charges abroad. It still makes sense, however, to keep transactions to a minimum, since there is a charge each time you withdraw money.

Always use credit cards for large purchases; you get the preferred exchange rate, and you have someone to come to your aid if there are problems with the purchase.

If you use traveler's checks, you probably know to keep the receipts separate from the checks, in case you have to make a claim. It is also a good idea to separate your credit cards and cash into two wallets kept in two different places; if one disappears, you have another resource.

Another money suggestion before you set out: Be sure you have small bills for tips and enough change on hand to use the telephone or mass transit systems. If you are traveling to a foreign country, "trip packs" of foreign currency for this purpose can be bought in major U.S. airports. If you exchange money in the airport on arrival, remember to ask for small bills and change; the tendency is to hand out larger bills. If you use a cash machine, ask the hotel to give you smaller change as soon as you arrive.

The practice of tipping puzzles many travelers. If you are going to a foreign country, read up on local customs before you leave home. In many countries, the tip is included in the price of the meal. In the United States, the usual percentage may vary in different parts of the country.

Handy Companions

Some terrific gadgets have been devised to help you feel and look cool and collected on the road. One valuable traveling companion is a compact clothes steamer to remove wrinkles in a hurry when you unpack; they really work. Just remember to have the right adapter plugs if you are traveling in a foreign country.

Other handy travel gadgets include inflatable hangers for drip-dry clothes; tiny sponges that expand in water when you find yourself without a washcloth; portable clotheslines and individual packets of laundry soap; portable alarm clocks; and tiny calculators that help you figure foreign currency rate in a flash. I love my unisex Gore-Tex hat that packs flat but can be popped into shape to ward off both sun and rain. Again, remember that folding umbrella. It's expecting too much to think a thundershower will wait until you're within convenient reach of shelter or an umbrella store. Christine Columbus (see page 282) has a model that folds absolutely flat.

Tipping Guide

Here are typical tipping practices:

Bellmen, porters, skycaps carrying luggage: $1 per bag

Doormen hailing a taxi: $1

Restaurant waiters: 15 to 20 percent, depending on the level of service

Bartender: 10 to 15 percent

Room service waiter: Check the bill; a service charge is usually included. If not, 10 to 15 percent

Concierge: For special services, $5 to $10

Housekeeper: $1 per day (leave it on the dresser)

Parking valet: $1 to $2

Hairstylist, masseuse: 15 percent

Tour guides: Optional, but $1 for a day and $5 to $10 for a week of touring is usual

Shuttle van driver: Tip not necessary

Health club attendant: Tip not necessary

Shop your own department store notions department, or browse through stores like Brookstone and Sharper Image for these and many other intelligent travel items. If you don't have access to a good selection, here are four mail-order companies that specialize in travel gear; write for their catalogs or check their Web sites:

MAGELLAN'S
110 West Sola Street, Santa Barbara, CA 93101; (800) 962–4943; www.magellans.com. This company provides a comprehensive catalog of useful accessories.

TRAVELSMITH
60 Leveroni Court, Novato, CA 94949; (800) 950–1600; www.travelsmith.com. Official outfitters for many top adventure travel operators, this enterprise's catalog features outdoor gear, luggage, gadgets, and many clothes in wrinkle-proof fabrics.

CHRISTINE COLUMBUS

(800) 280-4775; www.christinecolumbus.com.

This online catalog is geared to women travelers.

LE TRAVEL STORE

745 Fourth Avenue, San Diego, CA 92101; (800) 713-4260 or (619) 544-0005; www.letravelstore.com, is stocked with everything a traveler might need, from guidebooks to gadgets to gear. They do not print a catalog but do take mail orders, and much of their stock can be browsed online.

Staying Healthy

When you are tired or not feeling well, minor problems loom twice as large. To maintain a feeling of calm and control, it's wise to do what you can to minimize the fatigue of traveling and to take sensible precautions to keep yourself healthy.

Air travel is particularly tiring because seating space is tight. Experienced travelers make the best of the situation by asking for seat assignments as soon as they make plane reservations. To be sure that you enjoy the most leg room available on board, ask for a window or aisle seat. Always avoid the squeezed-in middle seats if you can. Aisle versus window is a matter of preference—the aisle makes it easier to leave your seat, the window provides a headrest for napping. Inflatable pillows contoured to support the neck are a smart investment to rest better on planes, trains, or buses and to leave your transportation without a stiff neck as a souvenir of your trip. Use the little pillow given out on the plane as a back support.

On most planes, the lower-numbered seats near the front of the cabin get the quickest meal service on international flights and the best chance of getting your meal of choice; sometimes the most popular dish is no longer available by the time the meal cart gets to the back.

Some domestic airlines are now selling food on shorter flights, but to be sure, if you are taking a plane trip of less than four hours, remember to bring along a snack or sandwich.

Rows 10 to 20 are often the best choice for a quick exit; on many planes they are closest to the door.

As for jet lag, no one has solved the problem. Only time really helps your body clock to adjust when you cross several time zones. Some strategies may help to reduce fatigue, however. Begin a few days before departure to gradually shift your meal and sleep times to fit the new time zone. Adopt the new time immediately when you arrive at your destination, and spend time out of doors—daylight some-how seems to help adjust the body's rhythms. Avoid overeating or excessive drinking on the plane—as well as at your destination. Whether you are better off traveling by day or night depends a great deal on how well you sleep on a plane. Some travelers find that taking a mild sleeping pill helps them rest better and feel fresher at journey's end. In general, arriving at night is easier on the system because you have time to rest.

Don't leave your sunglasses and suntan lotion behind just because you are heading for a city; sightseeing often puts you out of doors for long periods.

Bring along bandages and medication from home. Be sure to include remedies for the most common travel maladies such as headaches and diarrhea. You'll be thankful you did if the need arises when pharmacies are closed. Just in case you might need them in the middle of the night, remember to look for extra blankets or pillows as soon as you check into your hotel room. The middle of the night may be too late.

If you are traveling to countries where hygiene is a problem, you no doubt have been warned to drink only bottled water. Remember to avoid drinks with ice as well. Eat only cooked fruits and vegetables or those that can be peeled, and eat only meat that is well done. Many people even play it safe by using bottled water for brushing their teeth.

Time for rest should be a must in your travel schedule. Travelers generally are better off seeing one less sight and getting more out of what they do see. Being tired is a special problem when you are alone. It magnifies the difficulties and gets you down, making you less willing to reach out to meet other people. Allow plenty of time for sleep and plenty of rest breaks in your day. If you are traveling to a high-altitude destination, remember to allow extra rest time until you adjust.

Be good to the feet that are doing extra duty getting you around. When you return to your room after tours of sightseeing, elevate your legs to give them a rest. Even if you are a confirmed shower-taker at home, you'll find that a soak in the tub does wonders for a travel-weary body.

Playing It Safe

When you are traveling alone, safety in hotel rooms is a concern. Ask for a room near the elevator; don't accept a room at the end of a long corridor. In a large hotel, someone from the front desk should always escort you to your room when you check in. The employee should unlock the room door, check to be sure no one is in the bathroom, and pull back curtains over any sliding glass

Safety Tips on the Road

- Use the peephole in your hotel room door to identify visitors. If you don't recognize the person, call the front desk to verify identification.
- Don't accept delivery of items or services you did not request; ask that the items be left at the front desk.
- When you ride in elevators alone, stand next to the floor button panel. If you sense any problem, press the button for the next floor and get off as soon as possible. Don't press the emergency stop button; it could leave you trapped inside the elevator waiting for assistance.
- When you leave your room, leave a light on and close the curtains if you plan to return after dark.
- Ask hotel personnel to point out unsafe areas on your street map so that you can take care to avoid them.
- Don't keep all of your cash and credit cards in one place; otherwise, you may be left without funds if a pickpocket strikes. Keep your main stash of cash and your passport (when traveling abroad) in a money belt or a safe travel pouch that can be worn out of sight.
- Have keys ready when you get to your guest room door so you won't have to fumble for them in a corridor. Ditto for cash to pay for cabs or bus fare.
- Don't let a stranger touch your belongings. A common travel scam starts with spilling coffee or ice cream on a tourist and offering to clean it up. While the traveler is distracted, the thief or his partner is cleaning out the victim's wallet. Another distracting ploy: a big "welcome to my country" hug at the airport; the accomplice comes up behind and startles the victim with a punch in the back so the hugger can get the loot.

doors. Sliding doors should have a secure lock, preferably in the floor track. If not, ask for some type of rod to put into the track. The hall door should have a chain as well as a bolt lock and a peephole so that you can see who is outside the door.

Never hang the MAKE UP MY ROOM sign on the door; it announces to the world that the room is unoccupied. If the maid is needed, phone housekeeping instead. To discourage intruders, when you are not expecting the maid, hang out the DO NOT DISTURB sign as you leave the room and leave the radio or television playing softly.

It's also wise to check the location of the fire exit nearest to your room. A helpful booklet published by the federal government, *A Safe Trip Abroad,* suggests that a room between the second and seventh floors is the best bet, high enough to prevent easy entry from outside but low enough for fire equipment to reach.

Chances are that nothing will happen to spoil your trip, but you'll sleep easier away from home if you take intelligent precautions.

Worry Insurance

One final matter to think about before you travel is insurance. Most tour companies and several independent companies now offer trip cancellation insurance. The average cost is low compared to the price of a trip and can prove a worthwhile investment whenever you plan far ahead for a very expensive journey. Cruises, for example, offer sizable discounts for early booking, but if it's necessary for you to cancel your plans at the last minute, you can lose your entire payment without insurance. Insurance also includes coverage for any costs that may occur due to travel delays en route.

Your U.S. health insurance probably will not cover you outside the United States, but travel insurance is available. Access America, Inc. (866–807–3982; www.accessamerica.com), Travel Guard International (877–248–8992; www.travel guard.com), and GlobalCare (800–821–2488; www.globalcare-cocco.com) are among several organizations providing this service. Travel agents and tour operators can supply names of other groups that will provide coverage. If you are traveling to remote places, be sure that emergency evacuation coverage is included.

Holders of gold Visa, MasterCard, and American Express cards also may be entitled to many travel benefits, from life insurance to car rental discounts to a helpline abroad with an English-speaking operator who can advise on medical or legal problems. It pays to check what your card offers, as it may be worth upgrading if you travel often.

Be Ready for the Blues

Vacations serve a great many important functions. They are our best chance to rest from routine and revive the spirit, to hone old skills and acquire new ones, to learn about other lifestyles and appreciate other cultures. However, many of us have the fantasy that vacations will be happy and exciting from beginning to end. That is not reality, whether you travel alone or with a companion.

Leaving familiar surroundings creates stress—pleasant stress, yes, but a strain nonetheless as you learn your way around a new place. You may not sleep as soundly, for instance, in an unfamiliar bed. Add the fatigue of unaccustomed exercise, and it's easy to understand why solo vacation emotions tend to be uneven, sometimes shooting from exuberant highs to lonesome lows. There will inevitably be moments when you may wish there were someone close to share a beautiful sunset or a wonderful experience.

The best way to cope when those feelings arise is to let your feelings out in writing—write to a friend back home or spill it out to your journal, the solo traveler's best companion. It's okay to write about your blues, but make a point of writing about the better side of the trip as well. It really helps to put good and bad in perspective.

One other suggestion: In addition to guidebooks, take along the most engrossing books you can find about your destination, either nonfiction or novels set in the locale you are visiting. You'll be learning and building excitement for the next day's outing even while you are distracting yourself from loneliness.

You will discover that traveling on your own will yield a bonus when you get home. With the knowledge and confidence gained as a successful traveler, you will be a more aware person—and you'll never feel quite as fearful or dependent on others again.

Probably none of us would choose to spend all of our vacations alone, but that does not mean that we cannot reap the special pleasures and rewards that come with solo travel. With the right preparation and an optimistic outlook, single can be a singular way to go!

Driving Safety

Just you in the car? Chances are you'll be just fine, but don't take chances. Here are some tips to keep you rolling along safely:

- *Keep the doors locked and the windows up. Use the air conditioner if necessary. Be extra-sure the windows are up when you stop for a light.*

- *Keep the gas tank full. When the gas level gauge reaches the halfway mark on your dashboard indicator, fill up. Don't wait for the gauge to read "empty."*

- *Park only on well-lit streets or parking lots. Check for loiterers when you get out, even in your own neighborhood.*

- *Have keys out and ready so you can get into the car quickly.*

- *Never stop if a stranger signals that something is wrong with your car—not even if two or three cars go by with the same message. They may be working as a team. Keep going to a service station to check it out.*

- *If you think you are being followed, head for the nearest police or fire station or a well-lit grocery store or gas station. Hit the horn hard in short, insistent beeps. If you can't find a place to stop, keep moving and keep beeping. You'll attract attention—maybe even the police, which is just what you want.*

- *If you have car trouble in the daytime, lift the hood and tie a cloth to the antenna or outside door handle to signal for help. In the nighttime, turn on headlights and emergency flashers and get back in the car and lock the door. If a stranger stops, lower the window slightly and ask him to call for help.*

- *If you are arriving at an airport late at night, stay at an airport hotel and get your car in the morning rather than trying to make your way to an unfamiliar destination on dark roadways.*

Appendix

Travel Information Sources

Other Books for Solo Travelers

Travel Alone and Love It: A Flight Attendant's Guide to Solo Travel
Sharon B. Wingler, Chicago Spectrum Press, Evanston, IL, 1996.
Practical advice on health, safety, packing, and traveling along with firsthand enthusiasm about the pleasures of solo travel.

A Journey of One's Own: Uncommon Advice for the Independent Woman Traveler
Thalia Zepatos, Eighth Mountain Press, Portland, OR, 1996.
More practical advice, this time with emphasis on extended budget travel to offbeat destinations. Good suggestions on safety and socializing and firsthand accounts from women travelers.

Gutsy Women: Travel Tips and Wisdom for the Road
Marybeth Bond, Travelers' Tales, Inc., 2001.

Mail-Order and Retail Travel Book Sources

INDEPENDENT TRAVEL STORES ASSOCIATION (ITSA)

www.travelstores.org

This Web site of a nationwide organization of independent booksellers specializing in travel has addresses and links to stores across the United States.

The Internet

If you have access to the Internet, you have a world of additional travel information at your fingertips. Books on all kinds of specialized topics can be ordered from Amazon.com, an online bookstore with more than a million titles.

Shawguides.com offers free the updated text of the most comprehensive guides published to cooking schools, art and craft workshops, and photography workshops and schools. Many of the operators listed in this book have current information on their programs under their own names on the Internet.

This is only the beginning of the vast resources to be tapped. Almost every state, city, and country now has a page on the Internet, which also carries Zagat restaurant listings and many guidebooks, including Fodor, Frommer, and Lonely Planet. You can browse through pictures of bed-and-breakfast inns, get transportation information, and even make reservations via computer. And you can ask for tips from travelers who have recently visited your destination. Wherever possible, Web sites have been added throughout this book.

European Travel

The European Travel Commission (www.visiteurope) has a useful Web site that includes highlights of their thirty-three member countries and names and addresses of their U.S. tourism offices. You can also sign up for a free online monthly newsletter with up-to-date events and special travel offers.

U.S. State Offices of Tourism

These offices can also supply contacts for tourist information in specific cities in the state.

Alabama Bureau of Tourism and Travel; (800) ALABAMA or (334) 242–4169; www.touralabama.org.

Alaska Travel Industry Association; (800) 667–8489 or (907) 929–2200; www.travelalaska.com.

Arizona Division of Tourism; (888) 520–3434 or (602) 230–7733; www.arizonaguide.com.

Arkansas Department of Parks and Tourism; (800) 628–8725; www.arkansas .com.

California Tourism; (800) 862–2543 or (916) 322–2881; www.visitcalifornia .com.

Colorado Tourism Board; (800) 265–6723; www.colorado.com.

Connecticut Tourism Division; (800) CT–BOUND or (860) 270–8080; www.ctbound.org.

Delaware Tourism Office; (800) 441–8846 or (302) 739–4271; www.visit delaware.net.

Visit Florida; (888) 735–2872 or (904) 487–1462; www.flausa.com.

Georgia Tourist Division; (800) VISIT–GA or (404) 656–3590; www.georgia.org/tourism.

Hawaii Visitors Information; (800) 464–2924 or (808) 923–1811; www.go hawaii.com.

Idaho Travel Council; (800) 635–7820; www.visitid.org.

Illinois Bureau of Tourism; (800) 226–6632; www.enjoyillinois.com.

Indiana Tourism Development; (800) 289–6646; www.enjoyindiana.com.

Iowa Tourism Office; (888) 472–6035 or (515) 242–4705; www.traveliowa .com.

Kansas Travel and Tourism Division; (800) 2KANSAS; www.travelks.com.

Kentucky Department of Travel Development; (800) 225–8747; www.kentucky tourism.com.

Louisiana Office of Tourism; (888) 225–4003 or (225) 342–8119; www.louisianatravel.com.

Maine Office of Tourism; (888) 624–6345 or (207) 287–5711; www.visit maine.com.

Maryland Office of Tourism Development; (800) 634–7386 or (410) 767–3400; www.mdisfun.org.

Massachusetts Office of Travel and Tourism; (800) 447–MASS or (617) 727–3201; www.massvacation.com.

Michigan Travel Bureau; (888) 784–7328 or (517) 373–0670; www.michigan .org.

Minnesota Office of Tourism; (800) 657–3700; www.explore minnesota.com.

Mississippi Department of Tourism; (866) SEE–MISS; www.visit mississippi.org.

Missouri Division of Tourism; (800) 877–1234 or (573) 751–1433; www .missouritourism.com.

Nebraska Division of Travel and Tourism; (800) 228–4307; in state, (800) 742–7595; www.visitnebraska.org.

Nevada Commission on Tourism; (800) 638–2328 or (775) 687–4322; www.travelnevada.com.

New Hampshire Office of Vacation Travel; (800) 386–4664 or (603) 271–2343; www.visitnh.gov.

New Jersey Division of Travel and Tourism; (800) 847–4865 or (609) 292–2470; www.visitnj.org.

New Mexico Tourism; (800) 545–2040; in state, (505) 827–7400; www.newmexico.org.

New York Department of Economic Development, Tourism Division; (800) CALL–NYS or (518) 474–4116; www.iloveny.com.

North Carolina Division of Travel and Tourism; (800) VISIT–NC; www.visit nc.com.

North Dakota Tourism Promotion; (800) HELLOND; www.ndtourism.com.

Ohio Division of Tourism and Travel; (800) 282–5393 or (614) 466–8844; www.ohiotourism.com.

Oklahoma Tourism and Recreation; (800) 652–6552; www.travelok.com.

Oregon Tourism Division; (800) 547–7842; www.traveloregon.com.

Pennsylvania Tourism; (800) VISIT–PA or (717) 787–5453; www.experiencepa.com.

Rhode Island Tourism Division; (800) 556–2484 or (401) 222–2601; www.visitrhodeisland.com.

South Carolina Division of Parks and Tourism; (800) 346–3634 or (803) 734–1700; www.travelsc.com.

South Dakota Department of Tourism; (800) 732–5682; www.travelsd.com.

Tennessee Tourism Development; (800) GO2–TENN or (615) 741–2159; www.tnvacation.com.

Texas Tourism Division; (800) 888–8839 or (512) 462–9191; www.traveltex.com.

Travel Montana; (800) 847–4868 or (406) 444–2654; www.visitmt.com.

Utah Travel Council; (800) 200–1160 or (801) 538–1030; www.utah.com.

Vermont Travel Division; (800) VERMONT or (802) 828–3236; www.vermontvacation.com.

Virginia Division of Tourism; (800) VISIT–VA or (804) 786–4484; www.virginia.org.

Washington, D.C. Convention and Visitors Association; (800) 422–8644 or (202) 789–7000; www.washington.org.

Washington State Department of Trade and Economic Development; (800) 544–1800 or (206) 586–2088; www.experiencewashington.com.

West Virginia Tourism Division; (800) CALL–WVA; www.wvtourism.com.

Wisconsin Division of Tourism Development; (800) 432–8747 or (608) 266–2161; www.travelwisconsin.com.

Wyoming Travel Commission; (800) 225–5996; in state, (307) 777–7777; www.wyomingtourism.org.

General Index

Special Index

About the Author

ELEANOR BERMAN WON THE LOWELL THOMAS BRONZE AWARD FROM the Society of American Travel Writers for *Traveling Solo*. She is a widely published travel writer whose journeys have spanned sixty-five countries and six continents. Eleanor is the author of fourteen travel guides and six nonfiction titles. Her other guidebooks for Globe Pequot are *Recommended Bed & Breakfasts New England* and *New York Neighborhoods,* winner of the Independent Publishers IPPY Award for best travel guide of the year.